UPSTREAM

Adjudicating the the Snake River Basin

Randy Stapilus
Publisher and editor
Snake River Basin Adjudication Digest
National Water Rights Digest

RIDENBAUGH PRESS
Carlton, Oregon
www.ridenbaugh.com

For more information, contact Ridenbaugh Press, P.O. Box 834, Carlton, OR 97111.

Printed and bound in the United States of America.
First edition June 2009
10 9 8 7 6 5 4 3 2 1

Library of Congress Cataloging in Publication Data

Stapilus, Randy 1955 –
The Snake River Basin Adjudication Digest
Bibliography
Includes Index
1. Idaho-History. 2. Idaho Politics and Government. 3. Idaho-Economy.
I. Stapilus, Randy. II. Title.
ISBN 0982466811 (softbound)

Front cover photo by Linda Watkins
Back cover photo by Randy Stapilus

Ridenbaugh Press
P.O. Box 834
Carlton OR 97111

Phone (503) 852-0010
www.ridenbaugh.com

| Contents

Introduction

Daniel Hurlbutt, who was presiding judge of the Snake River Basin Adjudication for 11 years, liked to say that water rights are not an especially complex area of law.

Nevertheless . . . the permutations are amazing.

When we began to publish the *Snake River Basin Adjudication Digest* newsletter early in 1993, we wondered whether new developments would arise on a frequent and regular enough basis to justify the periodical. We needn't have worried: We've never had to tell our readers, "Nothing happened this month."

Quite the contrary.

In 1997, we compiled some of the material from the SRBA Digest into a book called *SRBA: The First 10 Years.* That helped us (and the readers who picked up on it) to follow, chronologically, the developments in the Adjudication (at least since the newsletter began publication). We updated in 1999, but the 10-year mark since that book suggested that time has come for a new edition, to overview the important contours and developments in and around the case.

We hope this book will help untangle some of the questions.

We owe thanks to all the people who have helped us over the last numbers of years as we've been following the SRBA. That includes many of the parties and attorneys in the case.

In particular, though, we should point out the Natural Resources Division of Idaho Attorney General's office, which has been very helpful with access to its records; the staff of the SRBA Court, which has often gone above and beyond its obligations in helping us; and David Tuthill and the staff of the Department of Water Resources adjudication division, which has provided no end of help over the years.

And, of course, to Linda Watkins, who helps edit the monthly *Digest*, as well as this publication.

Randy Stapilus
May 2009

Two items:

SRBA Digest, December 2007:

The Snake River Basin Adjudication turned 20 years old in November, and IDWR Director David Tuthill decided to throw a birthday party.

Held at the Owyhee Plaza in Boise, the event drew two of the presiding judges (including current Judge John Melanson), four Supreme Court justices, several legislators, a large portion of the water bar and a number of other participants.

The event included a number of recollections from long-time participants in the case. It also included special musical numbers, notably a folk song written for the occasion called "Talkin' SRBA." ☒

SRBA Digest, July 2008:

All four SRBA judges – Daniel Hurlbutt, Barry Wood, Roger Burdick and John Melanson—appeared for a panel discussion on June 16, at an Idaho Water Users Association water law seminar.

Hurlbutt, speaking of his selection as the first judge, a post he held for about 11 years, "The truth is, I did draw the short straw."

The Twin Falls *Times-News*, in its report on the conference, noted as the judges looked toward the adjudication's wrapup: "Looking forward to the end of the SRBA, Burdick emphasized the need for good administration from the state once the court is gone. But Melanson suggested preserving it in some way as a court for appeals for other water-rights disputes. 'It would be a shame to finish the adjudication and have that expertise not utilized,' Melanson said of the staff expertise that goes back 20 years."

Melanson also remarked, "The end really is in sight." ☒

The **Snake River Basin Adjudication** is the largest water adjudication Idaho has ever seen, and may be the largest ever undertaken in the United States. It involves the determination, and legal battles surrounding, about 140,000 claims of water across most of the state.

Launched in 1987, it is at present (2009) heading toward conclusion – which actually makes it a relatively speedily-handled water adjudication.

☒ From an article which originally appeared in the SRBA Digest.

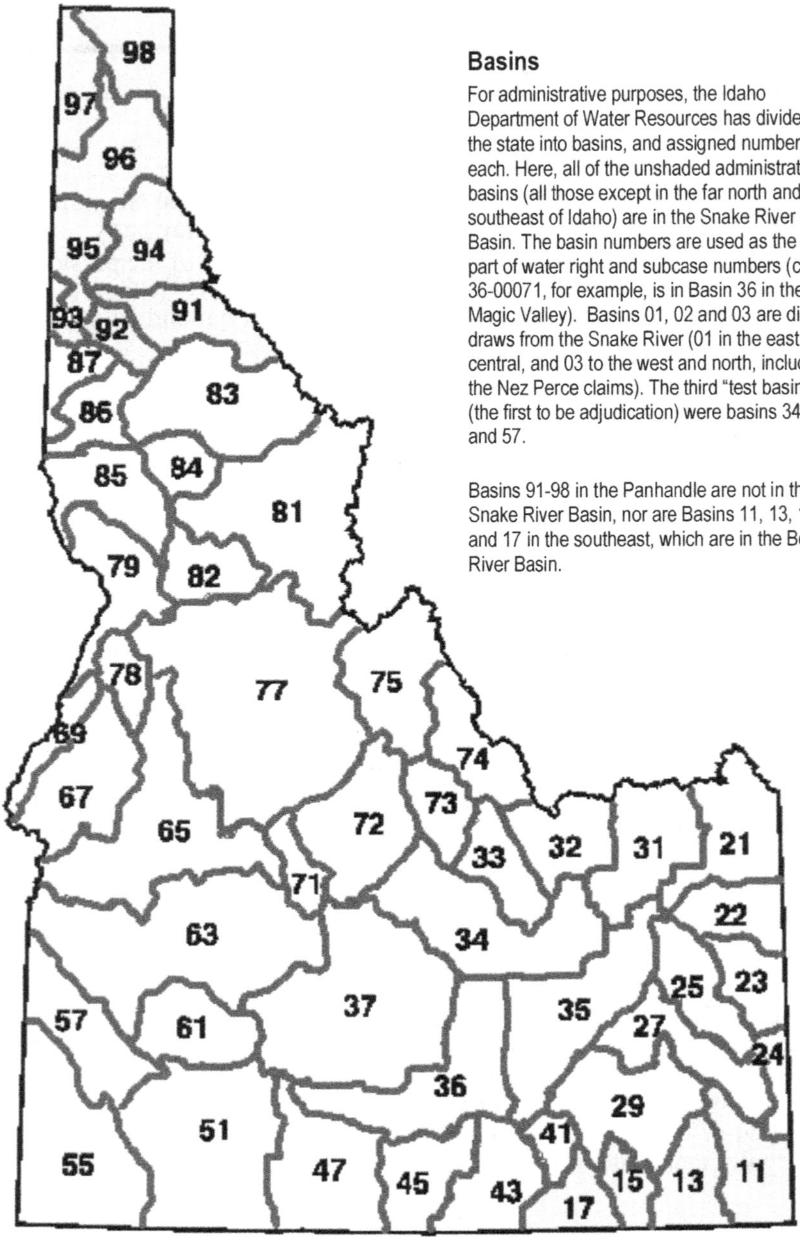

Basins

For administrative purposes, the Idaho Department of Water Resources has divided the state into basins, and assigned numbers to each. Here, all of the unshaded administrative basins (all those except in the far north and southeast of Idaho) are in the Snake River Basin. The basin numbers are used as the first part of water right and subcase numbers (case 36-00071, for example, is in Basin 36 in the Magic Valley). Basins 01, 02 and 03 are direct draws from the Snake River (01 in the east, 02 central, and 03 to the west and north, including the Nez Perce claims). The third "test basins" (the first to be adjudication) were basins 34, 36 and 57.

Basins 91-98 in the Panhandle are not in the Snake River Basin, nor are Basins 11, 13, 15 and 17 in the southeast, which are in the Bear River Basin.

1 | Water

The basin

About 87% of Idaho is located in the Snake River Basin. The Snake River originates in Wyoming near Grand Teton National Park, flows into Idaho south of Jackson, Wyoming, and winds across the southern part of the state to Oregon. It then turns north, forming part of Idaho's border with Oregon and Washington. At Lewiston, it leaves Idaho and flows into Washington state, where it eventually merges with the Columbia River.

Apart from the Bear River area in extreme southeast Idaho (in Bear Lake, Franklin and parts of Caribou and Oneida Counties), and the Spokane River system and related waters in Idaho's Panhandle, all of Idaho's waters are part of the Snake River system. The Snake is the main stem for many other rivers in the state. Its tributaries include:

• ***The Clearwater***. The basin runs from Lewiston east; the river splits about 60 miles upstream into the Lochsa and Selway. It drains parts of Nez Perce and Idaho and most of Clearwater counties.

• ***The Salmon*** (often called "The River of No Return"). Said to be the longest river contained entirely in one state, the Salmon deposits into the Snake River at Riggins. East of there, through several forks, it drains much of central Idaho, as far away as Stanley and Salmon.

• ***The Weiser***. Drains into the Snake just south of the city of Weiser; it drains much of Washington and western Adams counties.

• ***The Payette***. Entering the Snake near the city of Payette, this is one of the larger river systems, its forks draining the area from McCall to Horseshoe Bend (named for a twist in the river) to east of Lowman.

• ***The Boise***. Another large system that runs mostly east to west, from the mountains in Boise and northern Elmore and Camas counties down to the Ada and Canyon county flatlands. It enters the Snake River near Parma.

• ***The Owyhee***. The Owyhee leaves the Snake on the Oregon side of the river, but tributaries to it do flow in the southwest corner of the state in Owyhee County.

• ***The Bruneau***. Enters the Snake River near the C.J. Strike dam. Its origins are to the south in Owyhee County, and its tributaries have origins as far south as across the Nevada line.

• ***The Wood***. From its link to the Snake River near Bliss, this river's route runs north into Gooding, Lincoln, and Blaine counties, north through the "Wood River Valley" (Ketchum-Hailey-Sun Valley) area.

• ***The Raft***. A relatively small river system running north-south in eastern Cassia County.

• ***The Lost***. An oddity in that this small river system appears to the untrained eye to be self-contained. Water runs from the Sawtooth Mountain areas in central Custer and Lemhi counties south and east of Arco, where the flow seems to disappear. Scientific consensus is that it runs into the Snake River Plain Aquifer, which feeds springs 100 miles and more to the southwest near Hagerman; these pour into the Snake River at that point.

• ***The Portneuf***. Runs through northwestern Caribou and northern Bannock counties, entering the Snake at the American Falls Reservoir.

• ***The Blackfoot***. Back of its link to the Snake near the city of Blackfoot, it twists through the relatively remote mountains of eastern Bonneville and Bingham and northern Caibou counties.

• ***Henry's Fork***. Just north of Rigby, the Snake River takes a turn; its upstream path heads southeast to Wyoming. At that bend, Henry's Fork enters the Snake. The Fork runs through Fremont County (not far from Yellowstone National Park) south toward Rigby. This drainage includes the Island Park area.

• ***The Teton***. A tributary of Henry's Fork, the Teton (site of a dam which collapsed in 1976) straddles the Fremont-Madison County line, and east of that runs north-south through Teton Valley.

The Aquifer

The surface waters are only the more visible part of the story. Underground runs another massive flow of water, the Snake River Plain Aquifer. Fed by water from surface streams, general drainage (including from irrigation) and a host of other sources—some obscure—the aquifer is a prime source for water throughout southern Idaho. It runs from most of the eastern part of the state heading west until it gets just past the Twin Falls area. At the Thousands Springs area near Hagerman, much of the water from the aquifer is disgorged and joins the Snake River. The aquifer and the water it carries have been increasingly heated points of contention in Southern Idaho water debates. One key point is this: While many surface water right holders have older priority rights, many of the groundwater users, obtaining water through wells, are relative newcomers. When water expected at Thousand Springs or other outputs, for use by surface water right holders, doesn't appear, conflict (generally of the legal and administrative variety) usually does.

The aquifer has been studied intensively by regional hydrogeologists. Much about its flows and mechanisms remain obscure, but much more detailed information has become available in the 2000s than could be had when the adjudication began.

PAYING FOR THE STUDIES (3/1/1993) The Idaho Legislature's budget-setting Joint Finance Appropriations Committee voted unanimously on Feb. 25 to help pay for the Snake River Basin Aquifer Study. . . . A total $287,000 was appropriated; of this, the state provides $187,000 from the Resource Conservation Fund (administered by the Soil Conservation Commission) and the remainder to come from non-state public and private entities, in a virtual match arrangement. "To the extent possible, non-state sources of funds are to be solicited," the lawmakers wrote.

The hydrologists committee included Charles Brockway, Kimberly; Jerry Hughes, Boise; Rep. Jack Barraclough, Idaho Falls; Sherl Chapman of the Idaho Water Users, Boise; Keith Anderson, Boise; Gary King, Boise; and Dale Ralston, Moscow. ☒

AQUIFER INFO IN THE SRBA (5/24/1993) Two motions that would have had the effect of slowing—prospectively, for a long time—water adjudication action in Basin 36 were rejected by Judge Daniel Hurlbutt on Wednesday. The judge did, however, provide for a special late objection procedure for Basin 36 water right parties.

. . . The issue centered around a state-funded study by the Department of Water Resources of the relationship between ground and surface water in the Snake River Aquifer, which runs roughly from St. Anthony to King Hill, primarily north of the Snake River. The study was generated by a lawsuit involving the Twin Falls and Northside Canal Companies and their concerns about groundwater pumping, and funded with $322,00 by the Idaho Legislature last session. The state Department of Water Resources, with assistance from the University of Idaho plans to begin an intensive study in July of the flow of water in the Snake River Plain Aquifer. Completion is expected in 1996.

Water right owners in the Hagerman area, in the region where much of the Aquifer water emerges in the Thousand Springs area and in Snake River recharge, said that until that study is complete, they don't have the information they need to know which water rights upstream to which they should object. . . . Deputy Attorney General Peter Anderson said the state of water science is such that specific groundwater uses upstream cannot be specifically connected to water rights or springs downstream. If such connections have to be established before working on the adjudication, he said, "We're essentially going to be staying this case forever. Every well impacts a spring. It's a matter of gradation."

Both hydrologists who testified essentially agreed, though they left different impressions of the detail the study would provide. University of Idaho hydrologist Charles Brockway, subpoenaed by the Hagerman attorneys, said the study could provide information useful to the Hagerman interests, but would not identify the flow of water from a specific upstream user or well to another user or spring: "It may not be as detailed as you are envisioning . . . It will certainly help them [Hagerman water users] but it may not answer all of the questions."

Several witnesses from the Hagerman area reported declining water levels over the last several decades. John "Bill" Jones, Hagerman, who owns a ranch and fish hatchery which has been in his family since 1898, said the Department of Water Resources measured 73 cubic feet per second (cfs) at his property in 1972, but now only 30 cfs are available. ☒

STUDY RESULTS *Adapted from a 1999 address by IDWR Director Karl Dreher:* A study was published by the Idaho Department of Water Resources in January 1997. This hydrologic study was the result of a settlement agreement between IDWR and complainants concerned with diversions from junior ground water and surface water users in the Supper Snake River Basin. This study identified significant impacts on aquifer levels and spring flows resulting from land use changes. The magnitude of these impacts is sufficient to require the State to develop and implement mitigation policies in the context of conjunctive surface and ground water management.

A review of current data showed that there is no justification for redefining the 1986 trust/non-trust ground water line. Ground water flow lines representing spring and fall 1993 conditions showed only minor differences from those used in 1986. . . .

Aquifer discharge and water levels on the ESPA have not reached equilibrium and are still responding to historical development. In 1992, over the modeled area of the ESPA approximately 611,000 acres were irrigated from surface water sources, and 818,000 acres were irrigated from ground water sources. By holding net recharge reflecting this level of irrigation constant over many years, a model run was made to simulate equilibrium conditions for a "base study" from which to measure the impact of each "what if" study. At equilibrium, the base study simulation produced an annual average aquifer discharge in the Shelley to Neeley and Kimberly to King Hill reaches of 2,665 and 5,526 cfs, respectively. . . . ☒

LOOKING AHEAD *This is taken from a report delivered in 1997, "Where We Go From Here: A Framework for Planning Mitigation," by Karl J. Dreher, director of the Idaho Department of Water Resources.*

Idaho's constitutional and statutory implementation of the prior appropriation doctrine requires that water rights of senior appropriators be protected. However, that protection does not extend to the point of denying junior appropriators use of water that is beyond the amount necessary to meet the rights of senior appropriators. So, how can the rights of senior surface water appropriators be protected from injury by junior ground water appropriators? I believe this protection can be provided through adequate management of the resource, which includes regulating water diversions and the implementation of mitigation plans. . . .

It is well known that the hydrologic regime of the Eastern Snake Plain Aquifer has been enhanced by the widespread irrigation of lands above the aquifer. Whether or not impacts to a particular senior appropriator in a hydrologic regime enhanced by the historic water use of other appropriators fully constitutes injury is an issue that needs to be considered. Any diversion of water from either a ground water source or a surface water source can impact other diverters, but such impacts do not always constitute injury.

. . . In some instances, for example situations involving injury to senior appropriators such as the North Side and Twin Falls Canal Companies who rely on spring flows tributary to American Falls Reservoir, it will be more effective for junior ground water appropriators to provide mitigation water directly to American Falls Reservoir, or other reservoirs, than to use water available for mitigation in a recharge project. . . . In such cases, the senior appropriators benefit from using storage water leased by junior ground water appropriators from the water bank in lieu of storage water not placed in the water bank because the latter can be carried over for use during future drought periods and compensation has been made by the junior appropriators for the storage water provided through the water bank.

Eventually, there will be dry-year sequences during which: (a) direct or natural flows in the Snake River are not sufficient to fill the rights of senior appropriators; (b) those senior appropriators do not have sufficient storage water to provide for their necessary water supply; and (c) water is not available for lease from the water bank. During such dry-year sequences, it would not be consistent with the prior appropriation doctrine and Idaho's constitution and statutes for junior appropriators of ground water from an unconfined aquifer to have a full water supply while the water rights for senior surface water appropriators which rely on discharges to the river from the same unconfined aquifer could not be met.

Hypothetically, mitigation during such a dry-year sequence could be offered to senior appropriators for irrigation uses in the form of cash payments for loss of crops, reduction in crop yields, or even dry-year fallowing. Since the senior appropriator is not bound to mitigation in the form of cash payments, an alternative form of mitigation could be to fallow acreage under groundwater irrigation, and the groundwater that would have been supplied to the fallowed acreage could be pumped to supply mitigation water to the senior appropriator (mitigation wells).

Some might question the concept of depleting a reduced supply of ground water, as measured by decreased spring discharges, to provide mitigation for injury to surface water supplies already reduced by diminished spring flows. However, these depletions could be countered over the long term through managed recharge. Obviously, there are numerous issues, such as how water would be delivered from mitigation wells for use by senior appropriators, that require further consideration before this approach could be viewed as feasible. Nonetheless, this concept for mitigation is consistent with the prior appropriation doctrine and Idaho laws.

A NEW GROUNDWATER ERA 10/2001 The Idaho Department of Water Resources in September took more direct control of groundwater diversions in two large regions of the Snake River Plain. That followed an unveiling of a new analysis of the relationship between groundwater flows and water levels in the Snake River—an analysis that allows for an unprecedentedly precise determination of cause and effect.

IDWR Director Karl Dreher, speaking at the September 18 SRBA information meeting at Pocatello, told court and other officials that "The steps we took have ramifications on water rights administration. ... There will be some procedural things that will occur because of this."

The steps were triggered by an increasingly severe drought—surface water drought, at least—around the state.

The subject of groundwater flow has long been shrouded in mystery; the exact flows of that water never has been precisely determined. But comparisons between discharges into the Snake River with groundwater use (and recharge) in nearby areas have begun to yield some answers.

Dreher said that across the Snake River Plain Aquifer, "two-thirds to three-quarters of the groundwater levels are down where they were 22 years ago." Those levels generally are standard across the Snake River Plain, except for some areas near Burley and Oakley, where larger declines have been reported. Dreher noted that groundwater in the Oakley farm area, which has had some of the biggest declines, isn't connected directly to the Snake River Plain Aquifer.

"All in all the picture for groundwater looks pretty good," Dreher said. "The problem is at the margins."

Dreher said that some reaches of the river connect very directly with the aquifer and others appear to connect hardly at all.

The area of the Snake River from Milner Dam to King Hill doesn't link directly to the aquifer at all. In four other areas the connection is direct and observable: in the Henry's Fork area, in part of the Upper Valley (in the Madison and Jefferson County area), in the "American Falls" reach (from Blackfoot to Minidoka) and in the Thousand Springs area.

Asked how close is the model to precision, Dreher estimated, "plus or minus 10%."

Idaho law has allowed for some department action regulating groundwater. One law (Idaho Code 42-233a) says that "any groundwater basin or any part thereof, not having sufficient ground water to provide a reasonably safe supply for cultivation of irrigated lands, or other uses in the basin at the then current rates of withdrawal … as may be determined and designated, from time to time, by the director of the Department of Water Resources" can be designated a critical ground water area.

Section B says that any area designated as a critical area can be declared (by the director) a ground water management area. There, the director could order curtailment of junior groundwater right holders.

On August 3 he took just such an action, designating two groundwater management areas, the American Falls and Thousand Springs Groundwater Management areas. American Falls runs roughly from Blackfoot to Minidoka, and Thousand Springs from Milner Dam to King Hill. Groundwater users in those areas, Dreher said, agreed to provide replacement water for senior surface users, for two years, equal to what the groundwater users would use. And they agreed that if they can't come up with the water, they would voluntarily reduce groundwater diversions. ☒

AQUIFER PLAN DEVELOPED (3/2009) A comprehensive plan to improve the health of the Eastern Snake Plain Aquifer approved on January 29 by the Idaho Water Resource Board has hit the Idaho Legislature.

If passed by the legislature, it would provide for a variety of actions aimed at enhancing the underground water supply.

The Department of Water Resources described the proposal: "In light of declining aquifer levels and reduced spring and river flows, the plan is an effort to adjust water supply and demand in the ESPA over the short and long term, and to identify opportunities to manage the available water to meet current and future water needs. The plan is a culmination of almost three years of work by stakeholder representatives, agency staff, and consultants. An Advisory committee comprised of representatives from irrigation companies, ground water users, spring water users, hydro power, land developers, well owners, environmental/conservation interests, county assessors and mayors of cities within the ESPA, have been working on the plan for the last 18 months." ☒

2 | Water Rights and the State

SECTION 3.WATER OF NATURAL STREAM -- RIGHT TO APPROPRIATE -- STATE'S REGULATORY POWER -- PRIORITIES. The right to divert and appropriate the unappropriated waters of any natural stream to beneficial uses, shall never be denied, except that the state may regulate and limit the use thereof for power purposes. Priority of appropriation shall give the better right as between those using the water; but when the waters of any natural stream are not sufficient for the service of all those desiring the use of the same, those using the water for domestic purposes shall (subject to such limitations as may be prescribed by law) have the preference over those claiming for any other purpose; and those using the water for agricultural purposes shall have preference over those using the same for manufacturing purposes. And in any organized mining district those using the water for mining purposes or milling purposes connected with mining, shall have preference over those using the same for manufacturing or agricultural purposes. But the usage by such subsequent appropriators shall be subject to such provisions of law regulating the taking of private property for public and private use, as referred to in section 14 of article I of this Constitution. – *Idaho Constitution, Article XV, Sec. 3*

A water rights primer

This section is adapted from an Idaho Department of Water Resources paper on water rights policy and procedure in Idaho.

A complex system of water rights has been developed over the years by which appropriation and use of Idaho's public waters can be managed. Article 15, Section 3 of the Idaho Constitution provides: Priority of appropriation shall give the better right as between those using the water; but when the waters of any natural stream are not sufficient for the service of all those desiring the use of the same, those using the water for domestic purposes shall (subject to such limitations as may be prescribed by law) have the preference over those claiming for any other purpose; and those using the water for agricultural purposes shall have preference over those using the same for manufacturing purposes. And in any organized mining district those using the water for mining purposes or milling purposes connected with mining have preference over those using the same for manufacturing or agriculture purposes.

The general rule of thumb for Idaho water rights is: If you intend to put public waters to some form of beneficial use, it is against the law to do so without a valid water right. The exception is water for domestic use where, under specific conditions, a recorded water right is not required. Idaho law provides for civil penalties for appropriating water without a valid water right.

What is a water right? The constitution and statutes of the State of Idaho declare all the waters of the state, when flowing in their natural channels, including the waters of all natural springs and lakes within the boundaries of the state, and ground waters of the state, to be public waters. They also guarantee the right to appropriate the public waters. When a private right to the use of public waters is established by appropriation, a water right is established that is a real property right much like property rights in land.

A water right is the right to divert the public waters of the state of Idaho and put them to a beneficial use, in accordance with one's priority date.

A priority date is the date the water right was established. The priority date is important because the priority date determines who gets water when there is a shortage. If there is not enough water available to satisfy all of the water rights, then the persons with the oldest (or senior) water rights get their water rights satisfied first and so on in order until there is no water left. It is the persons with the new (or junior) water rights who do not get water when there is not enough to satisfy all the water rights.

Beneficial uses include such uses as domestic use, irrigation, stock watering, manufacturing, mining, hydro power, municipal use, aquaculture, recreation, fish and wildlife, among others. The amount of the water right is the amount of water put to beneficial use. Due to the beneficial use requirement, a water right (or a portion of a water right) may be lost if it is not used for a continuous five-year period.

A diversion is a structure for capturing the water before it is put to use. Typical diversion structures include pumps, head gates, ditches, pipelines, and dams, or some combination. A diversion is generally required to establish a water right. Some public agencies are authorized to acquire water rights without diversions. These water rights are called 'in-stream flow' water rights, and are typically authorized for purposes of protecting some public interest in a natural stream or lake, such as recreation, wildlife, or natural beauty. A water right may also be acquired to water livestock directly from the stream, which are called "in-stream livestock" water rights.

Water law in Idaho is called the appropriation doctrine, because water rights in Idaho are based upon diversion and-beneficial use of water. The appropriation doctrine has also been called "first in time is first in right," because the priority date determines who gets water when there is not enough to go around. The water night is also called an "appropriation", and someone who has a water right is said to have "appropriated" water.

A water right under the law of the state of Idaho can be established only by appropriation, and once established, it can be lost if it is not used.

How is a water right established? Surface Water: Prior to May 20, 1971, there were two ways in which a right to surface water could be established. The first way was to simply divert water and apply it to beneficial use. These water rights are called 'beneficial use', 'historic use' or 'constitutional' water rights. The priority date for a water night established by this method is the date water was first put to beneficial use.

The second way to establish a right to surface water was to comply with the statutory method in effect when the water night was established. The current statutory method is an application/permit/ license procedure. The priority date for a water night established by this method is the date of filing the application with IDWR, and this priority date is shown on the license is issued when the process is complete.

As of May 20, 1971, there is only one way to establish a right to and that is by application/ permit/ license. The one exception to this rule is for water rights used solely for in-stream watering of domestic livestock.

Ground Water: Prior to March 25, 1963, there were two ways to establish rights to ground water, which are the methods described above. Since then there is only one way to establish a right to groundwater, by the application/permit/license procedure.

There is one exception: A "beneficial use" right to ground water may still be established for domestic purposes.

Can a water right be changed? The point of diversion, place of use, period of use or nature of use of a water right may be changed so long as the change does not result in injury to the rights of other appropriators. However, after May 26,1969, any person wishing to make a change in use of the water right must file an application with IDWR for approval of the change. IDWR may approve the proposed change if it will not result in injury to the rights of other water users; does not constitute an enlargement of the original water right; and is in the local public interest.

How do I get a water right? If you wish to establish a new water right, then there are certain procedures you will need to follow.

First, an application for a permit must be filed with IDWR, which is required to publish notice of the application. Other persons may file protests to the application with IDWR; if that happens, IDWR must hold a hearing. IDWR must then review the application (including any hearing record), and if the application meets the legal requirements, a permit is issued. The permit describes the appropriation to be made and the deadline within which the appropriation must be completed.

Prior to the end of the period in which the appropriation must be completed, IDWR sends the permit holder a notice that the deadline is approaching and that the permit holder must submit proof of beneficial use. "Proof of beneficial use" is a form sent to the permit holder by IDWR, that the permit holder fills out and returns to IDWR. In the proof form, the permit holder states that he has completed his appropriation.

After filing the proof form, a field examination must be made. The purpose of the field examination is to insure that water is in fact being used as described in the permit. If so, then IDWR issues a license that describes the appropriation that has been completed.

What is a claim? There are two different types of filings that are often called "claims." The first is a "statutory claim" filed with IDWR to make a record of an existing beneficial use right. In 1978, a statute was enacted requiring persons with beneficial use rights (other than water rights used solely for domestic purposes as defined above) to record their water rights with IDWR. The purpose of the statute was to provide some means to make records of water rights for which there were previously no records. However, these records are merely affidavits of the water users.

The other type of claim is a "notice of claim" filed with IDWR in water rights adjudications. An adjudication is a court action for the determination of existing water rights, which results in a decree that confirms and defines each water right.

When an adjudication of a particular source is commenced, IDWR is required to notify the water users of the commencement of the adjudication, and notify the water users that they are required to file notices of claims for their water rights with IDWR. IDWR then investigates the notices of claims and prepares a report that is filed with the court. Claimants of water rights are notified of the filing of the report, and objections to the report may be filed with the court by anyone who disagrees with it. If no objection is filed, then the court decrees the water right as described in the report. If an objection is filed to a water right described in the report, then the court determines the water right after a hearing and decrees the water right. A general adjudication of the Snake River Basin in Idaho is currently ongoing.

Other water "rights": Some rights to receive water are not an appropriation. For example, some persons have the right to receive water that is represented by shares in a ditch company; here, the ditch company has the appropriation, and the water users have a right to receive water from the ditch company. People who receive water from a city, an irrigation district, or a water utility company, again, may have a right to receive water from the city, district, or utility (usually on payment of a fee), but they do not have an actual appropriation.

Water rights: Some tricky questions in the SRBA

FORM AND CONTENT OF DECREES (2/14/94) When the SRBA Court issues its water right decrees, what should those decrees look like, and what should be included on them? That apparently ministerial but highly practical matter is headed toward resolution in the next couple of months, and the first deadline toward its resolution passed January 11 when just two proposals for former and content of decrees were submitted to the SRBA Court.

Those proposals came from the state of Idaho (prepared in substantial part by Deputy Attorney General David Barber) and from the United States (submitted by Department of justice attorneys including Peter Monson, Leif Johnson, Jack Haugrud and Daria Zane). Both were submitted just before the deadline.

The federal proposal noted that the decrees originally were expected to look much like the forms in the "director's reports" (the details of water rights as ascertained by the director of Department of Water Resources, which already have been underway). But in December 1993 Judge Hurlbutt asked whether a water right decree ought to include remarks, or extra information, about a given water right.

State officials said they were concerned about the information being such that they can maintain it all on their existing computer databases. The U.S. attorneys said that "with one notable exception, the United States believe that the format used in the director's report for recommendations can be used for the decree of state-based rights. The exception is the 'remarks' section currently found in the recommendations." The remarks could be narrowed, they suggested, to include only information necessary to identify the right, rather than including as well data that is simply explanatory. ⊠

MISSING UNCONTESTED ELEMENTS (5/22/95) The SRBA Court also has concerns about other water rights elements: the annual volume of consumptive use. The absence of these figures could slow down resolution of many of the 12,484 uncontested subcases now before the court. Some 11,284 of these are considered incomplete by court officials, because the annual volume of consumptive use (listed as an element of a water right in Idaho Code 42-1411) was not included. The absence was discovered by an SRBA Court official in the process of preparing partial decrees.

At his May 16 status conference, Judge Hurlbutt asked, "Can this court enter that (decree) absent that element?" And he asked if this might turn into a basin wide issue. ☒

RIGHTS AND ENTITLEMENTS (9/96) A special master decision issued August 28 cuts to the heart of what constitutes a water right in Idaho. The decision, by Master Fritz Haemmerle, led to immediate talk of appeal – possibly to the Supreme Court. The dispute grew out of review of subcases in Basin 57 (part of Owyhee County) covered by a 1932 decree, *New International Mortgage Bank v. Idaho Power Co.* That case decided water rights in an area, but did not include in the decrees questions of consumptive use, period of use and the amount of irrigated acreage involved.

In making SRBA recommendations, the IDWR suggested reducing elements of some claims. Claimants had said they thought this was because of the concept of "partial forfeiture," or reduction in right because of reduced use; but on April 26 the SRBA Court said partial forfeiture was not (yet) a legal doctrine in Idaho law. The IDWR then tried to apply the idea of reduced beneficial use in defining the rights.

So Haemmerle said the issues concerned "whether elements of a previously decreed water right may be reduced based on beneficial use where there is no evidence of forfeiture, abandonment, adverse possession or estoppel." Haemmerle said the rights could not be reduced for any of those reasons. He noted that "the state and claimants disagree as to whether a change in beneficial use or better evidence of beneficial use, by itself, is a basis to reduce an established or vested water right. The most widely accepted rule is that once a water right is vested, the user may use some or all of the water within the appropriation."

It caused an immediate uproar. Officials in the Department of Water Resources were busy in the latter part of the month evaluating the decision to see if it may (if upheld) mean changes in the way the department recommends water rights. ☒

WHAT IS A WATER RIGHT: LEASE OR PROPERTY? (11/96) An angry and dramatic confrontation in SRBA Court October 15 led to a pronouncement from Judge Hurlbutt that neither party expected: An informal conclusion that the nature of a water right in Idaho may be at stake.

Along the way, Twin Falls attorney Patrick Brown sought sanctions against Deputy Attorney General Cheri Copsey. That request was denied.

The debate started with a request by the state of Idaho for a stay on actions relating to Basin Wide Issue 10, in light of a special master's ruling that relates to it. "It doesn't stop the sub-cases from going forward," Copsey said. But she said that if the SRBA Court is overturned on Basin Wide Issue 10, the state would try to reopen a number of SRBA subcases. In BW 10, Hurlbutt ruled that current Idaho law does not allow for "partial forfeitures" of water rights. That decision has been appealed.

Brown said that, in requesting the stay, Copsey had failed to make "reasonable inquiry" into the matter, and that Issue 10 questions did not impact any of the subcases at issue – and even that Department of Water

Resources personnel had indicated as much. "The [request for] stay is based on nothing more than misrepresentations of fact ...I think that what this is about for my clients is more obfuscation than enlightenment."

Hurlbutt gave neither side what they wanted: he denied the state its stay, and denied Brown (and the Hagerman Water Rights Owners he represents) their sanction. But his concluding remarks carried import far beyond those issues. In rejecting the stay, he said that "the concern of the state is a little difficult for me to understand" – that the parties involved should be the movers for a stay, if anyone is. But he went on to say that the state's raising the issue of partial forfeiture prompts other important issues if the Department of Water Resources has based its recommendations on "reasonable beneficial use" and not on partial forfeiture.

He blasted the state: "Unlike the state, this court starts with the constitution."

Hurlbutt said that he sees water rights as actual property rights, use of which can be limited in only certain ways. The implications of the state's position on "reasonable beneficial use," he said, is that water rights actually are like a license, which can be amended unilaterally by the state any time, in any way.

If the Supreme Court takes the latter view, he said, there would be no finality to any water right decree since it could be endlessly amended; and little consequent point to the SRBA itself. That basic point, he said, has been widely misunderstood and many parties in the SRBA "have been like they are passing in the night."

Parties in the case later petitioned to have Judge Hurlbutt's comments included in the documentation before the Supreme Court on the Basin Wide 10 appeal. "In some respects," they wrote, "life would be simpler if the District Court's effort to eliminate the uncertainty and complexity inherent in the forfeiture statute were achieved by limiting its application to the most egregious cases in which no part of the water right has been exercised. Then people could be issued water rights fixed in quantity and certain in duration . . . [But] were it implemented the increased certainty and value placed in the hands of holders of under-utilized senior paper water rights would come at the expense of efficient, junior appropriators who have invested millions in reliance on current stream and aquifer conditions . . ." ☒

PROOF OF OWNERSHIP (6/97) Again the question of ownership of a water right was raised and not fully answered. IDWR Adjudication Chief David Tuthill brought up the point, which had been discussed in April, at the May 20 SRBA information session in Twin Falls. He noted that water rights in the director's reports – the starting point for SRBA water right subcases – are in the name of whoever claimed them. That might not be the same as whoever owns the property to which the right is attached, so Tuthill asked: "What is to happen if we discover that the property is actually in the name of husband/wife?"

Hurlbutt in April raised the question of whether decrees would suffer from inaccuracies under these conditions, and returned to the subject in May. "I can't make a finding of ownership on that [basis], can I? Can I?" he asked. "So we're not decreeing ownership in this case?"

Attorney James Tucker, of Rosholt, Robertson & Tucker, asked, "Am I to understand that a decreed water right will not reflect ownership?"

Tuthill indicated that conditions will vary in subcases. Although he said that a water right can be an attribute of a piece of property, he said that the department has checked into ownership mainly in contested cases; where two parties each claim a right, the department will side with the property owner.

But those cases involving only one claimant for a right generally aren't pursued. To which Hurlbutt asked: "Is this a riparian [doctrine] state or a prior appropriation state?", referring to the two main approaches in water rights. (Most western states, including Idaho, use prior appropriation.) "I'm serious. I'm really troubled by this."

IDWR attorney Peter Anderson: "We're certainly willing to look at these issues."

But Tuthill warned: "I can tell you that as a practical matter, that [determination of property rights] would greatly change the cost of the adjudication." Not only would the cost of property determination run to $25 or more per parcel, but even that would only yield "a moving target" since property is bought and sold regularly. ☒

DIVERSION FROM OUT OF STATE (2/98) Roughly every other month, some new issue arises in the SRBA that, though simple on its surface, didn't occur to the major players before. The latest: Water diverted from a stream out of Idaho, but used inside the state. At least a few cases do exist, notably some 55 cases along the Wyoming border.

In a November 26 letter to Tony Olenichak, deputy water master in Water District 1 (Idaho Falls), Judge Daniel Hurlbutt said (in response to an inquiry) that the SRBA court had not issued an order or opinion on the subject. "While I cannot guess whether any claimants in the SRBA would challenge the jurisdiction of the SRBA Court to decree those 55 previously decreed rights, it is inconceivable to me that those people holding decreed water rights could be denied the right to file claims in the SRBA. Of course, by filing claims in the SRBA, I make no comment or decision about whether they can or will be decreed by the SRBA Court."

Later, however, the Department of Water Resources did weigh in with an opinion: Like Hurlbutt, Director Karl Dreher said the claims would be accepted for filing (provided the paperwork is donee and filing fee paid). ☒

MULTIPLE STREAMS, MULTIPLE FEES? (8/98) Stockwater rights have been considered among the simplest of water rights to resolve in the SRBA. But, as Twin Falls area rancher Bill Brockman suggested at an SRBA information meeting in July, they're not all simple. What to do, for example, about livestock wandering over a region, from stream to stream? Must the owner of cattle – the owner of the stockwater right –file separately on each stream accessed, a separate $25 filing fee on each one?

Idaho Department of Water Resources Adjudication Administrator David Tuthill said that in considering whether more than one stream can be included in a single water right, the department has generally come up with the answer: Yes. But in-stream flows are difficult to handle this way, he said. The question seems not quite resolved.

EDITOR'S NOTE: The IDWR, at least, has reached a resolution on this. It is noted in Adjudication Memo #12 (August 17, 1988) drafted by then-IDWR attorney Lynne Krogh-Hampe. She wrote: "The Adjudication Rules permit more than one source to be claimed if the claim is for a single water delivery system that has more than one source, in other words, if more than one source was developed as part of the same project, or the claim is for a single licensed or decreed right that covers more than one water delivery system. More than one source may also be claimed where the claimant developed an additional point of diversion after the water right was initiated. (An example is where a person is using water from an artesian spring, but the flow of the spring decreased, and the water user later dropped a well near the spring to be able to continue to get the full amount of the appropriation.) Note however that that where the additional point of diversion is used for additional uses, to irrigate additional acres, or to divert additional water than was originally appropriated, then there has been an expansion and there may be a second water right for the additional use, irrigation or diversion." ☒

INHERITANCE AND SPLIT RIGHTS (9/98) Inherited water rights, potentially among the most difficult and complex subjects for the SRBA, have arisen only seldom so far. But the Idaho Supreme Court on August 19 resolved several questions, in *Norman Riley v. Catherine Rowan*. It also upheld SRBA Judge Daniel Hurlbutt's decision in the subcase.

The case arose outside of the three "test basins" in the SRBA, where most legal issues have arisen so far. Its roots run back more than half a century.

It begins in 1944 when Lucille Howe was deeded a life estate in 756.5 acres of Madison County farm land. Remainder interests in that land were given to her two children, James Howe and Catherine Rowan. For decades after that, James Howe leased and farmed all of that land, both the portion in which he had an interest, and the part where his sister did. In 1978, the Department of Water Resources gave to "Lucille W. Howe and/or Jim Howe" a water right permit for developing a well on the southern part of the tract. Jim Howe built the well and filed a notice of completed development.

After Lucille Howe died in 1983, the land passed to James Howe and Catherine Rowan. Five years later, the brother and sister agreed to split the land: James Howe was deeded the northern half, and Catherine Rowan the southern half of the property. Jim Howe continued to farm both his half of the property and (under a lease agreement) Catherine Rowan's. They later agreed Howe would get a half-interest in the water from the south well, plus an easement to maintain delivery from the south well to his north land. In 1991, Howe sold his water rights, including those associated with the Rowan well, to his daughter, Robin Riley, and her husband Norman.

Howe died in 1992. In settling his estate, the Rileys filed a notice of change of water right ownership with the Department of Water Resources, saying water permit No. 22-07280 had been split. The IDWR agreed, and split the water permit into 22-07280A and 22-07280B (giving 4.270 cfs. to the Rileys, 6.540 cfs. to Rowan).

In December 1995, the Department issued a water right license in the name of Lucille Howe and Jim Howe, both by then deceased. On August 16, 1993, Rowan filed a declaratory judgment action against the Rileys, asking the court to decide the parties' rights and obligations connected to the ownership of the south well, the responsibility for certain debt, and the ownership of water right No. 22-07280.

Hurlbutt awarded the Rileys and Rowan half interest each in water license No. 22-07280. The Rileys appealed. But the Supreme Court concluded that James Howe had acquired no interest in the water permit until after Lucille Howe's death, and that his only interest in the permit was the one-half interest obtained following Lucille Howe's death and the partition of the property. Since Jim Howe could transfer to the Rileys no more than he owned, the Rileys and Rowan were each entitled to a one-half interest in the water license resulting from the permit. As for the naming of the water right by the Department of Water Resources, the Court said, "Regardless of when the IDWR issued the license, Jim Howe and Rowan each owned a one-half interest prior to Jim Howe subsequently selling his interest to the Rileys." ☒

INTERSTATE RELATIONS (5/2000) IDWR Adjudication Chief David Tuthill said at the April 27 information meeting that his agency is drafting prospective agreements with Idaho's neighboring states covering water that flows across state boundaries, and is claimed by users under state water law.

Tuthill said that he held a teleconference in April with water officials in Wyoming, Utah, Nevada and Oregon. As a result, he said, his staff is researching whether the state of Idaho could draft and execute a simple memorandum of understanding with the other states, rather than go through the more cumbersome compact process. "It's a little tricky, because these issues are not under compact," he said. ☒

60-DAY OBJECTION PERIOD (6/2001) The time for people who want to object to a water right recommendation is set in state law at 120 days, except that the presiding adjudication judge can lower it to 60 days.

SRBA judges have routinely done just that in recent years, holding that more time has almost never been needed.

"This 120-day period is kind of a relic of the earlier statute," IDWR Adjudication Chief David Tuthill said. He suggested the court issue a "global" order covering all subcases, reducing the comment period.

Judge Burdick quipped, "As fast as the courts work, couldn't you go to the courts quicker?" ☒

REVIEWING FOR QUANTITY (1/2002) One of the concerns in the SRBA is that the mass of water rights in the case be handled once and not revisited on frequent occasions – but people involved in the case have indicated some such instances are bound to happen. One arose in December, with a motion to set aside a partial decree so the water amount diverted could be increased.

"This is a perplexing procedural case," remarked SRBA Judge Roger Burdick, as a tangle of actions in the partial decree 72-10033 for Robin Wegner was laid out.

An original claim by Wegner was objected to by the Bureau of Land Management; after a settlement, former SRBA Judge Barry Wood in February 2000 issued a partial decree in the case.

Since then, evidence was found indicating that Wegner should receive a larger diversion. The BLM did not object, and on December 18 Burdick agreed to set aside the old partial decree.

That starts much of the partial decree process over again.

Court staffers said that several partial decrees in the SRBA have been set aside for technical or reasons of error, but this was the first they could recall that was set aside because of a matter of substance relating to the claim. ☒

SUPREME COURT ON TIMELINESS (2/2002) On January 18, the Supreme Court found that North Snake Ground Water District did not submit in a timely way an objection or response in a contested water right subcase.

Bradley and Linda Gay Gisler submitted an SRBA water claim in 1988. The Idaho Department of Water Resources' Director's Report recommended an amount less than that claimed by the Gislers.

In 1993, the Gislers filed the sole objection to the Director's Report. IDWR and the Gislers ultimately resolved the dispute in October 1997, and a Special Master's Report and Recommendation was issued recommending the rights they had stipulated.

On November 28, 1997, the North Snake Ground Water District filed a motion to alter or amend, claiming that the amount of water decreed was based on gravity/flood irrigation, although the Gislers were currently using sprinkler irrigation. NSGWD requested a remand to the special master for the presentation of additional evidence on the matter or in the alternative, provided qualifying language it wanted added to the decree. The special master denied NSGWD's motion and rejected the addition of the qualifying language. The district court upheld the special master's decision, finding that NSGWD did not timely file an objection or response in the subcase.

It also said the SRBA court was not the proper venue to challenge the policies used by IDWR.

Before the Supreme Court, NSGWD argued that the district court erred when it decreed the Gislers' water right, questioning the sprinkler/flood irrigation policies used by IDWR. It also appealed the district court's decision not to incorporate the proposed qualifying language into the decree. The Supreme Court rejected those arguments. *– adapted from Supreme Court documents* ☒

REST STOP CLAIM (12/2005) Motions to file late claims are common in monthly court status actions, but one in November was unusual for the claimant and the use.

The Idaho Transportation Department was seeking permission to use water for a highway rest stop, in central Idaho near the Salmon River.

The late claims for water right 72-04059 covers only a small run of water, .05 cfs. The land covered by the stop had been owned by a school district which had held it since 1981. The district transferred the property to the state, but no notice of water right claim was filed at the time.

This is not the first rest stop water right claim. Like most others, it has been considered a small claim. The late filing was approved.

LATE OBJECTIONS (6/2006) A battle over water claims between the federal government and several ranchers in the Cassia County area may be moving in the ranchers' direction, as in May they won a master's approval to lodge late objections in a string of subcases.

The Basin 45 cases involve 48 claims which were recommended in March 1998 by the Idaho Department of Water Resources in favor of the Forest Service. They were recommended "each for .02 cfs from various creeks, springs and ponds for stockwater use in Cassia County from May 1 to November 30, with a priority date of May 1, 1879, based on beneficial use."

The first objection, filed 10 days after the deadline, came from rancher Scott Bedke, who argued "The USFS/BLM should not be allowed to use a priority date that predates the organization of the Forest Service (1898 Organic Act) and BLM (1931 Taylor Grazing Act). They are not the successors in interest of these grazing allotments. The USFS/BLM do not own the livestock and therefore can not put the water to beneficial use as per Idaho water law."

The federal government countered, according to court records, that "1) the movants received sufficient notice of the proceeding; 2) since there is no evidence of equitable tolling, the objections are timebarred; 3) the *Motions* are untimely; and 4) the movants failed to allege facts showing a meritorious position and/or sufficient grounds for relief."

In January 2005 a special master denied the motion to file the objection. But in a similar case, Judge John Melanson reversed the master on a range of issues. The federal government argued that case and the current Bedkes case were different, but Master Terrence Dolan held they were insufficient. ☒

Moving and Splitting Water Rights

MOVING AND SPLITTING (3/1/93) The Idaho Department of Water Resources moved that a standardized form be used for parties who move from the location of their water rights, or sell their property. Clive Strong of the Attorney General's office noted that property is sometimes divided on sale, so the water right is divided also. On Feb. 25, Judge Hurlbutt said he will issue SRBA Administrative Order 3, to provide a standard form for notice of change in address or motion for substitute of party.

Filings of claims related to property sales are frequent. Statistically, Shaw said, property in Idaho tends to change hands every seven years. Judge Hurlbutt said "It's something we've got to confront procedurally as well as substantively." Sales of land or cars, he noted, are recorded in government offices, but "there's no standard certificate of title reflecting the water right, no single registry of all water rights so we see that rights are sold or transferred in all kinds of different ways." ☒

WHOSE RIGHT IS IT? (5/1997) At the April 15 information meeting, Tuthill pointed out a potential glitch department SRBA staffers have begun to consider. Usually, he said, the water right description which is used as the starting point for subcase activity is listed in the name of the person making the claim. But what happens, he asked, if it turns out the person who owns the property where the right is situated is not the same as the claimant? In some cases, he said, the claimant may be the husband but the land is owned by a husband and wife. Or divorce, inheritance or other family situations could make the situation far more complex; bankruptcies can muddy the waters; and in some cases, right claims were made by lessees of land, rather than land owners.

The point dropped like a small bombshell in the room. Hurlbutt, clearly taken aback, was evidently angry. "Well, we've always talked about accurate decrees. Why is this coming up 10 years after the case was filed?" he said. "Where are all my accuracy fans now ...What am I supposed to decree?"

Special Master Terry Dolan, who worked in adjudications in Wyoming before starting in the SRBA, said he's long held a clear view on the subject: the water right and the property ownership have to go together, and the names on each should match.

But Tuthill said that his agency didn't try to check on property ownership when water right claims were pouring in; from the IDWR perspective, only a "contact name" for each claim was really needed at the time.

"No question, it would be a huge project to do it right," Hurlbutt said. "[But] in fact, we're doing it inaccurately in a lot of cases." ☒

BIG MOVE (11/2004) The Idaho Department of Water Resources has completed its move from its headquarters at Orchard Street in Boise to the new Idaho Water Center at Broadway and Front Street near downtown Boise. As a result of the move, the department will participate in the Water Center with the University of Idaho, the Idaho Water Resources Research Institute and the U.S. Forest Service.

The new address will be 322 East Front Street, P.O. Box 83720, Boise ID 83720-0098. Mail will only be delivered, however, through the post office box, not directly to the building.

The new main phone number will be (208) 287-4800, and the adjudication main number will be (208) 287-4910. ☒

ORGANIZATIONAL STRUCTURE [*some of the material in this section is adapted from Department of Water Resources documents*] The Idaho Department of Water Resources is headed by a director appointed by the governor. The agency is divided into three operating divisions, each headed by an administrator. Each division has bureaus or teams organized around specific areas of responsibility.

• March 9, 1895 – Legislature creates Office of State Engineer. State Engineers:

Frederick J. Mills, Pocatello - 1895-1899
D. W. Ross, Boise - 1899-1903
Wayne Darlington, Mackay - 1903-1904
Jas. Stephenson, Jr., Boise - 1904-1908
D.G. Martin, Idaho Falls - 1908-1910
A.E. Robinson, Wallace - 1911-1912
Frank King, Boise - 1913-1914
J.H. Smith, Pocatello - 1915-1916
Fred A. Wilkie, Ashton - 1917-1918

• 1919 – The engineer's office becomes the Department of Reclamation, and the agency head the Commissioner of Reclamation:

W.G. Swendsen, Boise - 1919-1925
George N. Carter, Jerome - 1925-1930
R. W. Faris, Boise - 1931-1938
James Spofford, Mountain Home - 1939-1940
E.V. Berg, Idaho Falls - 1941-1942

• 1943 – Agency name changes again, to State Reclamation Engineer.

James Spofford, Mtn Home - 1943-1944
Mark R. Kulp, Moscow - 1944-1958
George N. Carter, Boise - 1958-1963
Carl Tappan, Boise - 1963-1966
R. Keith Higginson, Boise - 1967-1970

• 1965 – After voter approval of a constitutional amendment in 1964, the Idaho Water Resource Board was established by the Legislature for state water planning.

• 1970 – The agency goes through another change of name. This time, the agency is given a new name and becomes the Department of Water Administration.

R. Keith Higginson, Boise - 1971-1974

• 1974 – The Department of Water Administration and the Idaho Water Resource Board are combined to form a new agency called the Idaho Department of Water Resources, which it has remained since. The Water Resource Board becomes an eight-member body whose members are appointed by the governor.

R. Keith Higginson, Boise - 1974-1977	C. Stephen Allred, Boise - 1977-1981
A. Kenneth Dunn, Boise - 1981-1987	R. Keith Higginson, Boise - 1987-1995
Karl J. Dreher, Denver - 1995-2006	David Tuthill, Boise – 2007-present

WATER RESOURCE BOARD The Idaho Water Resource Board was created by the Idaho Legislature in 1965 following passage the year before of a constitutional amendment which established the Board. There are eight Board members, appointed by the governor, who serve four-year terms. The Board is provided for in Idaho's constitution to formulate and implement a state water plan. The Board initially was a separate agency with its own staff.

There are specifically mandated Board functions and responsibilities within IDWR. The Department provides administrative and staff support to the Board. The Board and IDWR are also interrelated in areas such as appeals, administrative rules adoption, water supply bank administration and water right negotiations with the Federal government and Indian Tribes. Board programs are divided into three general categories: comprehensive state water planning, water management activities and financial programs.

The Idaho Water Resource Board manages the operation of Idaho's Water Supply Bank. The purposes of the Bank are: to encourage the highest beneficial use of water; provide a source of adequate water supplies to benefit new and supplemental water uses; and provide a source of funding for improving water user facilities and efficiencies.

WATER BANK In its most simplistic sense, the Water Supply Bank is a water exchange market operated by the Board to assist marketing of water rights to natural flow water or water stored in Idaho reservoirs.

Using the Bank, water users who in any given year have rights to more water than they require can put the excess stored water or natural flow rights that will not be used in the Bank from which it can be sold or leased to people who do not have enough to meet their needs. This system helps make excess water available to other users for such things as irrigation or other authorized uses. Water Bank water also has proven valuable by providing stored water for downstream salmon recovery efforts. This Water Bank approach helps put the maximum amount of water to beneficial use.

Water in the Bank involves two distinct categories of water:

• **Natural flow water**. This generally involves rights to surface water diverted from a river, stream or groundwater. The Board directly controls the sale or rental of water covered under natural flow water rights.

• **Stored water** (in "rental pools" in reservoirs). There are currently four rental pools operated by local committees in Idaho. They involve water from the Snake River upstream from Milner Dam near Burley (including a separate bank operated by the Sho-Ban Tribes), the Boise River and the Payette River. The rental pool committees set the price, which the Board must approve, for which water can be rented or sold from their rental pool. This price is different for each rental pool and can be determined by where the water is to be used. For example, in 1997 the Upper Snake rental pool charges $2.95 per acre foot for stored water used above Milner Dam and $10.50 per acre foot for water used downstream from Milner Dam.

The Board receives a fee of 10% of the gross amount for the water sold or rented through the Bank. This fee first pays the administrative costs of administering the Water Bank with the remainder going to the Board's financial loans and grants program where it is used to help finance water projects around the state.

The Department and the SRBA

INTERROGATORIES (4/12/1993) A one-hour session turned into a hard-fought all-day session at the SRBA Courthouse on April 7, when the Hagerman Water Rights Owners asked the Idaho Department of Water Resources to supply information. A lot of information. It will take some doing. The April 7 round left some participants on both sides exasperated. The Hagerman group, through attorney Patrick Brown, filed an extensive request for information with the Department of Water Resources. Brown said the information is necessary in preparation of their case.

The Department said those requests were overly broad and vague, and could amount to a request for most papers in the department's possession, and beyond. "We said, we'll get you the information, and if you need it documented for trial basis, we'll get you that later," said attorney Lynne Krogh-Hampe of the IDWR. The Department argued that specific document discoveries should be delayed until after objections and responses are filed; until that point, officials said, there's no certain way to know what is relevant and what isn't.

But Judge Hurlbutt ruled the Hagerman request is not premature. ☒

COMMUNICATIONS BAN (5/16/1994) Judge Hurlbutt issued in writing on May 5 an order he had announced at the April 25 status conference: banning communication between the Department of Water Resources and claimants in the SRBA. The ban keeps the director of IDWR and "its agents and employees" from contact with any party to the SRBA about the case, including settlement discussions. The department was also banned from any further investigation of water rights in the three test basin areas.

Those points, also referred to in court action, drew a May 4 letter from IDWR Director Keith Higginson, who said that "a question has arisen that has substantial impact on the function of adjudication staff during the operation of the order."

He noted that "IDWR staff are limited to conducting field examination of most claims during the 'field season', when water is available and is in use. For this reason, adjudication agents concentrate on the investigation of the claims and the preparation of recommendations following field season. The field season is currently underway, and in some areas where claims are currently under investigation, the period of time water is available, and water use can be field examines, is very short." And, he noted, such inquiries usually need the presence of the water right holder. "I am greatly concerned because, if these and other similar types of communications are deemed prohibited negotiations, IDWR will effectively be precluded from proceeding with its statutory duty to investigate claims and prepare director's reports."

For now, Higginson said, IDWR staff has been told not to proceed with the work. ☒

● **(5/30/94)** The SRBA Court order banning some communications by the IDWR has been interpreted too broadly, Judge Hurlbutt said at the May 17 status conference. So he clarified his intent there and in a followup written description. And Director Keith Higginson followed up with a memo to his employees and watermasters on communications that are allowed, and those that are not. It says:

• "…the order is not intended to prevent communications that are necessary or appropriate for the purposes of IDWR's statutory duties outside the SRBA, even when the matters discussed may be relevant to the SRBA. IDWR's other statutory duties include, for example: water distribution, including communications by and with waster masters, and promulgation and implementation of water distribution rules; administrative proceedings on water rights, such as transfers, permits, licenses, etc.; other programs of water allocation and resource protection bureaus, such as stream channel alteration, dam safety, etc.; data collection and other data management activities of the technical services bureau."

• "Particular care must be exercised regarding communications with the Water Resource Board concerning any of the Board's or other parties' SRBA claims or the SRBA."

• "The Board is also designated as the state's negotiator for federal water right negotiations with the United States and the Indian Tribes. Communications with the Board relative to federal water right negotiations must be limited to responses to requests from the Board for public record information at this time. IDWR employees may communicate with the Board regarding to the Board's other statutory duties . . ."

Hurlbutt's view, though, was that his order was much too broadly interpreted. "I think there has been some overreaction," he said. "It's extraordinary the order be read that widely …I feel the order has been abused, quite frankly." He said that "any fair reading of the order would not dispossess the department of its statutory obligations." Suggestions he had heard that it might result in virtually shutting down the department are "not fair, not fair at all." ☒

STAY OUT OF LEGAL ARGUMENT (9/26/1994) To extrapolate (slightly) from a decision on September 20 by SRBA Judge Hurlbutt: the Idaho Department of Water Resources, under legislation passed by the 1994 Legislature, has no place in the legal arguments being made in the SRBA.

He that day refused to accept a 100-plus page report by the Department (and, on its request, by University of Idaho Professor Dennis Colson) on constitutionality of the 1994 legislation, which is the subject of the current Basin Wide Issue 3.

After hearing attorney Jeffrey Fereday suggest that he might submit Colson's report as part of his brief on the issue, Hurlbutt then blocked "the submission of, reference to or the use of any portion" of the IDWR materials.

Hurlbutt said that he hadn't read the department's submission, and won't.

The IDWR materials argued that the 1994 legislation was constitutional.

On hearing of it, three parties in the SRBA – the Hagerman Water Right Owners (represented by attorney Patrick Brown), the Big Lost Irrigation District (represented by attorney William Hollifield) and the federal government, through the Department of Justice – immediately objected to its use.

"The Department, by filing its submission, has directly violated this Court's orders," Brown said at the September 20 status conference. He noted that the current law (which is under dispute) defines the department's role in the case as that of a technical expert, and not a party in the case. The department has no interest, and no standing, on the issue, Brown said; but by submitting its report, the IDWR has helped some parties (those backing the statutes) and harmed others (such as his clients). Brown even sought financial damages (which the court did not approve) from the department to compensate his clients and other parties.

IDWR attorney Lynn Krogh offered a spirited rebuttal. "The parties have mis-characterized the orders," she said: Nothing in them restricts communication between the Department and the Court, provided due notice is given to parties in the case. The submission on Basin Wide 3 was a communication with the court, and notice was given to the parties.

Beyond that, she said, "It's common practice to submit an *amicus curiae* brief with other motions," and the Department followed procedures for appearing as an *amicus* (friend of the court). She said that the report submitted constituted neither evidence nor testimony, but was instead reference material, much like a law review article. The court, she said, was entitled to consult any material it chose in making a decision, and this material was simply being made available to the court. And, she said, "if we continue to obsess about what convenient label" to place on the Department, the Adjudication could well go on forever.

Asked by Hurlbutt whether the Department's position differed from that of the state's (presented by Deputy Attorney General Clive Strong), she said, pointedly, that "I've not been allowed to talk to Mr. Strong."

Krogh did get some support from attorney Fereday, who asked "What really is the problem? Too much good information? Too much legal argument?"

But Hurlbutt said he had concluded that the report was not part of the Department's responsibility "of an independent expert or technical assistant" since it did not relate directly to the claims. It was a departure from the Department's proper role, and therefore should not be considered, he said.

Hurlbutt did not have any comment about a brief filed with the court that same day (September 20) by attorney Scott Campbell, which includes discussion about Colson's report. Campbell said that he generally agreed with Colson's analysis that the statutes are constitutional, and makes references to that report. ☒

A PARTY FOR DISCOVERY (1/23/1995) The Department of Water Resources and its director will be treated as a party to the SRBA, and not as a witness or technical expert, for purposes of "discovery" – being required to provide information and answers – Judge Hurlbutt ruled January 17. The Idaho Legislature's 1994 SRBA laws said the director of the Department of Water Resources was no longer a party in the adjudication but a technical advisor instead. Judge Hurlbutt's December 7 ruling on Basin Wide Issues 2 and 3 reversed that, keeping the director — Keith Higginson — a party.

The state said, however, that the legal standard to be used in case of discovery should be that of a witness. In a memorandum from the attorney general's office, attorney Clive Strong argued that "to the extent discovery is necessary against the Director of IDWR, it should be limited to the method and scope of discovery that is available for non-party witnesses." ☒

DREHER NAMED DIRECTOR (4/17/1995) Karl Dreher, 46, the head of engineering for the Northern Colorado Water Conservancy District, will take over as director of the Idaho Department of Water Resources on June 1.

Keith Higginson, director since January 1987 and in that position for more than a decade in previous terms, is scheduled to retire at the end of May.

Dreher has extensive background with the U.S. Bureau of Reclamation in dam-building, and with water rights and resources developments in the fast-growing and litigious Colorado Front area. Gov. Phil Batt, who made the appointment, said he "selected Karl because of his long history dealing with water rights law and litigation in a state very similar to Idaho. I am confident that he will bring a new relationship with the courts, while maintaining the statutes of long-established Idaho water law." The Department of Water Resources, and sometimes Higginson personally, have bumped heads with the SRBA court on a variety of issues.

Dreher: "the critical elements of sound policy at the Idaho Department of Water Resources are already in place because of the contributions of the current staff and director. I plan a fine-tuning to improve the overall balance and efficiency in the competition for Idaho's water."

The new director received a bachelor of science degree in 1971, and a master's in civil engineering in 1973, from Colorado State University. He worked for the Bureau of Reclamation office in Denver from 1975 to 1982, specializing in dam design, and from 1982 to 1986 was a consultant and senior structural engineer for Stone & Webster Engineering Corporation in Denver. (During that time, he directed evaluation of a 500-foot high concrete arch dam in China.)

Since then he has been head of engineering for the Conservancy District, which includes much of the Front Range north of Denver. Dreher has been involved in with three major water rights litigations: One involving conditional water rights his district holds but challenged by a Denver suburb; a second in which that Denver suburb had purchased a block of land with the intent of transferring consumptive uses of water to municipal uses.

Colorado water policies, while driven by many of the same arid-state concerns as Idahoans, do have some significant differences. Water marketing, for example, is a major component of water policies in Colorado, while a much smaller one (the Idaho water bank excepted) in Idaho. ☒

THE DEPARTMENT'S ROLE (2/1996) The Idaho Department of Water Resources was in 1994 removed by the Idaho Legislature as a party in the SRBA and was re-designated as an "expert" in the case. The Supreme Court upheld that action in a ruling last summer. Now the SRBA Court is working on the fine print: what role exactly do officials from the department play when actual specific water right cases are thrashed out in settlement conferences and in court.

The department's role – pre-1994 – originally was set forth in the SRBA Court's Administrative Order 9, which covers a range of proceedings on settlements. Possible revision of that order was the subject of a motion by U.S. Department of Justice attorney Daria Zane at the January 16 SRBA status conference. She broke out three issues:

• Does the Department sign off on settlement agreements before they are submitted to the court? As non-parties, Zane suggested, they shouldn't, although up to this point parties have submitted reports and documentation to IDWR when they have disagreed over a water right. A better approach, she suggested, is to treat the IDWR as an advisor to the court, but not otherwise take a direct role, or speak up unless questioned.

• Settlement conferences, by court order, are supposed to be closed-door sessions involving only court personnel and the parties involved; they are not open to the public. Nevertheless, IDWR is supposed to attend, Zane noted. Presumably, the rules might have to be changed to allow IDWR to be present, to avoid a conflict with other rules; but beyond that, what restrictions should be placed on IDWR personnel who attend settlement conferences?

• IDWR formerly was a party in the SRBA, which meant that it could (and sometimes did) advocate positions on matters before the court. What might that aspect of the past mean now, when department officials are not a party but are there simply, presumably, "to ensure the technical expertise they are out there to render. That's what it's limited to."

While Zane suggested that a number of issues related to the department's role are unresolved, state attorneys saw less of a gray area.

Matthew McKeown, a deputy attorney general (and not directly representing the department), said that the language of Hurlbutt's existing Order 9 answers some of the questions Zane posed. He said that, for example, it clearly binds to confidentiality all of the participants in a settlement conference. But he acknowledged the affirmative when Judge Daniel Hurlbutt asked him, "Isn't the role of the Department one that will evolve?" ☒

NEW AT ADJUDICATION (10/1996) David Tuthill, a long-time manager in the Idaho Department of Water Resources Western Region, was on September named the new bureau chief of the IDWR Adjudication Bureau.

Department Director Karl Dreher, who made the appointment, remarked that Tuthill "is a superb water resources engineer and manager who has repeatedly demonstrated an outstanding expertise in various aspects of water management. His services as adjudication bureau chief will be a powerful asset to the adjudication effort in Idaho."

He is not new to the job. Tuthill has been acting bureau chief since late June. The job was held before that, for many years, by David Shaw, who saw the SRBA through most of its early stages. Shaw departed in June to become a consultant on the SRBA and other matters with a private company.

The state adjudication office employs 45 people, and many of them are directly involved with reviewing claims in the SRBA. The agency has been under intense pressure in recent years as court actions have often directly impacted how it does its work, and as the Idaho Legislature has stepped up pressure to move ahead more speedily on the Adjudication. ☒

RULES STOP (8/1998) New statewide water management rules will not go into effect for another few months at least, to allow for additional refinements, Department of Water Resources Director Karl Dreher said in mid-November. He said the action followed ongoing disagreements between water users over elements of the proposed rules, and because of the need to integrate more science into the proposed rules. Dreher said he also was concerned that many water users and the public in general were not aware of the issues involved and the potential impact of the rules.

Certain elements of the proposed rules, particularly regarding how groundwater rights would be administered to prevent injury to senior surface and groundwater rights, have been divisive issues throughout the negotiated rulemaking process.

"Pursuing adoption of the rules at this time would prematurely bring the remaining disagreements before the Legislature and could divide and distract water interests at a time that other critical water issues in the region need to be addressed," Dreher noted in a letter to water users.

IDWR water managers will spend the next two months developing approaches to resolve the disagreements based on new hydrologic and geologic information, some of which only recently became available. The revised rules would then be circulated for additional public comment and review in late January.

In March 1999, IDWR plans to ask the governor for approval to adopt the new rules as "temporary rules" effective April 1, the start of the 1999 irrigation season. That will give IDWR a full irrigation season to test the rules before promulgating them as permanent rules.

IDWR held four public hearings on the rules earlier this month, only two of which were reasonably well attended. Three additional public information meetings were also held in October with limited attendance.

The rules, which would implement additional enforcement of water use around the state, have been under development for more than a year. The rules will establish how enforcement of water rights will be handled, how conflicts between water users will be resolved and other similar crucial water management issues, according to IDWR officials.

Another element addresses use of water rights for surface water when it is available prior to using ground water rights. The proposed rules also provide guidelines for measuring and reporting of water use. *– Adapted from Idaho Department of Water Resources materials* ☒

DREHER STAYS ON (1/1999) The appointment roster of the incoming Kempthorne gubernatorial administration was incomplete at press time, but the new governor has made clear one of the holdovers from the Batt Administration will be Department of Water Resources Director Karl Dreher.

Dreher, who had been a water administrator in Colorado, was appointed to the post by Gov. Phil Batt about four years ago. He has been credited with (among other things) smoothing relations between his agency and the Snake River Basin Adjudication Court. ☒

NEW ADJUDICATION CHIEF (12/2005) The first major shakeup in the Idaho Department of Water Resources adjudication section in this decade was set for early December, when longtime-Adjudication Bureau Chief David Tuthill takes over as administrator of the department's Water Management Division. The adjudication bureau is part of that division.

Don Shaff, supervisor of the Technical Support Section, will replace Tuthill as the adjudication chief. The changes, announced in November, were effective in early December. ☒

DREHER OUT AS DIRECTOR (12/2006) The November elections have brought one big, direct shock to the Idaho water resource community: Karl Dreher, director of the Idaho Department of Water Resources for about a decade, will not be retained in the position under the new administration of incoming Governor C.L. "Butch" Otter.

Dreher was scheduled to leave his job at the end of December.

In a release, Dreher said that he had been interested in staying on under Otter, but the new governor decided to make a change.

"I very much appreciate having the opportunity to serve in a significant role and move Idaho's challenging water resource issues towards resolution," he said in a prepared statement.

Directors of the Department of Water Resources serve unusually – for a fixed term of four years, but at the appointment of a governor with confirmation of the state Senate.

In the years since, the department's work in the SRBA has speeded, and its basic research and reporting work in the adjudication is nearly complete. It is just beginning its work on the northern Idaho adjudications.

Former state Senator Laird Noh, the long-time chair of the Senate Resources and Environment Committee, told the Twin Falls *Times News* that Dreher may have been the best water director Idaho has had. He added, "It's one of the most high-pressure jobs in the state, maybe in the nation. I have the utmost respect and admiration for Karl Dreher and the work he's done."

Dreher has also taken controversial stands, notably in the last three years.

Faced with conflicts between senior surface water users and ground water pumpers in southern Idaho, Dreher finally issued calls and made a series of management decisions praised in some quarters and damned in others. ☒

TUTHILL NAMED DIRECTOR (2/2007) After declining to retain Karl Dreher, director of that Idaho Department of Water Resources for more than a decade, in that position, Governor C.L. "Butch" Otter in early January promoted one of Dreher's key lieutenants – David Tuthill – to take over the agency on an interim basis.

Tuthill said he would apply for the job of director on a permanent basis. A search for applicants for a new director also was underway, but Tuthill was not discouraged from applying.

He took over as director shortly after the turn of the year, just after Dreher departed.

He is a figure familiar to anyone involved in the Snake River Basin Adjudication in recent years. Until last year, he was for about a decade head of the adjudication bureau, which most specifically managed the department's work in the SRBA. In that capacity, he regularly toured the state and delivered monthly presentations on the status of the adjudication.

Tuthill's education credentials include a B.S. in Agricultural Engineering, Colorado State University (1974), an M.S. in Civil Engineering, University of Colorado (1975) and a Ph.D. in Civil Engineering, University of Idaho (Boise, 2002). He retired in July 2-4 as a colonel in the U.S. Army Corps of Engineers.

He is an IDWR veteran, starting with the agency in 1976. He worked on the Payette River adjudication and in the department's western regional office before becoming chief of the adjudication bureau.

Last year he was promoted to administrator of the Water Management Division (which includes the adjudication bureau), reporting directly to Dreher. ☒

➲ *Later in the year Tuthill was named to the job on a permanent basis.*

Delivering and distributing water

The Idaho Department of Water Resources, as the state's administrative agency concerned with water rights, is responsible for ensuring that the rights of water right holders are protected. That fact has had major import in the SRBA, and most notably in what's come to be called "the Musser case."

SHUTTING DOWN THE AQUIFER (7/5/1993) A filing by the Hagerman Water Rights Owners on June 22 could, if approved, have the effect of banning use of the aquifer by nearly all of its users to the north and east of the Thousand Springs area.

The motion, filed by John Lezamiz of the Twin Falls law firm Hepworth, Nungester & Lezamiz, is on its face simple. It concerns property owned by Alvin and Tim Musser and leased by Howard "Butch" Morris as agricultural, irrigated crop land. (It is located in District 36.) The water rights have a priority date of 1892.

The water source for the land is a spring which in turn gets its water from the Snake Plain Aquifer. Water levels have been dropping, and Morris has several times asked Keith Higginson, director of the Idaho Department of Water Resources, to ensure his access to the water noted in the water right. The most recent demand came June 16; on June 18, Higginson again said no.

The petition for a writ of mandamus filed by Lezamiz called for "a writ and/or order compelling defendants fully honor plaintiffs' call and demand for the delivery of water."

At the Water Users law seminar June 25, Higginson spoke on conjunctive management (of surface and ground water) and said that "all surface and ground water in Idaho is ultimately interconnected."

Generally, however, he also said that impacts of water loss in one specific point can't be traced to specific uses of aquifer water, because the flow of water in the aquifer is not well enough understood.

Higginson noted that while the first surface water diversions date to the 1850s, extensive use of groundwater did not really begin in Idaho for nearly a century later. Now, he said, Idaho law related to groundwater may need "retrofitting."

While many people believe that groundwater is self-replenishing, he said, the fact is that when an aquifer is used it is gradually drained to its lowest elevation (in Idaho, at Lewiston). And he said that a fundamental conflict in Idaho law, between "first in time, first in right" and requirements that beneficial development should not be impeded, and protection of the aquifer from depletion. That suggests, he said, there isn't an absolute constitutional protection of prior rights. "This is heresy, isn't it?" he told the audience. ☒

AQUIFER IN THE BALANCE (7/19/1993) Judge Daniel Hurlbutt has taken under advisement a request to deliver water that could, if granted outright, have the effect of shutting down most water use on the Snake River Plain Aquifer.

The motion was filed by John Lezamiz of Hepworth, Nungester & Lezamiz in Twin Falls, for Alvin and Tim Musser and Howard Butch Morris. The Mussers and Morris have an interest in property in Gooding County which is watered from a spring whose source is the Aquifer. The water received, they said, has dropped below their water right level; an 1892 water right priority date applies, impinging on Morris' ability to water crops he has grown there.

If all water users whose rights are junior to the Mussers and Morris, and who use the Aquifer, were bent to their right, those thousands of water users could theoretically be blocked from any use of the Aquifer. Higginson has said that water activities in ground and surface waters around the Snake River are interconnected. But Department officials and others have said no one is presently able to link losses of water at one point in the Aquifer to a specific water use in it somewhere else. A study of water in the Aquifer has been funded by the state effective July 1, however, and now is underway.

On July 6, Higginson wrote that their letter to him of June 16 should be considered a petition (under Water Resources rule 37.01.01.230.01.c) and they should amend their petition accordingly by July 9. But on July 8, attorneys for the Mussers and Morris, the Department and several other parties put in appearances to argue before Judge Hurlbutt. The extended hearing, to which some witnesses were subpoenaed, included allegations by Morris' attorneys that the loss of water was a direct result of inadequate control of ground water use by the Department of Water Resources and its director.

But Higginson responded that many factors besides groundwater use have contributed to depletion of the reservoir. ☒

JUDGE ORDERS DELIVERY (8/16/1993) In what may have been the most sweeping action yet in the SRBA, Judge Daniel Hurlbutt issued a very specific order – for the Idaho Department of Water Resources to see to it water is delivered to a water user. But that ruling opens a vast number of prospective impacts.

This has become the first ruling in the SRBA to be appealed to the Idaho Supreme Court by the state of Idaho. The appeal document hasn't yet been fully drafted, but a notice of appeal has been filed with the SRBA court. Depending on court decisions and scheduling, however, the water users who prevailed in this instance in Hurlbutt's court might seek a contempt citation if the IDWR doesn't soon deliver the water, somehow.

IDWR Director Keith Higginson rejected the call for water in letters dated June 8 and June 16. The water right owners maintained that Higginson is legally obligated to deliver the water, and they asked Judge Hurlbutt to require him to. In his August 5 decision, that is exactly what Hurlbutt did. But because that may have opened the door to many other requests, and because there is no certainty how the IDWR will try to comply, the consequences could be wide ranging.

Hurlbutt based his reasoning in part of a string of Colorado adjudication decisions which were cited in the ruling. Basically, he concluded:

• That a writ of mandamus (to compel) could be issued against the IDWR. He wrote that such writs carry a number of requirements; that the action to be compelled is part of the agency's or officers duties, if it is ministerial or executive, and where other forms of legal remedy aren't readily available. Hurlbutt held that all those conditions apply. The Director of IDWR has a clear legal duty to distribute water according to priority, he wrote, a point not contested by IDWR.

• The Mussers and Morris have a clear right to receive the water and are not receiving their full entitlement.

• Higginson's refusal was arbitrary and capricious and, therefore, cannot stand.

• The director is required to distribute water according to specific rules and regulations he is required to adopt – except that, Hurlbutt said, those rules haven't been adopted. "The record reflects that there are not now, nor have there ever been, rules and regulations for the distribution of water …"

The IDWR argued that it cannot distribute water through the groundwater system until the court addresses that matter; but Hurlbutt rejected that argument. "The duty and authority of the Director to conjunctively manage the resource he knows to be interconnected needs no judicial imprimatur. The duty is clear and unambiguous. Even so, such a finding has already been made in the SRBA at the director's own urging," Hurlbutt said.

• He also found that Morris' crops were suffering damage as a result of the lack of water, and no other judicial remedy was available (since he could not sue the state over the crop loss) other than the demand for water. Hurlbutt closed with a short order requiring the IDWR to deliver the water. ☒

MUSSER AT THE SUPREME COURT (2/28/94) A decision on the appeal of an SRBA Court decision on delivery of water and the private attorney general doctrine is thought likely to appear on a very speedy basis, possibly as early as Tuesday. That would follow an intense session at oral hearing before the Court on February 16. Justice Byron Johnson (who asked all the questions save one) blew large holes into the state's appeal of the SRBA decision, and undercut important parts of the Musser case argued by John Hohnhorst of Hepworth, Nungester & Lezamiz

Johnson started by asking whether, since the writ simply required the director to comply with the law, that the director need not comply. Deputy Attorney General Peter Anderson said that no, in fact the director had complied. In that case, Johnson asked, why is there a contested case? And, he asked, why are rules suddenly being developed in the SRBA if not to meet a hitherto-unmet legal obligation?

"The director had determined the rules are necessary," Anderson said. He also suggested there's a "great disconnect" between the basis for the writ and what it ordered.

As Hohnhorst delivered his case, however, Johnson seemed to focus on another kind of disconnect — involving the practical matter of carrying out the writ. Johnson asked what, exactly, Department of Water Resources Director Keith Higginson should have done on getting the request for water.

Hohnhorst said he should have said he would deliver the needed water. In a week, a month, a year? Johnson asked. If he had said you'll get your water, eventually, one day, the justice asked, would this case have been avoided?

"That is probably correct," Hohnhorst said.

Since no one has asserted the Mussers' diminished water is a result of a particular water user's use, Justice Cathy Silak asked, how should the director comply with the demand to deliver water? "I'm looking for a practical matter," she said.

Hohnhorst replied that "It's the director's job to get the water to the Mussers. How he goes about doing that is his decision." ☒

THE RULING (3/14/1994) Sen. Laird Noh, R-Kimberly, the chairman of the Senate Resources and Environment Committee, may have mixed his metaphors in calling it "another monkey wrench thrown into an already tangled web." But everyone at the legislative hearing where he and others tried to figure out of the impact of the Idaho Supreme Court's Musser ruling knew what he meant.

The Court decided on February 28 to uphold an SRBA Court ruling by Judge Daniel Hurlbutt, which on its most basic level said that the director of the Department of Water Resources has to comply with state law and deliver water to Idaho water right holders in accord with law.

Some say it could mean shutting down hundreds of ground water users on the Eastern Snake River Plain Aquifer, though Gov. Cecil Andrus vowed in a speech on March 10 that he would not allow that to happen.

In the unanimous decision written by Justice Byron Johnson (who had asked all but one question at oral argument), the high court said that Hurlbutt had properly issued the writ. "Although the details of the performance of the duty are left to the director's discretion, the director has the duty to distribute water." The Court made short work of Higginson's reference to Idaho code 42-226 (which concerned groundwater user rights), which was enacted in 1951 but which, the Court noted, exempted from its term water rights acquired earlier. (The Mussers' dated to 1892.)

On its face, the Supreme Court decision terms may be fairly limited. One interpretation is that, since the Supreme Court (like Hurlbutt) did not explicitly say how or when the water should be delivered, those conditions may be variable on a case by case basis. If the water were delivered in a water truck months after a call for water, for example, the conditions of the order could presumably have been met.

Terry Uhlig of the J.R. Simplot Co. said that the decision may be read narrowly, that the Musser situation may be distinguished from that of many other water right holders. He said he was concerned about the possible impact of a broad reading of the decision.

The prevailing view among many attorneys, legislators and state officials, however, was much more drastic and sweeping, and involved the prospective shutdown of large numbers of ground water right users on the Snake River Aquifer.

A notice "to all users of ground water from the eastern Snake Plain Aquifer" from the IDWR, noting a series of upcoming hearings on conjunctive (ground water/surface water) management and related subjects, included its take on the Supreme Court decision.

"The Court did not adopt the Department's position that junior-priority rights are subject to provisions of Idaho law relative to reasonable ground water pumping levels and that exercise of prior rights not block full economic development of ground water resources," it said. "The Court did not address the Department's argument that the interrelationship of the various rights must be determined before distribution and regulation of uses may occur. The purpose of this notice is to advise ground water users that curtailment of junior-priority ground water rights from the Eastern Snake Plain Aquifer may be commenced this year if senior-priority rights make a call for priority distribution of water. If the Department's investigation of a call by a senior-priority right determines that the senior-priority right is not being met, junior-priority rights will have to be shut off even if this results in under-utilization of the aquifer." ☒

WATER SUMMIT (5/2007) Governor C.L. "Butch" Otter convened a "water summit" at Burley on April 17, hoping to use discussions there to develop a framework for water use in the decades to come. Additional meetings may follow.

Otter spokesman Jon Hanian reported afterward – some of the meetings were closed-door – that "some sides gave and other sides didn't. I think we've got a basis for moving forward, but I don't think we'd call it an agreement."

The governor was quoted as saying at the conference the state should fix the problem because it allowed over-allocation of water rights. "For that, and for all the people who did that, I'm sincerely sorry. But we have to play the hand we're dealt, and we haven't been dealt a very good hand."

In an April 25 guest opinion in the *Idaho Statesman*, Norm Semanko, executive director of the Idaho Water Users Association, remarked, "Bottom line: The summit established a solid foundation for additional discussions and potential solutions. . . . The game plan: The governor announced plans for 16 months of meetings to diagnose the problem and prescribe a permanent cure." ☒

Water Districts

WATER DISTRICT 1 AND THE COMMITTEE OF NINE Relatively little known outside the Idaho water community, but powerfully important within, is Water District 1 – a regional entity that governs water use in the area upstream from the Milner Dam (roughly, southern Idaho east of Twin Falls).

Its policy activity is carried out by the "advisory" group the Committee of Nine, made up of water users from the area. (Members are chosen in what amount to caucuses at the District's annual business meeting in March.) ☒

WEST WATER DISTRICT (12/1996) The newly formed West Water Measurement District is now looking to hire a district hydrographer, and also has set the next meeting for its advisory committee, District officials said.

The West District held its first annual meeting Nov. 4 in Jerome. At that meeting the District Advisory Committee was formed and Conrad, of Murtaugh, representing the Idaho Irrigation Pumpers Association, was named committee chairman. ☒

GROUND WATER DISTRICT (4/98) The North Snake Ground Water District – a type of district that did not even exist in Idaho until legislative action a few years ago – has entered the SRBA, seeking to "alter or amend" certain subcases in the Hagerman area.

The filing said that in August 1995, before the formation of the District, that some of its constituents-including Faulkner Land & Livestock Co., May Farms Ltd. and Sand Springs Ranch Partnership – filed motions to file late responses in six Hagerman Springs area subcases. ☒

Water right holder organizations

Apart from public entities, many water users have organized into interest groups. The biggest, and oldest, and the one substantive statewide water users organizations, is the **Idaho Water Users Association**. Formed decades ago, it was led from 1974 until 2000 by geologist Sherl Chapman.

WATER MANAGEMENT (7/2000) Chapman has been executive director of the Idaho Water Users Association since 1974 – "I just found a job I liked," he said – but no longer: his last day at the association was June 30.

The new executive director – and general counsel as well – is Norman Semanko, who has been highly active in the SRBA with the Rosholt, Robertson & Tucker firm in Twin Falls. ☒

HAGERMAN WATER OWNERS (4/12/1993) One impact of the test basin approach to adjudication setting much legal policy for the whole Snake River Basin by running a few small basins through the process first has created an unusual situation for the people in those test areas. On one hand, legal costs for people in those first areas are likely to be higher because precedent is being set using those cases. By the time rights holders in other basins have their cases heard, much of the precedent already will have been set.

Not surprisingly, an organization is springing up to deal with it.

Representatives of water rights holders in all the test basins met in Twin Falls on April 2 to discuss the costs of being the first, including bearing the burden of precedent setting litigation. Part of the idea, said co-chairman Dan McFadden of Hagerman, is to find ways to "spread our base. We don't necessarily object to [being] test basins if we can get some help." Others who participate would get a say in precedent development.

Much of the organization is spearheaded by Hagerman area water rights holders, about 300 of whom have organized into an organization which has funded an aggressive legislative and legal arm on water rights matters. Many of those individuals, McFadden said, are retirees and others who would have a hard time supporting the legal action individually. ☒

HWRO DEPARTS (11/1997) The Hagerman Water Right Owners, for whom the Twin Falls law firm Hepworth Lezamiz & Hohnhorst has pushed basin wide issues and repeatedly shaken up the SRBA, is pulling out of the case.

An October 6 motion by Patrick Brown of the Hepworth firm said that it is withdrawing as attorneys for the organization. A letter from HWRO chair Daniel McFadden said that "Henceforth, it will be the responsibility of each member of HWRO to arrange for his or her own individual legal representation in that [SRBA] court." Brown said his firm will continue to represent five individual HWRO members. ☒

3 | The SRBA's Origin

Historical backdrop

This section is adapted from the book ***Paradox Politics: People and Power in Idaho*** *by Randy Stapilus (1988, Ridenbaugh Press, Boise).*

The first electric power in Idaho, in Ketchum and Hailey in the 1880s, came from string, glue, and baling wire operations. But the mom-and-pop companies died out. Most of the score or so of other private companies in southern Idaho were reduced to five by 1914, and by 1916 to just one – Idaho Power Co.

Instead of hotel turbines, IPCo used hydropower dam plants, many on the Snake River: American Falls in Eastern Idaho, Shoshone Falls in the Magic Valley, Swan Falls in the Southwest, and others. (Swan Falls was built by the Trade Dollar Consolidated Mining Co. for the mining community of Silver City. By the time it fired up, Silver City was becoming a ghost town. The dam came to Idaho Power in the consolidations of 1915.)

Hydro is cheap power, and Idaho Power's rates have always been among the lowest in the nation. While utilities elsewhere would be blasted by politicians as a matter of course, Idaho Power was for years loudly defended by them. But Idaho Power's dams also meant conflict in the making.

In the early seventies Idaho Power began importing small amounts of coal-generated electric power. In November 1974 IPCo asked the PUC for permission to build a coal-fired power plant in the desert 26 miles southeast of Boise, near a wide spot in the road called Orchard. It was near the Union Pacific rail, which would haul in coal, and the Snake River, which would supply water. The Pioneer case Idaho Power executives thought would get snap PUC approval became the longest utility case the PUC had considered until then. It lasted nearly two years. The PUC decision to reject Pioneer was based mostly on environmental concerns and partly on the enormous costs.

SWAN FALLS The next year, as Pioneer cooled off, 32 Idaho Power ratepayers filed a lawsuit to block future big power plants.

The state water plan, which governed flows of the Snake River, was nearing legislative approval. (It would be approved in 1978). The plan allowed drawing down the Snake to 3,300 cubic feet per second near Swan Falls Dam. The ratepayers said Idaho Power hadn't protected its water rights and that the failure squandered water and cost ratepayers money. (Swan Falls produced about 10.3 megawatts of juice, enough to power Eagle or Ketchum or Gooding.) In mid-summer 1977, in a drought season, water levels at the dam dipped to two-thirds of the plant's generating capacity. The 32 ratepayers said that meant Idaho Power had to buy more expensive out-of-state coal power than it should have. If IPCo had demanded its Swan Falls water, they said, rates would be lower. They insisted Idaho Power insist on its rights. But these ratepayers, many farmers, also had in mind a court ruling protecting their own water rights, and were confident they would get it.

Laird Noh, making his first race for the state Senate in 1978, was a friend of some of the key plaintiffs. "I used to go to lunch with them and say, But what if the decision [on that lawsuit] goes this way [in your favor]? And they would all say, there's no way in the world, no reasonable people could ever rule in that fashion, just don't waste your time worrying about it."

IPCo executives tried to get the complaint dismissed. Failing that, and realizing that not acting meant stockholders could hold the company legally liable, they did two things. First, they got the PUC to stop new electric hookups for irrigation; at a stroke, that froze farm expansion in southern Idaho. Second, IPCo sued to get the Fourth District Court to say its Swan Falls rights were not subordinated – that no one had rights superior to Idaho Power's – and the state water plan was a "taking" of rights.

District Judge Jesse Walters ruled Idaho Power subordinated at the Hells Canyon Dams in the early fifties (to curry favor with Len Jordan and the irrigators). He reasoned that the Snake and the dams on it were one system, and that when Idaho Power subordinated at the end of the system at Hells Canyon, it had agreed to subordinate the whole works. Since Idaho Power had agreed to all that, it could not argue that the state water plan took away its assets; the utility, Walters said, had already signed them away. His ruling was the conventional wisdom of the time.

But in November 1982 the Supreme Court overturned him in a unanimous decision that threw Idaho into turmoil. The supremes said that the federal Hells Canyon license referred to Hells Canyon as "one complete project," not Swan Falls or anything else. "We find therefore no intent to subordinate water rights at other projects," the court said. Idaho Power, the court said, had the right to 8,400 cubic feet per second at Swan Falls Dam (subject to some continuing court action on related issues).

"It came as a real shock to everyone," Noh recalled.

Now the moratorium on irrigation power hookups expanded to a third of the state: All of the Snake River drainage east of Swan Falls. State officials worried farmers might have to quit irrigating 200,000 acres to free enough water for IPCo's water rights. Hundreds of water permits issued since 1919 were at risk.

Early in 1983 IPCo President Jim Bruce warned that "if we ... don't file a suit to uphold the decision granted to us by the Supreme Court of the state of Idaho, I would have a serious question in my mind that we might be subject to a number of suits." That meant suing individual water right owners, and in March 1983, IPCo did sue 7,500 of them. Farmers no longer saw a friend on the other side. The area hardest hit was the Magic Valley, where irrigation came later than in the East and Southwest.

The shape of things took focus when Ken Dunn, director of the state Department of Water Resources, went on the road to explain Swan Falls in rural communities. If Idaho Power won, critics said, it could decide who and what could have water. Evans, scion of a ranching family, backed subordination, warning the Snake was Idaho's "jugular vein" and Idaho Power might clamp it. Evans had an ally in Jim Jones, the attorney general elected in 1982. Jones was a protégé and former staffer of Idaho Power's old friend, Len Jordan. But Jones came from a farm family and knew well that side of the picture.

But there was another side. Idaho Power did not need all its water to keep Swan Falls at full steam. The year 1977 brought drought; July and August – the months the 32 ratepayers complained about – were its pits, and even then water levels did not fall drastically short. Not much of the water farmers had been using really needed be at risk. More to the point was water sought by new developers - and the water which would be used at the Hells Canyon dams, which produced four-fifths of IPCo power. Although water rights there technically were subordinated to irrigation and other use, in practice once water got past Swan Falls little was used for other purposes until it got to Hells Canyon. The reality was that a water right at Swan Falls was almost the same as a water right at Hells Canyon. At moments that long-term impact seemed less important that the immediate situation, but precedent was highly valued in Idaho.

Legislators started questioning the precedent: If the Legislature erased Idaho Power's water rights, whose were next?

The most potent point, though, was again economic.

Idaho Power's rates would rise if it lost hydropower water, a prospect increasingly significant as more water was diverted for irrigation. A PUC study said customers could wind up paying $54 million above normal rate increases, or $200 per customer per year. That was especially poignant for farmers. Consumer groups said the higher rates would hurt senior citizens and others on fixed incomes; business groups said they would hurt the economy. Al Fothergill, executive director of the Idaho Citizens Coalition, argued that "the question is whether we want to irrigate more land at the expense of all power consumers in the Idaho Power service area."

The coalitions were bizarre. Idaho Power, which had fought so hard to go coal-fired, now defended cheaper hydro with all its might. The PUC was on its side. So were the conservation and consumer groups who so often fought the utility.

Many farmers bought their logic for a time. Jones recalled that when he traveled the Magic Valley and Eastern Idaho in 1983, "I had numerous people saying, 'You're cutting your throat politically, because you're not going to get anywhere on this'." Jones worked with the Committee of Nine and other farm groups and hammered subordination into the public's consciousness. And in the next two years Southern Idaho public opinion changed in favor of subordination, and so against Idaho Power.

In the summer of 1984 Evans, Jones, and Bruce signed a 32-page compromise: Idaho Power would drop demands for 8,400 cubic feet per second and be guaranteed 3,900 in the summer and 5,600 from November 1 to March 31. The state agreed that the effect of new water permits on hydropower had to be considered. IPCo's lawsuit against water right holders would be dropped. Jones almost pulled out because of a provision saying Idaho Power could keep its water until the state issued permits for it, but returned to the fold when Rexburg attorney Rigby crafted a plan for putting IPCo water rights in trust by the state for the near term.

It was a complex settlement – so complex no one knew what it would do. The agreement seemed to lift most restraints on irrigation, but no one knew how much agriculture in Southern Idaho would grow. (Two University of Idaho economists guesstimated 195,000 acres by the year 2000.)

A special Snake River water rights adjudication court was set up in Twin Falls and energetic young Judge Daniel Hurlbutt assigned to preside.

But there was a snag. The Federal Energy Regulatory Commission (FERC), successor to the Federal Power Commission, kept the issue on its calendar ... and kept it there. Evans and Jones asked the congressional delegation to step in. With Sen. McClure taking the lead in the Senate and Rep. Richard Stallings in the House – each in the majority party – a bill shoving the agreement down FERC's throat cleared Congress in mid-1986. It had the bad luck to be tied to another bill President Reagan disliked. A few days after Reagan stopped in Twin Falls campaigning for Senator Steve Symms, then running for re-election, he vetoed the bill.

When a new federal bill emerged in 1987 Jones was convinced a report attached to it could lead to a federal water grab. McClure and Stallings agreed to revisions. The bill got through Congress in December 1987, and Reagan signed it.

It will shape the future of Idaho. ☒

Adjudications in Idaho

The SRBA is not the first adjudication in Idaho – far from it. Water has been adjudicated around Idaho for a century and more, in many adjudications. Most of them, however, have been small in scale and scope. Some of the largest have involved substantial parts of tributary river basins, such as the adjudications of the Payette and Lemhi rivers. Not all were done when the SRBA launched, and effectively superseded them.

PAYETTE ADJUDICATION ROLLS IN (2/2001) The decades-old Payette River Adjudication, which started in 1979, technically is still alive, even as the SRBA has been re-adjudicating water rights in that basin.

Most work in that smaller adjudication was done almost 20 years ago, but some subcases never have cleared, and the adjudication has stayed active.

On January 24, Deputy Idaho Attorney General David Barber asked SRBA Judge Burdick to effectively close out that old case. He noted that decisions in the smaller adjudication were used by the Idaho Department of Water Resources in developing its recommendations in that area for the SRBA.

There was no objection to the general proposal, and Judge Burdick indicated he would probably agree to it.

Two parties, however, did file to ensure that their rights would not be compromised by the decision. Attorney Dana Hofstetter, representing the Roseberry Irrigation District in Valley County, said that some errors had been made in the Payette adjudication, and she wanted to ensure that those still could be addressed in the SRBA. And attorney John Simpson, representing cattleman Jim Little, said that his client has a water right claim in the SRBA that wasn't covered in the Payette adjudication – because, he said, his client didn't file in it, figuring his case eventually would be resolved in the SRBA anyway. ☒

4 | Organizing the Adjudication

The Court's personnel

The Snake River Basin Adjudication Court, established in November 1987, is located at 253 Third Avenue North, Twin Falls, Idaho. Its phone number is 736-3011.

Melanson, John – Presiding Judge, the fourth presiding judge.
Bilyeu, Brigette – Special Master, one of the three original masters.
Dolan, Terrence A. – Special Master, one of the three original masters.
Booth,Theodore R. – Special Master, fourth master in his job.
Wildman, Eric – Staff Attorney
Swank, Marisa – Law Clerk
Delaney, Diana – Case Administrator
Connell, Janet – Deputy Clerk/Assistant to Special Master
Hall, Robbin – Deputy Clerk/Assistant to Special Master
Murphy, Julie – Deputy Clerk
Maureen, Newton – Court Reporter

HURLBUTT RESIGNS (11/98) SRBA Presiding Judge Daniel Hurlbutt, who has led work on the SRBA since his appointment on June 19, 1987, will leave the case and his judicial office as of December 31.

The contours and direction of the SRBA have been in considerable part set by Hurlbutt, who was assigned to the case by the Idaho Supreme Court as part of the process of setting up the case.

Hurlbutt delivered his resignation on October 14 to the Idaho Supreme Court. Chief Justice Linda Copple Trout said that "he has shouldered a tremendous responsibility. He has worked tirelessly to assure that the rights of claimants in the adjudication are protected and that their claims are handled expeditiously."

Public comment on the judicial changeover – by participants and close observers in the case – runs this way: The change of judges need not slow the case at all. Speaking at the October 20 informational meeting, Judge Hurlbutt even held out the prospect that the case might move faster after he leaves.

Certainly, as Hurlbutt noted, the case is in some regards at a dividing point. Large-scale settlement of many water rights is well underway; Department of Water Resources determination of all domestic and stockwater claims may be finished (or nearly finished) by the end of this year. Work in the three "test basins" – so called because they were set up as test cases to help work out procedures and legal issues – is mostly done.

Hurlbutt said, too, that he will try to wrap up (within his court) a number of loose ends in legal issues, before his resignation takes effect.

Those include questions about general provisions on irrigation (where he said a state Department of Water Resources proposal looks promising) and conjunctive water management.

On the other hand, a string of issues involving reversals by the Supreme Court of Hurlbutt decisions remains essentially unresolved. So do a series of critically important federal and tribal water right issues, including the massive Nez Perce tribal claims, which are tentatively set for trial in 2000.

Such a judge may not be easy to find. Since the introduction of the SRBA, district judges other than Hurlbutt have virtually been banned from consideration of water rights issues within the Snake River basin (which includes 87% of Idaho). While a few judges around the state have background in water rights law, none have in the last decade had any substantial judicial experience with it. The last district judge other than Hurlbutt to work on a water rights case in the area, Seventh District Judge James Herndon, saw one case reassigned from him to Hurlbutt as soon as it came to the Idaho Supreme court.

Idaho does not lack for water lawyers; but many of them are, or have been, involved in the SRBA, and so probably could not be assigned as a judge in the case.

Hurlbutt's background was not in water law but in complex litigation. Since the work of an SRBA judge is management-heavy, the Supreme Court may look in that direction again.

Hurlbutt's position as a Fifth District judge, and his assignment to the SRBA (which has been his only assignment for only a few years) are separate issues, and his replacement in those two positions will proceed separately. When a district judgeship becomes vacant, the first step is taken by the Idaho Judicial Council, which announces the vacancy and invites applications for filling it. The Council receives public and bar comment on the applicants, conducts public interviews of applicants, then votes to send up to four names to the governor, who makes the final selection.

The Judicial Council has begun its work on filling the judgeship, but no applications have as yet been received.

The assignment of a judge to the SRBA is more unusual. It has only one precedent: the Court's assignment of Hurlbutt to it, 11 years ago. The Supreme Court was then acting under a mandate of the Idaho Legislature, which had ordered that the adjudication be filed with the Supreme Court. The high court had considerable latitude about deciding the specifics, however. It could have assigned the case to any of the district courts, and could have assigned more than one judge to it.

It considered options in location of the court; a site in Canyon County was considered, as well as the ultimate choice of Twin Falls.

Theoretically, the Court could move the SRBA again, though because of the financial investment in the Twin Falls site, that's considered unlikely.

The assignment of the judge was handled internally and quietly. Hurlbutt recalled that he had heard about the upcoming SRBA but had not sought it, when one of the justices visited him and asked him to take the case. Hurlbutt agreed, and the assignment was made.

There's never been any public word whether any other judge was ever considered for the assignment.

Now, with Hurlbutt's departure, the Idaho Supreme Court has sent letters to the state's district judges informing them of the situation, and inquiring whether any are interested in taking the case. (In the years since Hurlbutt has had the case, none, apparently, has said – publicly at least – that they would be interested in taking it.)

"I never intended to leave this job in a pine box," Hurlbutt said in an interview after his announcement. "From a personal standpoint, it was the right time." He pointed out that he turns 50 in December, and reached a time when he needs to pursue other interests, or not at all.

Is there more to the resignation?

Much of the organizational work of the SRBA – an area where, because of his background in complex litigation, Hurlbutt was keenly interested – has been completed. Beyond that, Hurlbutt has expressed frustration about the case repeatedly and publicly over the last year.

In January, at budget hearings before the state legislature's Joint Finance Appropriations Committee, he remarked: "I go too fast, I go too slow. I do too much. I do too little."

He has been reversed by the Idaho Supreme Court on a number of key rulings over the last two years. And he has warned about the impact of those decisions, several times during court proceedings.

For example, at SRBA Court hearings on September 16 about an Idaho Supreme Court ruling on conjunctive management, Hurlbutt remarked that as a result: "The mission for this court is far broader than I had contemplated, a far, far more massive undertaking than this court ever envisioned … and it will not be in my lifetime the case will be completed … [That Supreme Court ruling] is a rejection of everything I've said this case is about and is not about. I have said for the record and say again this is my worst nightmare in the case … I'll probably be dead before anyone figures out what this case is all about … You don't like it, I don't like it. Many people here don't like it. [But] I think the command here is clear and explicit … Maybe the legislature will overturn this in some measure. But that's not my job."

He has made other warning comments in court about the scope and longevity of the case over the past year. ☒

THE INTERIM, AND THE APPLICANTS (1/1999) The next presiding judge in the Snake River Basin Adjudication is … 5th District Judge Barry Wood. But only for a short time: Probably only until late February or early March.

With 11-year Judge Daniel Hurlbutt's December 31 departure, and the process of replacing him only in its middle stages, the Idaho Supreme Court ordered that another judge will sit in to take care of necessary business until the spot is filled.

Hurlbutt took his leave December 31, after conducting business through the month. His last open court event was a December 21 hearing on Nez Perce tribal claims mediation and litigation.

There, U.S. Department of Justice attorney Peter Monson told the judge that "we haven't agreed on all issues, but we've respected your decisions and I think you've treated us fairly. And I want to say, thank you your honor, and we'll miss you."

Hurlbutt said, "I'll miss all of you. It's been a privilege to work with everyone in this case. I know it's going to go forward and it's going to be successful. There are too many good people working on it, for it not to be."

Wood was elected a district judge in 1994 and 1998. ☒

WOOD STAYS A LITTLE LONGER (3/1999) 5th District Judge Barry Wood is still the interim, not permanent, presiding judge in the Snake River Basin Adjudication. But on February 15, Idaho Supreme Court Chief Justice Linda Copple Trout said that he'll be presiding over the case a little longer than had been expected.

Up to that point, the widespread presumption was that the adjudication would be handed over to the new district judge in the fifth district. Three nominees were chosen by the Idaho Judicial Council after interviews on the 15th, and forwarded to Gov. Dirk Kempthorne for a final selection.

The Idaho Supreme Court first asked the district judges around the state if any were interested in presiding over the SRBA; none indicated they were. Still, Trout said the high court would feel most comfortable if an incumbent, experienced, district judge were handling the SRBA for a while.

At the interview sessions, she said Wood had over the weekend agreed to continue presiding in the case "for some period of months into the future" – probably about 12 to 15 months, she said. But she said the time period was not specific or absolute.

During that time, she said, Wood will continue to carry out many of his ongoing regular duties as a district judge. (He also is administrative judge for the 5th District.) She said the new judge would need to help out with general court work, as well as presumably take some SRBA work as assigned. In some respects, she said, the new judge will be "an assistant to Judge Wood."

How that work might be divided, she said, will be up to Wood. "I would say it's up in the air," she told one applicant. "I know he will be delegating some of the work out."

She said the 12 to 15 month period would also allow the Supreme Court and others (including the Idaho Legislature) opportunity to review the SRBA process and decide whether to keep it as it is now, or change it in some way. Some talk still is ongoing, she noted, about installing a three-judge panel at the adjudication.

About the new arrangement, Wood simply and briefly remarked at the February 16 information session, "It's what I learned over the weekend." ☒

WOOD REMOVED FROM SRBA (9/2000) Judge Barry Wood will be removed as presiding judge in the Snake River Basin Adjudication, the Idaho Supreme Court decided August 31.

That big shift in the oversight of the case, only the second of its kind in the 14-year history of the case, results from Wood's close relationship with state Supreme Court Justice-elect Daniel Eismann.

Wood, who has presided over the SRBA since January 1999, is expected to transition off the massive case over the next few months.

The Supreme Court decision was delivered by telephone, and SRBA court staff said they've not yet received a written order. A written order may not be delivered until a decision is made who will next take over the case.

There was no immediate indication who that might be.

That followed an August ruling by the Idaho Judicial Council that Supreme Court Justice-elect Daniel Eismann would have a conflict of interest in reviewing SRBA cases from the court of brother-in-law Judge

CANDIDATES The vacancy following Judge Hurlbutt's resignation is the only time the SRBA judgeship appeared to be thrown open to applicants rather than filled unilaterally by the Supreme Court. Even then it didn't work out that way: The applicant chosen to fill Hurlbutt's seat on the 5th district bench wasn't assigned to the SRBA. But it was the closest we've come. Here's who applied for the job:

· **Patrick Costello**, Orofino, a former magistrate in Clearwater County.

· **Nathan Higer**, Burley, a magistrate (21 years) in the 5th District, Cassia County. [Higer was ultimately named to the 5th district judgeship.]

· **Gregory P. Meacham**, Idaho Falls, a 25-year attorney with Meacham & Decker, working half in litigation and half in general business practice. (He was a law classmate with one of the Council members, 5th District Judge Roger Burdick.)

• **Brigette Bilyeu**, the only one of the three current special masters in the SRBA to apply. Bilyeu said, however, that she always had considered the job to be that of a district judge, not necessarily the SRBA judge..

• **Cindy Campbell**, a Blackfoot attorney who has been a Bingham County deputy prosecutor.

• **Patrick Costello**, Orofino, a former magistrate in Clearwater County who departed that position after losing his retention election in November (by two votes).

• **Michael Gilmore**, Boise, a deputy attorney assigned to the civil litigation division; he previously was assigned to the Public Utilities Commission.

• **Carolyn Minder**, Boise, an Ada County magistrate (for three years) – formerly Hurlbutt's counsel (who worked on developing many decisions, working on legal research and much more) for several years.

• **Philip Rassier**, Boise, a deputy attorney general (a section chief) assigned to the Department of Water Resources. Although he has worked in that department many years, he hasn't been actively (or at least visibly) involved in SRBA matters.

Three applicants withdrew before the interviews:

• **Jerry Reynolds**, Idaho Falls, a private practice attorney.

• **Karl Shurtliff**, Boise, an attorney who has been a state representative and a member of the Board of Education. He ran for an open 4th District judgeship last year, but lost that election in November.

• **Gary Spackman**, Boise, who is in charge of the water distribution section at the Department of Water Resources.

Barry Wood, Eismann said August 30 that he would recuse himself from acting in any SRBA cases.

Eismann, who had said he thought there would not be a conflict, personally asked the Council for a ruling on the matter after the May 23 primary election when he defeated incumbent Cathy Silak. The Council said the family relationship creates a conflict. It warned of the potential that SRBA cases could be moved from state to federal court if a conflict of interests were found. Eismann said that he would abide by the ruling and back off cases in the SRBA, where Wood is presiding judge.

"I guess it's news to me," Chief Justice Linda Copple Trout told the Twin Falls *Times News* shortly after Eismann's comments. She said the Court would meet soon to review the situation, and added, "I guess there's still a question as to who will be sitting, Judge Eismann or Judge Wood."

➲ *At this writing, almost a decade later, Wood is still on the 5th district bench as a judge, and has delivered several substantial water-related decisions over the years.*

BURDICK TO LEAD SRBA (11/2000) The Idaho Supreme Court on October 27 assigned the Snake River Basin Adjudication to Fifth District Judge Roger Burdick, who will become the case's third presiding judge. He will take over the case effective December 15. The order indicates that Burdick will be named presiding judge on a permanent, not an interim, basis.

Burdick has been a district judge since 1993, when he was appointed to fill a newly-created seat located at Twin Falls. Previously, he was a magistrate judge at Jerome County. He also has served on the Idaho Judicial Council, and served on it when it made recommendations for filling the bench seat Hurlbutt left vacant.

"I think it's going to be a really hard job," Burdick told the Twin Falls *Times News*. "I'm going into it as optimistically as I can."

The Twin Falls *Times News* had said in an editorial that Burdick should be appointed to the case.

Burdick is expected to retain his current cases while preparing to take over the SRBA. He may retain a few cases for a more extended period, as Wood did when he moved into the SRBA.

At a regular monthly meeting in Dubois on October 25, Wood delivered what amounted to a good-bye, when he delivered thanks to the attorneys, staff and other participants in the case. IDWR Adjudication Chief David Tuthill said "his tenure has been a time of solid case management, well-written decisions, and productive relationships with claimants, agencies and the legal community. He has done an outstanding job and will be missed both personally and professionally." ☒

BURDICK'S DISCLOSURE (12/2000) Incoming Judge Burdick got ahead of the curve November 2, filing – before his arrival at the SRBA – a statement disclosing his interests in water rights. It was a short statement.

"I own and occupy a single residence within the City of Twin Falls. The City supplies all of my domestic water. In addition, I pay a yearly irrigation fee to Twin Falls City for irrigation water which I do not use on my residential lot. I own no other real property in Idaho and neither own nor claim any water rights in Idaho," he wrote.

"My sister, Linda Baker Tylka, resides in Rupert, Idaho, in a single residence within the city limits of Rupert, Idaho. Additionally, she owns a half undivided interest in an undeveloped building lot in Pelican Point Subdivision, Minidoka County. That subdivision has a domestic communal well for property owners within the subdivision. There has been no claim on that water by her."

He added, "I have no other relatives living in Idaho as my parents live in Denver, Colorado, and my sons live in Alaska and California." ☒

BURDICK MOVES IN (1/2001) Fifth District Judge Roger Burdick on December 15 became the third presiding judge in the Snake River Basin Adjudication. The Idaho Supreme Court had on October 27 assigned the case to him.

Burdick, 53, has been a district judge since 1993, when he was appointed to fill a newly-created seat located at Twin Falls. He is scheduled in January to become administrative judge in the 5th District. Both Wood and Hurlbutt also had that role. Burdick is expected to retain his current cases while preparing to take over the SRBA.

“What I’m left with is a well-seasoned staff and special masters who are hitting on all the right cylinders,” he said. He said that he plans no major changes, at least any time soon. And he said he plans no personnel changes.

He said that he plans to continue a program Wood started, periodically holding monthly SRBA sessions around the basin, not just in Twin Falls. “That proved very popular,” he said.

Burdick said he will look at “fine tuning” some technical and procedural areas. “We also will try to continue what Judge Wood started, a comprehensive review of the technology.”

He said he wants to continue to move toward a computer system that integrates the SRBA’s system with other courts and the Idaho Department of Water Resources.

At present, he said, “there are a lot of different incompatibilities.”

Burdick made his first appearance as SRBA Judge at the December 19 information meeting and status conference. That session was attended by former SRBA Judge Wood, marking the first time a current and former SRBA judge have appeared together at an adjudication event.

At the meeting, Idaho Department of Water Resources Director Karl Dreher gave Wood a plaque as “an expression of our appreciation for the work you’ve done in the last couple of years.”

He advised Burdick, “Don’t give up … Keep plugging along and you’ll see you’re making a difference.” ☒

BURDICK TO SUPREME COURT In July 2003, Supreme Court Justice Jesse Walters (who more than two decades before as a district judge had written the decision overturned by the Idaho Supreme Court that launched the SRBA) rsigned from the court. SRBA Judge Burdick applied for the position and was appointed to it by Governor Dirk Kempthorne.

His replacement at the SRBA by now followed an established pattern: It went to an experienced judge in the 5th district: John Melanson.

MELANSON TAKES CHARGE (11/2003) The Snake River Basin Adjudication’s fourth presiding judge, 5th District Judge John M. Melanson of Rupert, took charge of the case in October.

District judge at Minidoka County since his appointment in December 2000, he began to split his time between ongoing case work at Rupert and the SRBA at Twin Falls.

At his first monthly information meeting, on October 21, he said that “I appreciate the work of the director and the staff. … I have tons to learn here and am humbled by that, but I think I can do it. We’ve had a whole bunch of progress made in the last few years, and this is a doable endeavor. I’m very pleased to be on board, and I look forward to the cooperation that’s been developed in the last few years between the court and director.”

Melanson practiced law for 14 years in Buhl, serving as a city attorney and sometimes representing farmers and ranchers in bankruptcy and other matters, providing, he noted, some familiarity with the importance of water rights in the area. He said that he did not practice water law himself, though one of his partners, Bob Weaver (now deceased, and not a participant in the SRBA), did. He was named a magistrate judge in 1995 and a district judge in 2000. Melanson earned a Bachelor of Business Administration degree from Idaho State University and his J.D. degree from the University of Idaho College of Law.

Melanson said that he has no plans for any change in the adjudication effort, but hopes to keep it moving ahead. "I can't think of anything I would change at this point," he said.

Asked by the *Digest* about his interest in the adjudication, Melanson noted, "In the past, this position hasn't been seen as particularly something a person would seek out. When it started, especially, it was seen as something that was too gargantuan a task. Now, particularly because of the efforts of the last few years, you really can see the light at the end of the tunnel. ... I could be the person who signs the final decree. ...

"Another thing that made me think this would be an interesting position was the cooperation that now exists between the director and the court ... The court has an obligation to investigate the legality of the claims but it's much better to have the director involved, than otherwise." The experienced SRBA staff, he said, also provided a positive incentive.

He said that he was excited about being able to concentrate his efforts on a major, far-ranging case.

He said that he plans to divide his time between Twin Falls and Rupert.

"I want to maintain a presence in Rupert anyway, because when the work here is done, or as it winds down, I'll still be the 5th district judge in Minidoka County; I'll still live there and try to be their judge as much as possible. But my impression right now, and perhaps for the next couple of years," is that his time in Minidoka County could be limited.

Time may be freed for the SRBA, he suggested, once the current vacancy on the 5th District bench is filled. ☒

The Court's role in the SRBA

McDEVITT, THE COURTS AND THE SRBA (10/24/1994) Idaho Supreme Court Chief Justice Charles McDevitt told a legislative interim committee on October 24 that the Idaho Legislature cannot direct a court action — specifically, the SRBA. In a discussion that covered many aspects of the SRBA, McDevitt spoke to the adjudication interim committee in Boise. He started by apologizing for a mix-up that last summer left a group of legislators who had expected to meet with SRBA Judge Daniel Hurlbutt instead meeting no one, on McDevitt's orders. He said the actions should have been better coordinated, but that a careful line between legislative and court responsibilities has to be maintained.

That theme arose most directly through a musing by Sen. Stan Hawkins, R-Idaho Falls, a persistent SRBA critic. After McDevitt noted that the SRBA is just seven years old, while many previous (and much smaller) adjudications in Idaho went on for decades, Hawkins noted that "none of them had the complexity or the numbers involved in the current adjudication. This is such a monumental task that we cannot even see the problems that will arise." Close interactive contact between legislators and the courts, he suggested, may be necessary.

McDevitt replied that "It's fully appropriate the legislature retain an overview and inquire into the progress of the SRBA," and said that he would be willing to make regular reports on it. But, he said, if Hawkins was suggesting that the legislature should participate in directing a court action, "then you and I part company."

When lawmakers become involved in a litigation, he said, "we destroy your independence from us as well as our independence from you."

But he was optimistic that the SRBA is basically on track and "it can be handled."

Later, Hawkins said that since the SRBA started as a legislative action, lawmakers might want to take action in the case if it moves in a direction different from that legislators originally expected. "I have the distinct impression the court ...would now have us positioned to where they would like us to stay out now. I'm getting the impression the court is saying, we have the law now, stay out and let us run with it."

McDevitt said that some subjects (such as the components of a water right) are properly legislated topics, but court procedures and rules "are the province of the court." And he noted that each time the Legislature changes the law, relevant legal cases will have to grind to a halt while they try to figure out their new place within it.

As regards the costs of the adjudication, McDevitt noted that only a small percentage of the spending has been by the SRBA court, and the courts are examining procedures (including alternative dispute resolution, simple forms and speedy settlements) to keep costs down.

He was also asked, by Rep. Golden Linford, R-Rexburg, about the sometime testy relationship between the SRBA Court and the IDWR. (He spoke of "a lack of cooperative effort which is a perceived cause of lack of progress.")

McDevitt said the relationship "is not atypical" and usually is more difficult in the early stages of an adjudication. "I think that's being resolved," he said. ☒

ADMINISTRATION REMANDED (10/2000) The Idaho Supreme Court on September 6 remanded to SRBA Court a case concerning the Department of Water Right's administration of a water right.

The case, which had been handled by 7th District Judge James Herndon, was vacated and remanded to the SRBA Court. The Supreme Court said that the SRBA Court had sole jurisdiction over the water rights case.

The origin of the case stemmed from 1989, when Sagewillow, Inc., bought the Knollin Ranch in Butte County; the ranch came with surface and ground water rights. Four years later, the firm obtained more land near the ranch. The case stemmed from Sagewillow's claims in six water rights. Those rights, providing for irrigation of 2,383 acres, mainly have priority dates 1950 to 1960, though one dates from 1972.

In its summary, the Supreme Court noted, "In October 1990, Sagewillow filed an application for transfer, seeking to transfer the place of use and point of diversion for water right number 33-02091. No protests were filed to the transfer, which was formally approved in October 1992. In 1993, Sagewillow filed seven additional applications for transfer with the IDWR, proposing a change in the place of use for its water rights. Protests to several of the applications were submitted by respondents James Mays, Mays Land and Livestock, and Blaine County Canal Company. A recommended order was issued by the IDWR on May 22, 1995."

After Sagewillow filed objections to the proposed IDWR order, the department in April 1996 amended its order – but not to Sagewillow's liking. It held that a significant part of Sagewillow's right had been forfeited because 20 years had passed since much of the land in question had been irrigated. And, the high court noted, "the order voided the previously approved transfer of water right number 33-02091, which Sagewillow had been using to irrigate 320 acres of its property, and stated that as a result of the forfeitures, no more than 1,412 acres could be irrigated under Sagewillow's water right."

The next month, Sagewillow took the IDWR to court – Herndon's. The district judge sided with IDWR, and Sagewillow appealed again. But the Idaho Supreme Court said that non-SRBA Court was the wrong venue.

The court held: "Sagewillow's claim falls clearly within the exclusive jurisdiction of the SRBA district court. The waters involved are within the scope of the SRBA because they are part of the Snake River water system. See generally, In re Snake River Basin Water System, 115 Idaho 1, 764 P.2d 78 (1988). The IDWR decision involved a contest to Sagewillow's water right and transfer of the same.

"Accordingly, because Sagewillow's request for review of the IDWR decision falls within the exclusive jurisdiction of the SRBA district court, we hold that the district court below lacked jurisdiction to review the decision of the IDWR." ☒

SUPREME COURT ON SAGEWILLOW (5/2003) The Idaho Supreme Court on April 10 held that the Idaho Department of Water Resources wrongly applies a resumption-of-use defense in the contested Sagewillow, Inc., water rights.

The decision written by Justice Daniel Eismann noted, "The Department contends that resumption of use only applies if there are no junior appropriators in the same or an interconnected water source. If there are junior appropriators, then the resumption of use will not apply. According to the Department, as a matter of law the resumption-of-use doctrine only applies to the most junior appropriator."

But the Supreme Court said its interpretation was flawed, and it vacated the order. It also noted that forfeiture doesn't occur if the water – because of drought or other conditions beyond the water user's control – simply isn't available. Sagewillow had raised that point as a defense, and the Supreme Court said that the IDWR had not shown that water was available through the 20 years of diminished use.

The case was sent back to the Department of Water Resources for reconsideration. ☒

Administrative Order 1

The SRBA Court uses the normal rules of civil procedures … usually. But because it is an unusual court (not the same as a normal trial court), it also has its own set of rules of practice and procedure. These were laid out in Administrative Order 1 by Judge Daniel Hurlbutt, and have been amended from time to time. A current text is posted on the SRBA Court web site at http://www.srba.state.id.us/AO1NC.HTM.

Currently, its scope and purpose are stated as:

"The litigation of the SRBA will be governed by the Idaho Rules of Civil Procedure (I.R.C.P.), Idaho Rules of Evidence (I.R.E.) and the Idaho Appellate Rules (I.A.R.). These procedures supplement the I.R.C.P., I.R.E., I.A.R. and any other applicable laws or orders of this court only to the extent necessary to allow for the fair and expeditious resolution of all claims or issues in the SRBA. Provisions setting forth the manner of service and notice are adopted under the authority granted by Supplemental Order Granting Additional Powers to District Judge, Idaho S.Ct. 99143 (February 20, 1988)."

Procedures

ALLOCATING CLASSES (10/97) Major revisions to Administrative Order 1 – the SRBA Court's rule of procedure – are in the works and considered likely to be adopted by the end of September. The revisions divide subcases (individual water right cases) into two classes.

Class I subcases generally are considered to be the simpler cases, notably those where the difference between the claimant's request and the Department of Water Resources' recommendation is less than .8 cubic feet per second of flow, and where the Department felt would involve "miminal impact" on the system generally. An attempt will be made, the rule suggests, for quick and simple resolution of these cases at the claimant's hearing with the special master. A Special Master report might be drafted – even in handwriting – at the meeting. Absent a settlement, a trial would be scheduled for within 45 days. Class II cases would include most of the rest: larger and more complex cases where IDWR involvement is likely to be intensive, and where a larger possibility of litigation exists. These cases involve more procedures within the SRBA Court system, but Judge Daniel Hurlbutt said the new rules even here are aimed at greater informality and more flexibility.

"The factor is going to be the amount [of water] that's in dispute," Hurlbutt said. He said the changes reflect the actual practice special masters have encountered in subcase activity, and so won't mean any major changes in actual procedures. (The AO1 document itself, includes a massive revision to incorporate the new material.)

In many cases, the "preliminary recommendations" from IDWR would be dropped, and cases would go directly to the special master.

The revisions were drafted by Special Master Fritz Haemmerle and IDWR Attorney Peter Anderson. Anderson said that some of the ideas for the two-class approach came from a successful approach used in the Yakima River Adjudication in Washington state, on which he once worked. ☒

WHO IS NOTICED? (7/1999) Department of Water Resources officials said at the June 15 SRBA information meeting that several questions have arisen concerning providing proper notice to a number of parties in the SRBA.

IDWR Adjudication Chief David Tuthill pointed out that the last "notice handbook" for the SRBA is a decade old, updated mainly through the early 90s, and several issues have arisen since.

• Many original notices, Tuthill pointed out, said that "in-stream and stockwatering rights did not have to be claimed because of potential general provisions. The firefighting general provision was accepted … [but] the Court's order regarding deferring stockwatering rights only defers for small stockwater [claims]. So, large stockwatering rights need to be claimed, but notice was inadequate."

Those large rights refer to operations with more than 1,000 head of cattle, Tuthill said. He said the numbers of such operations is small, and the department will try to identify them and serve new notices on them.

"The ones we're concerned about are those that weren't claims because the operator thought it was deferrable," Tuthill said.

Smaller claims (under 1,000 head of cattle) are "deferrable" and claims on those in-stream uses may never need to be filed.

• The department's new computer mapping technology has allowed it to pick out irrigated lands for which no claims have been filed, but current SRBA procedures do not provide any course of action the department should take.

Tuthill said that he plans to submit a proposal to the SRBA Court at the July status conference.

• In a related area, Tuthill also raised this question: "Does Idaho Code 42-1408(4) require second-round service on 'claimants' who have not filed or does it require service when a 'water use' has not been claimed?"

• Many people who buy property after the initial round of notices go out, may never receive notice of their case in the SRBA, Tuthill said.

"Notice is not showing up on title reports," he pointed out. He asked: "Is the statutory requirement that the filing of this notice with the county recorders … constructive notice of its contents enough for due process?"

He said: "The question is, how does notice filter down to the buyer?"

Judge Barry Wood asked: "What do you suggest?"

Tuthill said, "Well, it's a tough one, your honor." He has said that the department does not have enough personnel to track all the property changes in the state. ☒

STOCKWATER NOTICE (8/1999) Department of Water Resources officials have prepared a new plan for "second round service" to provide notice of SRBA progress to many water right claimants.

IDWR attorney Peter Anderson noted that state law requires the department to provide both an initial "round of service" (of a notice of commencement of the SRBA) and a second pass as well. "The department now is moving on to new basins where the second round service hasn't been completed," Anderson said.

He said that as in the case of the plan for the first round of service, the department would plan to "locate potentially unclaimed water rights; determine the places of use for such rights; determine the owners of such places of use; [provide] service by certified mail on those owners."

A draft proposal on second-round service also notes "A problem arises because places of use are identified in IDWR's water right records only by quarter-quarter section. IDWR may attempt to determine which portion of the quarter-quarter section is the place of use for the unclaimed water right where this can readily be done."

There's also a plan for unclaimed portions of water rights: these "will be identified by comparing split claims with the water right record to determine if all of the water right record was claimed. If IDWR determines that the owner of the unclaimed portion of the water right record has filed claims in the SRBA, that claimant will not receive second round service."

"What we've done is to streamline the second round service plan," Anderson said. ☒

LENGTH OF DEFERRAL (6/2001) Another of the unsettled questions in the SRBA: When the adjudication began, many users of very small amounts of water were told that they did not have to file claims in the SRBA, at least not right away. The question now: Do they ever have to file, and if so, by when?

Department of Water Resources attorney Nick Spencer said the question goes back to the early days of the SRBA.

Many small claims in the Snake River Basin generally were considered too small to merit the expense and effort of full-scale involvement in the SRBA, Spencer suggested, but said federal agencies were concerned that if they were not involved in some way, the SRBA would not be a "general" adjudication. (If it were found not to be general, it would fall outside the scope of the congressional McCarran Amendment, which requires federal participation in general stream adjudications.)

The compromise was to serve all claimants, even the smallest, with a notice that they would be bound by the SRBA, and allowing them to participate in the case. They were formally "joined" as parties, but given the option not to file claims in the case, at least not right away. That approach was established through an order issued by former SRBA Judge Daniel Hurlbutt in 1989.

Spencer noted that even now, small-scale domestic and stockwater claimants can file but are not required to, and do not face losing their rights by failing to file. Such small claims, he said, must be filed only if the claimant wants to transfer them or have them administered.

The process was adjusted in 1995, "streamlined," Spencer said, allowing claimants to come to the court to file notice of late claims. ☒

NEW APPEALS PROCEDURES (7/2001) SRBA Judge Roger Burdick on June 25 established a clarified list of procedures for filing appeals from his court.

The order, he said, was intended to supplement Idaho appellate rules.

Most of the rule changes note what information must be included in an appeal, and what documents should accompany an appeal to the Idaho Supreme Court.

"To file a notice of appeal for multiple subcases or for consolidated subcases, parties must consider how those subcases were decreed by the court," Burdick wrote. "If the court treated the subcases as one group and issued one partial decree or one interlocutory decision for the group, the appellant need only file one notice of appeal listing all the subcases in the group. There would be only one appellate fee and one record on appeal. If the multiple subcases or consolidated subcases were treated as a group by the court, but were decreed individually or if an interlocutory decision was entered in each individual subcase, then the appellant must file an individual notice of appeal for each subcase. Each notice of appeal would require a separate appellate fee and record on appeal." ☒

NO COMPROMISE? (2/2005) In many cases the SRBA Court has urged parties to develop their own language on water right definitions, and has adopted a number of compromises. (The Nez Perce agreement, which is still in process, may be the single most substantial of these.)

But not always has everyone been able to develop a compromise solution.

That is what led to this court order, signed by SRBA Judge John Melanson and released on January 7:

On September 1, 2004, this Court issued a *Memorandum Decision and Order on Cross-Motions for Summary Judgment*, Consolidated Subcase 91-63 (Sept. 1, 2004). At the conclusion of the opinion, the Court ordered the parties to attempt to agree upon a remark to be included in the partial decrees for the subject water rights, which defines the ownership of the rights consistent with the Court's opinion. The remark establishes how the ownership element will appear in the partial decrees and also determines how future water rights involving the same issue should be recommended by IDWR. The date for submittal was extended until January 3, 2005. Ultimately the parties did not agree upon specific language, albeit the proposals appeared to all be legally consistent with the Court's ruling.

THEREFORE, the following are hereby ordered:

1. The name of the United States of America acting through the Bureau of Reclamation shall appear in the "*Name and Address*" element of the partial decrees.

2. In the "*Other Provisions Necessary for Definition or Administration of Water Right*" section of the partial decrees, the following remark shall appear:

Although the name of United States of America acting through Bureau of Reclamation appears in the Name and Address section of this partial decree, the ownership of this water right is divided. The United States Bureau of Reclamation holds nominal legal title. Beneficial or equitable title is vested in the landowners using the water. Pursuant to Idaho law, the landowners' interest is held in trust by the various irrigation organizations contracting with the Bureau of Reclamation for delivery and/or storage of this water, in quantities and/or percentages specified in the respective contracts between the Bureau of Reclamation and the irrigation organizations.

Document management

The idea of a practical difficulty in handling large volumes of information seems almost odd in these days of tiny iPods and desktop computers handling terabytes of information. But at the time the adjudication began, and for a decade or so after, the handling and distribution of the immense amount of information the SRBA was sure to produce, seemed an enormous obstacle.

Begin with the 150,000 or so subcases destined for action.

DOCUMENT PRESERVATION (3/1/1993) Hagerman Water Right Owners, Inc., filed a request on Feb. 9 that the court set up a procedure for managing SRBA documents. A week later, at the Feb. 16 status conference, Twin Falls attorney Patrick Brown (of Hepworth, Nungester) asked Judge Hurlbutt to issue an order preserving relevant (discoverable) documents. He told Hurlbutt that in some past complex cases businesses and others have sometimes destroyed, as a matter of course, documents 5 or more years old; and the Adjudication now is 5 years old. Hurlbutt agreed to proceed.

Brown also asked Hurlbutt to set up a central document repository for the Adjudication. Hurlbutt said he would convene a committee to determine how such a repository could be established. ☒

ORDERING PRESERVATION (4/26/1993) While the details and a wide array of proposals for handling and preserving documents in the SRBA are yet to be worked out, Judge Hurlbutt took a preliminary step April 23 when he issued a sweeping order on document preservation.

The one-sentence order said: "It is ordered that no party to the SRBA may destroy any document or evidence kept in any medium which relates to a pending claim to the use of water in the SRBA or any document prepared to be used in the SRBA, except on motion and order of approval" by the court. Hurlbutt told the attorneys at the status conference that "all of you should caution your clients [that] this is a very broad order." He indicated it could be narrowed in future. ⊠

LITIGATION BY FORKLIFT? (9/25/1995) Everyone seemed to agree that there's got to be a better way, but they couldn't agree on what that way should be.

Boise attorney Jeffrey Fereday brought a widespread problem to the SRBA Court at its September status conference. In many areas, large numbers of water right claims, especially those involving federal and tribal claims, often involve only a few and simple issues — the same issues for each of hundreds or even thousands of claims. Fereday proposed service of what would amount to consolidated documents by the objectors to claims, listing the water rights involved and the common issues for that group. Serving full sets of identical objections on a large number of rights held by the same parties, he said, means unnecessary duplication. "We are definitely moving toward a litigation by forklift situation," he said.

(He also noted an irony: the client who prompted the proposal was Potlatch Co., "and yes, my client sells paper.")

Federal and state attorneys, however, opposed the idea, suggesting that Fereday's proposal would simply mean shifting the paperwork burden from objectors to claimants. Each claim has to be settled individually, said U.S. Attorney Daria Zane, and someone has to wind up filing claims and objections on each. Whatever such work the objectors don't do, the claimants will have to.

The workload and cost at stake is considerable. Idaho Deputy Attorney General Clive Strong noted that the objections to in-stream flow claims could run to 300,000 pages, at a print cost of around $20,000. ⊠

STREAMLINING (10/9/95) Judge Daniel Hurlbutt partly approved a request to streamline the water claim objection process. That came in response to a proposal made at the September 19 status conference by Boise attorney Jeffrey Fereday. Fereday proposed service of what would amount to consolidated documents by the objectors to claims, listing the water rights involved and the common issues for that group. Serving full sets of identical objections on a large number of rights held by the same parties, he said, means unnecessary duplication. "We are definitely moving toward a litigation by forklift situation," he said.

Federal and state attorneys, however, opposed the idea, suggesting that Fereday's proposal would simply mean shifting the paperwork burden from objectors to claimants. Each claims has to be settled individually, said U.S. Attorney Daria Zane, and someone has to wind up filing claims and objections on each. Whatever such work the objectors don't do, the claimants will have to.

The workload and cost involved is considerable. Idaho Deputy Attorney General Clive Strong noted that the objections to in-stream flow claims could run to 300,000 pages, at a print cost of around $20,000.

In his October ruling, Hurlbutt indicated that he saw validity to both arguments. He noted that "parties opposing the motion have done so on the basis that, as the court is required to do, they prefer to maintain separate files for each water claims in order to best represent their clients. Therefore, the suggested procedure would shift the burden of copying objections for those individual files onto the claimant. …The proposed streamlining process would, in fact, result in far greater confusion and add both time and expense to the process of sorting out the impacted rights. For example, an objection which is filed to scores or even hundreds of rights raises some difficulties for parties, including the claimant, who wish to respond to that object. Confusion will arise as to whether the responding party must file one single response to the multiple-objection form or individual responses for each water right named in the objection."

What Hurlbutt did, in agreeing in limited part to Fereday's request:

In connection with all those federal and tribal non-consumptive claims filed March 31, 1994, all objections can be served on the federal department of agency filing the claim by mailing one to the U.S. Department of Justice (at Environment and Natural Resources Division, 550 West Fort Street, MSC 033, Boise ID 83724), except for service on the three tribes.

And, he said, "the owner of the water right section of the objection form must be completed indicating the owner of the right as listed in the Director's Report. It is intended that this change in the service requirement will eliminate service of duplicate copies of objections on federal entities." ☒

WEB SITE (6/97) The SRBA Court is officially on the web. It's been a long time coming, since the spring of 1996, when Judge Hurlbutt decided to move many of the court records which have bee available on the IWATRS bulletin board computer system onto the World Wide Web, available through the Internet.

The web site has been up and available for review for more than a month. But on May 29, Court Administrator Jeff Runkel sent a letter for distribution noting that the site is available for general use. The URL for the site is www.srba.state.id.us .

It is available just from 7 a.m. to 7 p.m., for security reasons, Runkel said.

He also noted that "for those users who are currently accessing IWATRS using the dialup service, things will remain as they are for the time being. However, the court is planning to discontinue the dialup service, due to resource limitations." ☒

RECORDS RETENTION (3/2003) The Idaho Department of Water Resources is reviewing, and may change, its policies on records retention in the SRBA. The action comes as the department begins planning toward a move, in another 18 months or so, to a new Water Center building.

"It's a healthy opportunity to consolidate records," Adjudication Chief David Tuthill told the SRBA Court at a February 18 information meeting. At the same time, he said, "We want to make sure we're in compliance with the court on records keeping."

He said he plans to set up a committee to review the records retention policy, and report back to the court in March.

He indicated his interest is less in destroying documents than in moving some of them off site, away from the IDWR office. Some could go into "cold cold" storage, at the State Historical Society archives, and others into "medium cold" storage at the state records center.

Special Master Terrance Dolan cautioned that the records be stored in a way that individual documents can be located when needed – a problem he said he observed in a Wyoming adjudication – and that they be protected from theft or distribution.

The SRBA Court, which has a records policy of its own, reviewed about six months ago the possibility of changing its procedures to incorporate more electronic scanning and storage of documents. No document-storage changes have been made yet, however, or are contemplated in the short term. ☒

RECORDS AVAILABILITY Since the 90s, when electronic storage space was still expensive, both the court and the department have placed massive volumes of SRBA records on the web, available for general access. Through the court's IWATRS system, accessible on the court's main web page (www.srba.state.id.us), thorough lists of water rights, claims, objections and documents are posted. The department's SRBA-related web pages are less massive, but still extensiuve. ☒

The Idaho Legislature and the SRBA

The Idaho Legislature established the SRBA in the first place, ordering that a lawsuit be filed with the Idaho Department of Water Resources as plaintiff. It has been active in the SRBA several times since, too, changing the rules in mid-case.

ANTI-SRBA LEGISLATION? (1/10/1994) The Snake River Basin Adjudication goes to a different kind of court – the Idaho Legislature – this week, as lawmakers consider what to do about an SRBA that has become unpopular in some quarters. The first action on the SRBA is a hearing before the Joint Finance Appropriations Committee (JFAC, which drafts the state budget, including for the SRBA court) on January 12, reviewing the funding shortfall generated by the U.S. Supreme Court decision last March exempting federal agencies from adjudication filing fees.

But more is expected to come.

One senator, Republican Stan Hawkins of Ucon, tried several years ago to persuade legislators to impose a moratorium on adjudication action. Now a member of JFAC (he was appointed to it last summer), Hawkins plans to try again.

"We had a lot of breaches in the adjudication agreement," he said. "I think there's a lot of work being done that under the strictest definition of the adjudication, is not necessary." He noted that some concern has arisen that the SRBA may result in restricting use of water in the state, and if that had been understood at the time the adjudication bill was in the legislature, it never would have passed.

A moratorium, he said, might allow time for many informal agreements and settlements before a court imposes action. "It might be good to see how it works for five years," he said.

He brought up the idea again at a JFAC hearing January 12, after pulling up a budget report from former Water Resources Director Ken Dunn in 1985 – including a projection for relatively modest funding needs and a 12-year plan for completion of the adjudication. (By most conservative estimates, the SRBA is expected to last at least 16 years from start to finish, and probably substantially longer.)

"Where are we headed with this thing?" Hawkins said. "I think it could go on for 40 years."

Water Resources SRBA Administrator David Shaw replied that the shorter estimate was based on earlier adjudications, while this one has run into different problems and conditions. Shaw showed the committee "red light" and "green light" options for the SRBA, the former showing impacts of closing down the adjudication, the latter discussing the Department of Water Resources' recommendation that it continue and be fully funded. Funding shortfalls, he noted, do not arise until the 1995 fiscal year (which begins July 1). Over the eight years that follow, he said, total SRBA funding shortfalls would reach $32 million under the current revenue structure.

One possibility for resolving that, he said, is imposition of a water use fee.

Hawkins acknowledged that "we'll lose this time, probably." In any event, he said, he won't vote for more funding for the SRBA this year, and a split vote on the SRBA budget is likely in JFAC this year. ☒

AN SRBA REDESIGN? (1/31/1994) Key Idaho legislators have asked the Idaho Attorney General's office to draft legislation which would change the procedures used for determining water rights in the Snake River basin Adjudication.

The request followed extensive hearings throughout the first three weeks of the Legislative session concerning the SRBA, presented primarily by the Department of Water Resources. Director Keith Higginson and others outlined the status of the massive case, and the mounting costs involved.

Lawmakers have particularly noted the U.S. Supreme Court ruling of last March, exemption federal agencies from fees in the SRBA, and a more recent SRBA Court ruling that under some circumstances the private attorney general doctrine could be invoked, providing payment for legal fees for some private parties, from state coffers.

As those hearings came to an end, on January 24, Sen. Laird Noh, R-Kimberly, and Rep. Golden Linford, R-Rexburg, chairs of the Senate and House Resource committees respectively, wrote EchoHawk to ask for a rewrite of the SRBA law.

"Some issues have evolved which appear to require legislative attention," they wrote. "The U.S. Supreme Court decision relieving the federal government of payment of filing fees, the imposition of the private attorneys' doctrine by the court and a much greater volume of litigation tha[n] anticipated have caused great concern over costs. The perception of the legislature at the time of initiating the adjudication was that much of the conflict resolution and factual determination would be made through administrative processes of the Department of Water Resources so as to minimize litigation. It appears, however, that many such conflicts are moving directly to court with the attendant costs and delays to participants and the state.

"We believe," they added, "it is time to modify our adjudication statutes so as to bring the process back in line with original legislative intent. We need your assistance and guidance to accomplish this and how you can work with us to these ends."

The job of drafting legislation to match the intent of the letter was given to Clive Strong, the lead state attorney in the SRBA. Strong, who has been busily at work on a state Supreme Court appeal from the SRBA court among other matters, said he plans to have proposed legislation ready for examination sometime this week.

Strong said he expects to base part of the proposal on the Oregon water adjudication system, which places greater emphasis on administrative resolution of water cases. ☒

SRBA REDRAFT (2/28/1994) Legislation that would greatly re-route the Snake River Basin Adjudication, into a more administratively-oriented operation, has been ordered drafted by key members of the Idaho Legislature.

The measure is based on a draft prepared by Clive Strong, chief of the attorney general's Natural Resources section and the lead state attorney in the SRBA. "This is one concept, and not the only concept," Strong said. As drafted, it was based around concerns expressed in a January 24 letter.

At a February 24 meeting, Linford said "there is a feeling [among legislators] this thing has become bogged down, expensive and out of hand." Unless greater progress and less cost is shown soon, he warned, legislators will be reluctant to continue funding the SRBA. He also asked attorneys present at the meeting (including about a dozen of the most active SRBA attorneys), "Is this particular court part of the problem? If no one [here] wants to speak to that, that's fine."

Several attorneys suggested that was not the case. Attorney William Ringert, who was on the losing side of the court's recent decision to rule the "presumption statute" concerning irrigator water rights unconstitutional, said, "Frankly, I think the judge did the state a favor."

And Ringert, who as a senator in 1985 was involved in preparing and passing the SRBA statute, said that while some changes probably should be developed, "we shouldn't abandon the investment we already have."

Others said the problem is serious enough that immediate action is needed. Rexburg attorney Jerry Rigby said "it's imperative it be done in this session," and Noh said he was beginning to think about the possibility of a special legislative session this year to consider the SRBA.

Strong's 32-page draft, dated February 17, responds to the concerns about high costs and a movement away from administrative action. It makes numerous changes to existing law and adds some new sections. The core of the bill is built, Strong said, around expanding the use of the director's report of water rights. It also covers a wide range of other subjects.

• Prohibition of application of the "private attorney general doctrine" in water adjudication cases. The doctrine has been invoked in two cases by the SRBA court, and involves state payment for legal expenses for certain types of private-party actions seemed to have widespread benefit.

• All claimants would be required to pay fees for exceptions.

• The draft does not include a rewrite of the presumption statute (42-1416) which was recently ruled "void for vagueness" by the SRBA court, but it does include an extensive redraft of the associated "accomplished transfer" statute (42-1416A) which was also thrown out by the court. The rewrite changes the emphasis of the statute from the rights of a water right holder to the procedure to be used by the Department of Water Resources.

A statement of intent says the lawmakers find "some water users . . . have changed the place of use, purpose of use, point of diversion, nature of use or period of use of their water rights without compliance with the transfer provisions of sections 42-108 and 42-222, Idaho Code . . . [and] that the present water use patterns resulting from these changes is in the public interest if they do not cause injury to another water right. One of the purposes of the adjudication is to develop an accurate description of all water rights. Denial of a claim based solely upon a failure to comply with sections 42-108 and 42-222 where no injury or expansion exists, would cause significant undue financial impact to a claimant and the local economy." The provision says the changes to 1416A are designed to avoid this impact.

• Changes the impact of the adjudication, from being binding on "all persons" to being binding "in the adjudicated water system." Parties such as conservation groups have used the "all persons" language to try to leverage access to the SRBA.

• Specifically says "the director [of Department of Water Resources] retains jurisdiction of all decreed water rights under chapters 2, 3 and 6, title 42, Idaho Code" and of all beneficial use water rights. Outlined some procedures for alternative dispute resolution. Attorneys present noted that the SRBA court has proposed ADR methods and fostered a recent Boise workshop on the subject; but Department of Water Resources SRBA Chief David Shaw suggested the court has given "lip service to ADR."

The draft gained general distribution at two meetings on February 24, one involving private and state attorneys and another also including Noh, Linford and Rep. Bruce Newcomb, R-Burley, the House majority leader.

The proposal drew sharp criticism from a number of quarters. Richard Simms, now a Hailey-based attorney practicing *pro hac vice* in the SRBA and formerly a court-appointed master in the case, said it could run afoul of the federal McCarran amendment in several ways. (Simms said that he was speaking for himself, not for a client.) The amendment waives federal immunity in the case of a state water adjudication lawsuit; Strong said that since the SRBA is already underway as a court case, that should not be a problem. But Simms said that a change in procedures could cause federal courts to view the SRBA as basically an administrative proceeding, and insist federal water rights be adjudicated in federal court. "The supreme courts of at least five states in the west have defined the suit in such a way as to render this one [the SRBA] outside the [McCarran] definition if the legislation were passed." ☒

THE 1994 SESSION (4/11/1994) In the final hours before the Legislature adjourned sine die on April 1, it passed a whole tribe of water-related legislation that will have a big impact on the SRBA.

A part of one measure may render moot (or not) the basin-wide issue now under consideration by Judge Hurlbutt: the role of the Department of Water Resources in the adjudication. The legislation limits the role to that of technical assistant.

But other aspects were intended to address concerns considered more pressing, especially exemption of federal agencies from SRBA filing fees, and the impact of a Supreme Court decision ordering delivery of water (by the IDWR). The measures were signed into law on April 7 by Gov. Cecil Andrus, who expressed concerns about them even as he did so. "We probably are financing the careers of another 15 to 20 water lawyers for the next decade," he said. The measures went into effect on that day.

The key legislative movers behind the legislation were Resource Committee chairs Sen. Laird Noh, R-Kimberly, and Golden Linford, R-Rexburg, and House Majority Leader Bruce Newcomb, R-Burley.

More than a dozen private water law attorneys worked on the measures, and so did Clive Strong of the Attorney General's office, who coordinating the drafting.

The effort resulted from "a very bad hand dealt to water management and the agricultural and financial community," Noh said. The resulting compromise, he added, included "a broad package of decisions by the water user community."

The measures had broad support and easily passed Senate and House. "It's going to correct the problems we need to have corrected," said Rexburg attorney Ray Rigby.

But they had critics too, including attorney Pat Brown (whose legal actions led to some of the court decisions these laws seek to turn back) and, in one specific area, conservation groups (who expressed concern at the narrowed limitations, and sometimes omissions, of local public interest as a component in SRBA action).

While the conservation groups pushed for a wider view of the adjudication, others said it should simply be a determination of water rights. "This adjudication should not be used as a vehicle for establishing state water policy," said William Ringert, a Boise attorney and former state senator.

Asked by Sen. John Hansen, R-Idaho Falls, whether the bills would be challenged in court, Strong replied, "It's certainly a possibility."

The key bills for the SRBA were House Bills 696 and its "trailer bill," 990; at press time, the governor had not acted on them but was thought unlikely to veto either. They would go into effect as soon as the governor acted on them.

Strong said that the overall intent of the measures is to help preserve the status quo among water right holders.

• Role of the director of Department of Water Resources (42-1401b, new). Simply: "as an independent expert and technical assistant to assure that claims to water rights acquired under state law are accurately reported . . ." He can also make recommendations. But he is not a "party" to the adjudication. (Another provision explicitly says that "director" means both the person and the IDWR.)

• New accomplished transfer and presumption statutes (42-1425 and 42-1426, respectively). These effectively replace existing statutes which were ruled unconstitutional by the SRBA Court and the Supreme Court. Those courts ruled the measures, as previously written, were too vague to be enforceable; they were challenged also on other grounds, but the courts did not review (pro or con) to the validity of those challenges. The new provisions are certainly clearer to the lay reader and not appear to be vague; whether they would survive other challenges is unknown.

The new accomplished transfer statute says that some people entitled to use of water changed the place, time or purpose of use without complying with Idaho law. The measure said "the continuation of the historic water use patterns resulting from these changes is in the local public interest providing no other existing water right was injured at the time of the change." It also said that "examination of these changes by the director . . . would be impractical and unduly burdensome." It said that a use which occurred prior to the filing of the SRBA in 1987 "may be claimed in a general adjudication" if no other water rights were hurt.

The new presumption statute says that some users "enlarged the use of said water enlarged the use of said water without increasing the rate of diversion and without complying with the mandatory permit system adopted by the legislature." The statute declared that the public interest lies in waiving those requirements "to insure the economic and agricultural base in the state of Idaho as it existed on the state of the commencement of the Snake River basin adjudication and to maintain historic water use patterns existing on that date."

The existing statutes (42-1416 and 1416a) which were ruled unconstitutional, were repealed.

• *Test basin reports and new claims.* The director's reports developed for the three SRBA test basins (34, 36, and 57) will be amended though updated filings with the court. (That's the revision in HB990; the earlier bill provided they "shall be remanded back to the director" to conform with the changes in the law). Also, the SRBA Court is required to allow for new claim notices which might be allowed under this change in law.

• *Separate agency filings* (42-1401c, new). Judge Hurlbutt has said that he considers the state of Idaho to be a single party which must speak with a single voice through a lead attorney. But HB969 says that "each state agency [except Water Resources], and the Idaho water resource board may file a claim and appear separately in any adjudication through the attorney general."

• *Claim forms* (42-1409). Collapses the two standard claim forms, for state and federal claims, into one.

• *Describing water rights* (42-1427). This notes that water rights in Idaho are described in a various ways. To protect existing uses, the measure says, "the legislature finds that it is in the public interest to provide a mechanism to decree previously undefined elements of existing water rights based upon conditions existing on the date of the commencement of the adjudication...

• *Federal water rights* (42-1411a). While state water right claims are collapsed into one form some provisions are added for federal rights. A possibly significant line: "Since no independent review of the notice of claim has occurred as provided for water rights acquired under state law in a director's report, a claimant for a water right established under federal law has the burden of going forward with the evidence to establish a prima facie case for the water right established under federal law."

• *Federal payment of fees.* Several sections restructured elements of the process intended to force federal payment for somewhat more of the services receives in state courts.

• *Sovereign immunity/attorney fees* (42-1423). This bans any award of attorneys fees or costs against the state, which "expressly refuses to waive its sovereign immunity to the imposition of any judgment for costs or award of attorneys fees."

• *Who can participate* (42-1404). This more explicitly limits actions in the adjudication to claimants of water rights. This removes language to the "public interest and necessity." It also limits the possible appellants of court action from a previous "any party who is aggrieved by the decree of the district court" to "any party who has appeared and is aggrieved."

And, in the section on responses to objections (42-1412), the provisions change from allowing objections by any "party" (which presumably could include such participants as the conservation groups) to any "claimant" (which limits it to those claiming a water right).

• *Director's report* (42-1411). Current law specifies the required content of the director's report on water rights. The revisions say "the director may file the director's report in parts as the director deems appropriate," and include explanatory information (which, the provisions state, have no legal standing). This basically gives the director full discretion on what to include in the report. It does still require him to file the director's report with the district court. This makes one other critical change; it makes the director's report prima facie evidence, and more explicitly than before places the burden of providing evidence on whoever challenges it.

• *Alternative dispute resolution* (42-1412). Provisions governing how the court must set up pre-trial conferences and trial preparations have been stricken and rewritten to require the court to "order a settlement conference to determine whether the matter can be settled." ☒

SRBA COURT RESPONSE (4/25/1994) The first official response of the SRBA Court to the mass of new water law legislation passed by the 1994 Idaho Legislature was very simple: The SRBA has come to a complete stop.

How long that will last is unclear. But while that has slowed the progress of the case, it does not mean any lack of activity in the area. Following his April 19 stay of all SRBA action, Judge Hurlbutt said that he would appoint a steering committee to consider a plan to action for proceeding next – and taking the many issues raised by the legislation in the proper order.

That committee was expected to be appointed by the end of this week.

The stay of proceedings had been suggested by the state of Idaho, the federal government and some other parties, to allow the court and participants to get their bearings under the new state laws.

Hurlbutt said that "The best way to ensure that the law is properly interpreted is to give everyone a chance to understand it."

As he made the stay he also told a crowded courtroom that he would hold a second, special, status conference April 25, and asked for comments from attorneys and others on how to proceed. He concluded with a few more statements and actions:

• He said he would set up a steering committee and order it to develop a blueprint for proceeding; to propose a sequence order of events (or suggest some events occur simultaneously), and to suggest the best method to resolve issues, whether to litigation or alternative means. The committee, he said, would help the court "avoid running up blind alleys."

He said he hoped to make the committee "representative" of participants in the SRBA and could include non-lawyers as well as attorneys. He said it would not include anyone from the Idaho Department of Water Resources.

• He will assume the 1994 legislation is effective, and work within it, at least until such time as any of it is ruled unconstitutional.

• Because of that, he declared the Department of Water Resources and its director, Keith Higginson, to be a special expert and no longer a party to the case. That also means, he said, the Department and Higginson will be sharply limited in how and with whom they can discuss the SRBA. Pending litigation, he said, the director cannot communicate with anyone outside the department concerning the SRBA, without specific permission from the court.

"There are extreme dangers here that the role can be compromised," he said.

The ruling's first impact came as soon as the court session ended, when a Twin Falls television reporter asked Higginson for an interview. He declined, saying he could not discuss the case. The ruling had been anticipated by state attorneys. At the opening of the session, lead state SRBA attorney Clive Strong said that up to then attorneys in the office of the Attorney General and attorneys assigned to the IDWR had worked closely together. Now, he said, two IDWR attorneys – Phil Rassier and Lynne Krogh-Hampe – would be assigned specifically to the department, drawing a line between the department's attorneys and the "state's." Hurlbutt indicated he thought that approach a good idea, for the time being at least.

The director's reports on water rights will be considered *prima facie* evidence, Hurlbutt said.

The judge's request for comments on how to proceed drew relatively cursory responses, and none from some key players.

One of the most substantive came from Higginson, who wrote the judge in an April 22 letter that "the completion of the SRBA is a formidable but, I believe, a manageable project."

Several specific issues were raised by some attorneys. A sampling:

• Nearly all the attorneys supported a steering committee to resolve issues. Strong, for example, said that "it's clear there will be challenges with respect to the statutes . . . We need to have some mechanism for bringing some order." One attorney who opposed was Patrick Brown of Hepworth, Lezamiz and Hohnhorst in Twin Falls, who suggested that most matters would simply have to be litigated anyway.

• Strong said that key issues to be resolved included the status of director's reports and pleadings, the director's role in future proceedings, the effect of the new presumption statutes, and attorney fees (which were limited in the new statute).

• Department of Justice attorney Daria Zane agreed in general, and noted that federal attorneys are closely examining how well the new legislation squares with the McCarran Amendment, which makes the federal government subject to general state water adjudications. She said the statutes were being examined to determine if the SRBA is still a "general adjudication." Asked by Hurlbutt what impact a "jurisdictional defect" in the legislation could have, Zane said the outcome could be "as extreme" as a federal request to be dismissed from the case. But she said study of the new law was not far enough along to determine if that would be appropriate.

• James Tucker of Rosholt, Robertson and Tucker suggested looking at a general approach to handling the current "transition period," and suggested placing a priority on ascertaining the constitutionality of questioned legislation. ☒

STEERING COMMITTEE (5/16/1994) The SRBA steering committee ordered to devise a way of "working through the transition period" meets for the first time on May 18 in Boise; Chair Robert Bakes said it will start with a review of how the adjudication came to its present situation.

The committee's mission, delineated in a May 3 order by SRBA Judge Daniel Hurlbutt, covers broadly the question how the adjudication should proceed in the wake of major changes wrought by the 1994 legislature.

Specifically, Hurlbutt ordered it to:

• "Identify issues and sub-issues" raised by the legislation.

• Suggest a chronological order and time for deciding the issues.

• Determine how the issues should be resolved, whether by court litigation, referral to future steering committees, or through some other means. And, Hurlbutt said, "If litigation is the preferred avenue, to recommend, the best legal mechanisms for resolution; for example, motion, declaratory judgement action, designation as a basin-wide issue, or trial of pending subcases which raise the issue."

• Deliver a written report on areas of agreement and disagreement.

• Complete its work within six weeks, if possible; but he said that extensions could be granted if necessary.

The report will be sent to those people who ordinarily receive court mailings, and it will be taken up at a status conference (presumably, in July, if the schedule holds).

Bakes said that the first committee meeting will feature a historical review of the SRBA and an examination of the 1994 legislation, as not all the members will have been familiar with it. Legislators, including several members of the Resources committees, are expected to be present as well.

"It's going to take a little while to get up to speed," he said.

Bakes said the questions of where the adjudication should go next likely will be taken up at the second meeting, which has been scheduled for June 13. Additional work is likely to take place between the meetings, he said.

The 17-member panel includes many of the most active attorneys in the SRBA, but representation of others as well: some non-lawyers, and some attorneys who have not been active in SRBA matters.

The membership includes:

• **Robert E. Bakes**, Chairman. Bakes is a former justice (from 1971-1993) and chief justice of the Idaho Supreme Court, now associated with the Boise law firm of Moffatt, Thomas, Barrett, Rock & Fields.

• **Clive Strong**. Strong is the state's "lead attorney" in the SRBA and head of the Attorney General's Natural Resources Division.

• **Peter Monson**. A U.S. Department of Justice attorney, Monson was co-chair with Strong of the committee which earlier this year proposed a restructuring (generally adopted by the SRBA court) of the steering committee process.

• **Timothy Hopkins**. A partner of Hopkins, French, Crockett, Springer & Hoopes, in Idaho Falls, Hopkins is one of the best-known attorneys in Eastern Idaho.

• **Ray Rigby**. A partner in Rigby, Thatcher, Andrus, Rigby & Kam in Rexburg, Rigby has been one of the best-known water attorneys in Eastern Idaho for many years; he is a former state senator and served on the Water Resource Board.

• **Bobbi Killian Dominick**. An attorney at Elam Burke in Boise, Dominick has been peripherally active in the SRBA recently.

• **John Hepworth**. A partner of Hepworth, Lezamiz & Hohnhorst in Twin Falls, he is head of the firm that has most shaken up the SRBA in the last year - and was the leading critic of the 1994 legislation.

• **Rebecca Craven**. Deputy counsel for the Nez Perce Tribal Executive Committee at Lapwai, she has been active in the SRBA.

• **James C. Tucker**. A partner in Rosholt, Robertson & Tucker in Twin Falls and Boise, Tucker has been consistently active and involved in the SRBA for several years, and participated in drafting the 1994 legislation.

• **Jeffrey C. Fereday**. An attorney at Givens, Pursley, Webb & Huntley in Boise, Fereday is a well-known water law attorney often active in the SRBA.

• **Randall C. Budge**. A partner with Racine, Olson, Nye, Cooper & Budge in Pocatello.

• **Terry T. Uhling**. An attorney for the J.R. Simplot Co., which has a wide range of water interests in Idaho.

• **Herb Whitworth**, of Mackay, and **Edward Shokal**, of Hagerman. Both non-attorneys have agricultural interests and have been active in the SRBA.

• **Craig Lewis**. A professor of law at the University of Idaho.

• **Brigette Bilyeu**. A special master appointed by the SRBA Court.

• **Carolyn Minder**. Minder is the staff attorney for the SRBA Court; she lives in Boise and works there and in Twin Falls. ☒

STEERING REVISIONS (7/11/1994) The SRBA Steering Committee report on how to proceed in the case, in the wake of 1994 legislation, became unanimous July 6. In revisions from its draft report, and in some respects from the final steering committee meeting on June 13, the document finally drew general approval from a panel split on approaches during its last meeting. The major change, however, incorporates a concept that seemed to draw universal approval at the meeting: "that by joining the Committee Report, individual members will not be bound in court by the recommendations in this report as it relates to their personal water claims, or the claims of their principals or clients."

Most of the changes came about after "extensive discussions" with several key members of the committee, including attorneys James Tucker of Rosholt, Robertson & Tucker, Jeffrey Fereday of Givens Pursley & Huntley, and Clive Strong of the Idaho Attorney General's office. The changes picked up the support of committee members who had supported the earlier version of the report. Among the changes:

• In a section on the new amnesty statutes, the court originally was asked to "engage in an administrative mechanism to assist the resolution of this issue." That was changed to simply suggest the court "inquire of the director as to whether he intends to engage in rule making to implement the amnesty statutes. The committee recommends that the court allow the director 30 days to inform the court whether the director will engage in rule making under the APA (Administrative Procedures Act) regarding how the director will implement the amnesty provisions...."

• In a list on constitutional issues, the language was softened to indicate several matters (such as separation of powers, void for vagueness issues and others) "which could be" addressed under the umbrella of consideration of the amnesty statutes.

The report was requested by SRBA Judge Daniel Hurlbutt to give the court guidance on how to proceed in the wake of major changes in state law on the SRBA, made by the 1994 legislature. ☒

DID THE LEGISLATURE HAVE AUTHORITY? (8/1/1994) The issue proposed by SRBA Judge Daniel Hurlbutt as the lever to move the SRBA forward is simple and fairly basic: Did the Idaho Legislature have authority, last session, to change the course of an already-filed lawsuit?

That's the essence of the July 15 decision by the judge, who also ordered a lift of the general stay on SRBA so this issue could be considered. (A few other narrow issues, including action connected with the Fort Hall water agreement, have also been exempted from the stay.)

Designated as Basin Wide Issue 3, he drafted the issue this way:

"Can the legislature expand or reduce the court's jurisdiction in the SRBA after jurisdiction attaches to the parties and subject matter of the action following issuance of the Commencement Order and filing of the notices of claims. Specifically, can the following legislative changes to the court's jurisdiction be made during the pendancy of the SRBA: changes in party status, pleadings and relief to the decreed; modification of the Idaho Rules of Civil Procedure with respect to the award of costs and attorney fees and the use of mandatory settlement conferences; modification of the Idaho Rules of

Evidence with respect to the designation of expert witnesses, the rules governing expert witness testimony, the admissibility of evidence and the legal weight to be attributed to evidence; and expansion of the court's jurisdiction to decree provisions controlling the administration of water rights by the Director of the Idaho Department of Water Resources."

And, he said, resolution of those questions "requires determining whether the SRBA is a court or administrative proceeding."

That latter point raises "McCarran" concerns. If the SRBA should be found to be an administrative proceeding, the federal government probably could opt out of it. The McCarran Act binds the federal government to participate in a state water adjudication only if it a court proceeding, not administrative.

One quickly noted aspect of the decision was that it did not appear to follow directly from the report, filed two days earlier, of the Steering Committee which Hurlbutt had appointed. He had asked the panel to propose what actions should be taken to move the SRBA head.

Basin Wide 3 did not reflect directly on any of those issues. The panel did offer a general list of questions which the new legislation do raise in the SRBA, however, and the question of the validity of the statutes was indicated implicitly or explicitly in them.

In a press release, Hurlbutt said that "It is critical to address changes in the court's jurisdiction now in order to be judicially and fiscally responsible. I hope early resolution of the important issues which have been recommended to me will help get the SRBA back on track . . .

"I am lifting the stay only to consider some of the most pressing legal issues which have been identified by the court Steering Committee. I intend to address these issues quickly as that water users will know whether the new statutes are valid before they are required to spend more time and money pursuing their water right claims . . . I think the spirit of cooperation we have seen among the parties has been remarkable during this transition, and I am optimistic that we will be able to begin decreeing water rights soon." ☒

STOOD UP (7/1994) It evolved into a faux pas, at least.

The legislative interim committee on the SRBA in June designated a subcommittee to review the SRBA financial situation, and its chair, Rep. Maxine Bell, R-Jerome, proposed to meet on that subject with Judge Hurlbutt. They settled on a meeting to be held July 15. (It was announced in advance, and was open to the public.)

Michael Nugent, supervisor of legislative research and legislation (in the Legislative Services office), discussed the meeting with Hurlbutt about a week in advance. Hurlbutt said that if he were asked a question he could not answer (for ethical reasons, because it would be a matter before him), he would simply decline to answer. The meeting was reconfirmed the day prior, and subcommittee members converged on Twin Falls.

What they didn't know what that Idaho Supreme Court Chief Justice Charles McDevitt had just ordered Hurlbutt not to meet with the legislators.

In a July 12 letter (not received until after the meeting) to Bell, McDevitt said that "it's my understanding that one or more of the members of your committee wish to express to Judge Hurlbutt their understanding of the 'intent' of the amendments to the pertinent water law statutes that were effected in 1994....

"I do not believe it would be appropriate to permit Judge Hurlbutt to address the issue of procedures or to receive comments as to the intent of the amendments adopted by the 1994 Legislature. The state of necessity will be represented in the proceedings before the Court and will be directly affected by the decisions of the Court. For the Court to have a dialogue with a department of the state government would not be appropriate. The matter of the legislative intent is something that if the issues arises will have to be presented to the Snake River Basin Adjudication Trial Judge in an appropriate evidentiary manner."

McDevitt said that he would be willing to answer staffing and budgetary questions personally. The SRBA budget is included as a subsection of the Supreme Court budget, rather than as a normal district court budget.

Later, at the full SRBA interim committee meeting, Rep. Bruce Newcomb, R-Burley, remarked that "when you read the letter, the integrity of that committee is somewhat impugned. …It treats the Legislature with disrespect."

The subcommittee members were met by SRBA court administrator David Egar, who said that McDevitt's letter had been sent (but discovered that none of the committee members had seen it).

Hard feelings may have been slightly smoothed over by a coincidence soon after. Subcommittee member Sen. Stan Hawkins, R-Ucon, stopped on his way out of town for lunch at the Twin Falls Burger King — where he ran into Judge Hurlbutt. The two sat and talked for a while. Hawkins has been a leading legislative critic of financial support for the SRBA, and from his seat on the budget-writing Joint Finance-Appropriations Committee has even suggested eliminating its budget. He described the lunch as cordial.

The finance subcommittee did hold a meeting, however, to discuss financing options. Bell summed up, in a report to the full committee, that "We did not find a silver bullet. …Basically, what we came up with was the fact that we will pay it." ☒

LEGISLATIVE AUTHORITY (8/12/1994) The sides have squared off in initial filings on Basin Wide Issue 3 in the SRBA. And opinions are sharply split not only on the key question it poses — whether the Idaho Legislature had authority to impose some of the legislation it passed in the last session — but even on basic interpretations of the Idaho Constitution and specific cases cited for authority.

The question stands: The debates over the legislature's actions earlier this year spilled far and wide over the last few weeks. The question posed in Basin Wide 3 was even challenged by attorney James Tucker of Rosholt, Robertson & Tucker (representing Idaho Power Co. and the North Side and Twin Falls Canal Companies).

And he said the issue of jurisdiction had at least been brought to the court's attorney in filing in June by the Hagerman Water Right Owners and the federal government. He said that Basin Wide 3 "will wholly subsume the jurisdictional issues raised by HWRO's motion to designate [related to the role of the director of the Department of Water Resources], IDWR's motion to implement uncodified section 34, the director's questions on how to proceed in pending subcases in the test basins, as well as those raised by the State of Idaho in its statement of issues . . ."

For the legislation: Attorneys for the state (in separate responses from the office of the attorney general and from the state Department of Water

Resources) defended the statutes, as they are obliged to do. The short response from Peter Anderson of the AG Natural Resources Division noted that, since statutes are considered to be constitutional until a court declares otherwise, and since no specific challenges to it had already been filed, there was little to say.

The IDWR, however, had plenty to say, most notably in an analysis written not by a participating attorney but by University of Idaho Law professor Dennis Colson, who teaches a course on the Idaho Constitution and wrote a book on the making of the Constitution, *The Tie that Binds* (University of Idaho Press, 1991). Colson argued strongly that the Idaho Legislature had full authority to pass the legislation it did, and to change the course of the SRBA in mid-stream.

Krogh, who said the IDWR was submitted its report to the Court not as a party but as an independent expert, had asked Colson to consider the matter. His 50-page report concluded that "generally speaking, the 1994 Amendments return to an old idea, and define the role of the Director somewhat like the 1903 Act defined the role of the State Engineer. Instead of being a party filing pleadings, the Director is again going to be an independent expert filing (maps) reports. The Supreme Court has long recognized that the legislature has the plenary and express constitutional powers to enact these special proceedings. It would be unusual if that recognition were not extended to the role of the Director."

Colson argued that in some respects, Idaho's government is not divided into executive, legislative and judicial sections with completely distinctive powers; instead, he said Idaho's system is more a "blend." While the SRBA is mainly a court action, he said, administrative and even legislative elements are attached to it. And, he said, "the power to determine rules of proceedings in the District Courts is shared by the legislative and judicial departments." Like many of the other briefers, Colson focused on a handful of Idaho cases concerning the Supreme Court's control of rules governing the district courts, especially *R.E.W. Construction Co. v. District Court* (1965), *State v. Griffith* (1975) and *State v. Yoder* (1975).

But he also said that the 1994 laws "do not purport to modify the Idaho Rules of Civil Procedure or the Idaho Rules of Evidence. They should be read to work with these rules, not conflict with them."

The only private party attorney making a detailed case for the constitutionality of the 1994 laws was Scott Campbell of Elam & Burke, representing the Sun Valley Co., Thompson Creek Mining and others. Campbell argued that the 1994 measures did not really affect the jurisdiction of the SRBA Court (the main issue noted by Hurlbutt) but rather addresses other questions. And, he said, "under Idaho law on retroactive legislation the 1994 amnesty provisions do not violate any constitutional right to due process. The Idaho Legislature is permitted to enact and apply the 1994 statutory modification to the SRBA and they are not retroactive on their face nor as applied."

Many of the other attorneys who filed briefs, including Roger Ling (A&B Irrigation District), Ray Rigby (Fremont-Madison Irrigation District), Terry Uhling (J.R. Simplot Co.), Don Olowinski (irrigation districts), Jeffrey Fereday (Idaho Ground Water Appropriators) and Tucker, filed shorter documents which did not contest the constitutionality of the statutes but also did not engage in extended defenses. Most noted that they had not yet seen any detailed challenges to the statutes, and hence had no arguments yet to respond to.

Against the legislation: Three briefs — from the United States Department of Justice (by Lee Leininger), Patrick Brown (for the Hagerman Water Owners Association) and William Hollifield (for the Big Lost River Users Association) said flatly the laws are unconstitutional.

Hollifield said the new laws conflict with the court's rules of civil procedure; is invalid because the SRBA had already been underway before the legislation was passed; is not retroactive (noting that the legislation itself did not state it should be applied as such) and conflicts with four sections of the Idaho Constitution.

The somewhat more limited Department of Justice brief was more detailed. It noted that the new laws require the court to automatically decree water rights noted in Department of Water Resources director's reports which have not been challenged. This, the report, argues, means "the new statutes mandate the decree . . . without permitting the court the discretion to review the legal determinations made by the administrative agency. The new statutes also violate Idaho law in retroactively affecting a party's vested rights without providing an adequate remedy."

It also noted the new laws create "an inherent conflict of interest in transforming IDWR, previously an advocate in this proceeding, into a decision-maker of both fact and law."

Those points were expanded on most fully in the 36-page Brown brief, the most direct counterpoint to Colson's analysis, in that it also maintained that the legislation was a simple attempt to strip jurisdiction from the SRBA Court — and that the SRBA is a court-run lawsuit and not in any way an administrative proceeding. Brown appeared to accept none of Colson's argument of "blended" powers. ☒

LEGISLATIVE RESPONSE (12/5/1994) Members of the interim legislative committee on the Snake River Basin Adjudication – all legislators re-elected last month – agreed to a relatively modest set of legislative proposals for the 1995 session, at their meeting November 29.

That may have been their last meeting, but co-chairs Sen. Laird Noh, R-Kimberly, and Rep. Golden Linford, R-Rexburg, said they may ask the Legislative Council for permission to meet again before the regular legislative session convenes January 9.

The committee approved, with some language changes, the recommendations of the co-chairs, which were developed into a 13-page report.

In it, Noh and Linford noted "there is some sentiment for terminating the SRBA. We believe, however, that such action at this time is not appropriate. Idaho has a finite water supply and there are real disputes over the use of this supply that must be resolved now. If these disputes are ignored, they will simply become more difficult to resolve. In addition, one of the major reasons for originally creating a comprehensive general adjudication for the Snake River Basin was to adjudicate the looming federal claims. Discontinuing the SRBA would open the door to adjudicating those claims in federal court without a comprehensive review of all claims."

They also indicated that the Adjudication had been "derailed" and was in apparent need of change in direction.

In one instance, Noh and Linford seemed more reluctant than other committee members to make further legislative changes in the SRBA. One section suggested that "the [interim] Committee should be mindful of the need to avoid continuing changes to the adjudication procedures. Ultimately, we must allow the changes that have been made to be tested before considering any significant new changes."

Linford noted that "we should avoid, every time there's a court decision, reacting to it" in the Legislature.

But on a recommendation by Sen. Stan Hawkins, R-Idaho Falls, that section was stricken by the committee.

Goals and Deadlines — The major concrete proposal was "that the IDWR [Idaho Department of Water Resources] and Court develop a date certain for the completion of the SRBA." One of the major problems thus far, Noh and Linford said, is the uncertainty in the adjudication. "Because of the pressing demands on Idaho's water supply, the SRBA must not follow the route of most other general stream adjudication[s] — where the adjudications seem to go on indefinitely. Thus, the Legislature should require each branch of government to develop measurable criteria that demonstrate who these goals will be achieved and a time schedule for completion of their duties."

The SRBA, they said, should specifically define water rights in the basin, including federal reserved water rights, and a decree should be issued at the end of the process "that contains sufficient information for state administration of all federal as well as state water rights."

Some members of the committee, including Hawkins and Rep. Jim Christiansen, D-Aberdeen, questioned how completely and precisely each water right can be defined.

Non-adjudication matters and the court — Another concrete change would limit the overall jurisdiction of the SRBA Court. It would not affect the Court's authority over the adjudication as such, but rather over other water rights issues in the Snake River basin. The 1994 Idaho Supreme Court decision in *Walker v. Big Los River Irrigation District* indicated that all water rights issues in the basin should be settled by the SRBA court, even if not part of the adjudication.

Noh and Newcomb presented, but did not specifically endorse, a measure specifically exempting from the SRBA Court's jurisdiction any appeals of decisions from the Department of Water Resources. "My own preference would be not to deal with this legislation at this time," Noh said. He said the hopes SRBA Judge Daniel Hurlbutt will "more aggressively" farm out non-SRBA cases to other judges.

The committee did accept, in principle, a statement by Rep. Bruce Newcomb, R-Burley, that if the SRBA Court is bogged down by non-adjudication matters, they should be shifted to other courts.

Schedule of federal claims — The committee considered and discussed various options for scheduling various claims in the SRBA. Noh and Linford suggested in their draft that "by scheduling the federal reserved water right claims first, the 40 percent objection rate by the United States might be reduced. Given this fact, the Committee may want to recommend that the Court and IDWR consider adjudicating these claims first. Implementation of this recommendation would not require any significant modification of the current schedule. The federal in-stream flows are already filed as one

Director's Report. Thus, only consumptive use claims would have to be reported to implement this suggestion."

IDWR Adjudication Chief David Shaw told the committee he had "heard this discussed a number of times," particularly since some of the federal rights have early priority dates (and high seniority). But not all do, he said, and questioned whether this approach would speed up adjudication of rights by other parties, including private Idahoans.

Deputy Attorney General and lead state counsel Clive Strong said that the matter of adjudicating federal claims first has sparked a big debate in western states. He said the idea is worth consideration, but stopped short of suggesting it be approved or not. The committee agreed to look at it.

Paying for the SRBA — The fill interim committee agreed to the suggestion of a subcommittee (chaired by Rep. Maxine Bell, R-Jerome) for paying the mounting costs of the SRBA after filing fee revenues run out.

"Nobody wants to spend the money," Sen. Marguerite McLaughlin, D-Orofino, reflected.

But committee members agreed, without dispute, that the SRBA would have to be funded somehow. The proposal is geared to the current costs of $4 million per year (combined costs by the Department of Water Resources and the Court); it proposes that $10 million of the FY1995 state general fund surplus be used to fund half that cost for five years, and that the general fund be tapped for the remaining $2 million in each year. ☒

THE 1995 SESSION (1/23/95) The legislature made one last-minute change to funding for SRBA services. After having eliminated three SRBA-related positions earlier in the session, the Joint Finance-Appropriations Committee (JFAC) passed a separate budget item providing funding for two attorneys and one paralegal from the adjudication fee account for the IDWR SRBA program. The bill's statement of purpose also said the appropriation "is required to account for the Attorney General's unified legal services bill which takes effect July 1." The bill provides an extra $133,800 in all.

The session wound up, however, with the SRBA funded only through March 1996, at which point lawmakers will take another look at the cash flow and decide what to do next.

Lawmakers also cut the position of SRBA court counsel (held by Carolyn Minder), and three positions in the Department of Water Resources Adjudication Division which have been vacant.

A REDESIGN (7/3/1995) The Idaho Supreme Court ruling on June 23 struck a number of attorneys at the June 27 "global conference" with Judge Daniel Hurlbutt in Boise as raising almost as many questions as it answered. But for Judge Hurlbutt, much of whose decision on Basin Wide Issues 2 and 3 was overturned by the ruling, the decision seemed to offer few mysteries.

"I can only encourage you to read and re-read the Supreme Court's decision," he told the assembled lawyers, repeatedly.

On hearing a suggestion from Boise attorney Jeffrey Fereday that a steering committee be appointed to consider how to proceed now under the Court's ruling (a suggestion echoed by other attorneys as well), Hurlbutt responded, "Too slow. I don't think time will allow us a steering committee. … I guess I've read this decision more than others have."

Later, he added: "The train's leaving the station … I think we're going to be going very, very quickly."

He said that he does not want to slow down work in the subcases in the test basins, and plans to focus the July 18 status conference in Twin Falls mostly on how to keep that work underway. He rejected proposals for staying part or all of the case.

On June 30 the judge issued orders carrying out aspects of the Court's decision:

• Noting that up to now Deputy Attorney General Clive Strong has been designated lead counsel for the state of Idaho, and that the Supreme Court said that each agency of state government can participate in the SRBA separately, the judge rescinded Strong's designation and ordered the Attorney General's office to designate lead counsel for each agency.

• He ordered the Department of Water Resources to send a representative to each subcase hearing by special masters in the SRBA, in contested cases.

Hurlbutt did say that some questions remain to be resolved.

Attorney James Tucker of Rosholt, Robertson & Tucker, representing Idaho Power Co., pointed out that, "whether prudent or not," many parties in the SRBA have relied on the Department of Water Resources to carry out a crucial role it now cannot. Until the Supreme Court's ruling, the Department (and its director) was considered a party in the case, someone who could challenge questionable water rights assertions, and someone with whom a claimant could "settle" in reaching an agreement. The Legislature pulled the Department from the case as a party, making it a special expert instead. That leaves, Tucker noted, open questions: with whom does a party settle in negotiating a water right (one attorney later compared it to a one-handed handshake); and to whom can the parties in the case look as a "watchdog" over spurious claims?

"Your point is a good one," Hurlbutt said. "Now, what do you want me to do?"

That point was not thoroughly resolved.

Strong said that the decision still leaves open the question of what, exactly, will constitute a decreed water right. (He suggested that the proposals to come out of the Fort Hall water right agreement may provide some useful templates.) Hurlbutt said, however, that a careful reading of the Supreme Court's decision will yield many of the answers concerning the form of the decree. ☒

1997 LEGISLATION PLANNED (9/1997) The Idaho Department of Water Resources has submitted proposals for several new laws that would have some tangential effect on the SRBA.

That results from a requirement by Gov. Phil Batt that agencies submit to the state Division of Financial Management, by early August, a list of "ideas" the agencies have for 1998 legislation.

The measures may not yet have been drafted, and might go no further.

The SRBA-relevant IDWR ideas submitted in August include:

● Legislation intended to clarify the definition of a domestic groundwater exemption, and "limit its use in areas already fully appropriated." The requirements would not affect users who have developed their wells prior to passage of the legislation, and probably would not apply statewide.

● Legislation requiring irrigation districts to register their boundaries with IDWR, so that areas of water use can be more precisely monitored.

● A similar measure intended to make more precise the use of water within canal companies and similar organizations. ☒

SRBA ROARS AHEAD (2/98) Idaho legislators were told, in the opening days of the 1998 legislative session, that the Snake River Basin Adjudication really is moving ahead "fast and furious."

And for the first time, a target end date for the SRBA – the year 2005 – gained currency in the legislature, the court and the Department of Water Resources. (That doesn't necessarily mean the goal will be met, but it does suggest a rough target for completion, more than has been generally discussed before.)

But questions and doubts remained.

Hurlbutt at JFAC: It was Judge Hurlbutt's turn to amass evidence and show it to the decision-makers, when he spoke January 21 to the budget-writing Joint Finance Appropriations Committee. But the committee seemed to absorb only some of it.

"I'm pleased with your report today," said Rep. Jack Barraclough, R-Idaho Falls. "This is welcome news for what you're going to do in 1998, but it's a few years late. … We hear a lot about what the people think. There are some disturbing comments out there."

He said he heard about conflict between the SRBA court and the Idaho Department of Water Resources, and "We don't have room for personalities and vanities."

At which point Hurlbutt pointed out to the committee that varied people and groups have many different agendas for the SRBA, and that he winds up being criticized by many of them. Some people, he said, still would like to see the SRBA abandoned, and others would be like to see it pursue various specific missions.

"I stand alone in limiting this case to inventorying water rights," he said. "I have been bludgeoned. … I go too fast. I go too slow."

At a time, he said, when the case is moving ahead with considerable and demonstrable, speed.

He said the court has worked on 15,920 water right claims in the three test basins, and more than 80% of them have been decreed.

Work around the rest of the state has been speeded, he said, by the decision to break apart the domestic and stockwater claims – about 80,000 of them – and settle them first. About 79,000 are expected to be resolved by the end of 1998, he said.

And he said the SRBA court has been scrupulous with its cost savings, to the point of analyzing the per-piece cost (even the time spent in copying and stuffing envelopes) of sending out paperwork. He said the court has found ways to save $21,000 for 1998 by cutting the cost of issuing partial decrees by 30 cents each.

JFAC Co-Chair Sen. Atwell Parry, R-Melba, asked him, "Are you seeing light at the end of the tunnel?"

"Yes I do," the judge replied. "The time frames we have set out are realistic … We have moved through the test basins. We have resolved most of these legal issues."

Strong at Resources (House & Senate): "I can tell you right now it is going fast and furious," Clive Strong told the House Resources & Conservation Committee January 15, making use of the favored terminology.

He noted "we've resolved most of the basin wide issues," and tens of thousands of partial decrees (mainly domestic and stockwater) will be issued this year.

But he acknowledged that not all issues are settled. And Rep. Bruce Newcomb, R-Burley, the House majority leader and one of the most active legislators in SRBA matters, brought up one of those topics little-discussed so far in official SRBA fora.

Newcomb (who also remarked later that many of his constituents were "getting damned tired" of the adjudication) asked about the possible impact of Federal Energy Regulatory Commission hydropower licenses on the adjudication, and specifically their impact on hydropower season of use.

Strong said that question remains open to some extent, and also another one not yet significantly addressed at all. In and around some federal Army Corps of Engineers projects, he said, the Corps is asserting control of some reaches of water on the basis of federal law covering navigability of streams, rather than a reservation of water. He said that would mean no water rights are needed for navigation uses. ☒

SUNSET THE SRBA? (8/98) The SRBA reared its head at the Idaho state Republican Convention at Post Falls, June 18-20. And a proposal aimed at ending the lawsuit lost, decisively.

One of the dozen-plus issues proposals offered at the party's Resolutions Committee called for sunsetting – ending – the adjudication after an additional five years. Several speakers said that the adjudication has dragged on at great length, and it should be concluded.

The resolution was defeated in committee, however. Twin Falls attorney Norman Semanko (of Rosholt Robertson & Tucker), who was also a delegate to the convention, spoke against the resolution. He said that the SRBA is moving along and that trying to impose a fixed deadline would not move the process faster. ☒

2000 MEASURES (5/2000) The 2000 session of the Idaho Legislature was not an especially decisive session in water rights legislation, but it did pass a lot of water rights-related measures. The measures passed included:

• **House Bill 400** provides specifically an idea that's been generally adopted already by the Idaho Supreme Court: That water can be used any time for firefighting purposes, whether or not the user (for that purpose) has a water right. This bill was also backed by the Department of Water Resources.

• **House Bill 544** in part covers a topic which has been a frequent topic in SRBA Court information sessions in recent months: reducing the statutory response period for the petition to assert injury from 120 days to 30 days by owners of water rights. This measure was proposed by the Department of Water Resources.

• **House Bill 545** concerns the law requiring water right owners in the Snake River Basin to file a notice of change in ownership or owner's address for a water right; this bill would make the requirement apply statewide. This measure also was proposed by the Department of Water Resources.

• **Senate Bill 1337** would change the filing fee for transfer of a vested right from $100 per application to a variable fee based upon the quantity of water. The IDWR, which proposed the measure, noted, "The proposed fee for an application for transfer would use the fee schedule for applications to appropriate water, as provided in Section 42-221, Idaho Code. The additional revenues to the water administration account will provide resources for the Department of Water Resources to address a growing workload."

· • **Senate Bill 1351** clarifies and backs up the current division of responsibilities between the Division of Environmental Quality (water quality) and the Department of Water Resources (resources) in the State Water Plan.

• **Senate Bill 1419** concerns livestock watering diversion. Proposed by the Idaho Water Users Association, it "allows diversion of stock water under limited circumstances and quantities, and without losing priority date. Current law would require relinquishing a favorable priority date if water is diverted from a stream channel. Enactment would result in reducing the turbidity and erosion caused by in-stream watering of livestock with no loss of priority date. Withdrawal of water is limited to 0.02 cfs (9 gallons per minute) per diversion. The installation requires withdrawal in piping and must contain an automatic shutoff device or the return of overflow to the original stream through pipes."

• **Senate Bill 1447** provides exceptions and defenses in water right forfeiture cases. The IDWR said its bill "recognizes that a water right shall not be lost or forfeited by a failure to divert and apply water to a beneficial use if the reason for the non-use of the water is to comply with the provisions of a ground water management plan approved by the Director. The legislation adds a new Section 42-223 to codify in a separate statute the specific exceptions or defenses to forfeiture of a water right previously listed in I.C. 42-222." The bill also includes other water management provisions. ☒

REVIEW IN 2001 (2/2001) Idaho legislators convening for the 2001 session in January seemed to have a higher comfort level with the Snake River Basin Adjudication than in some years

"Certainly, progress is being made," said Sen. Laird Noh, R-Kimberly, chair of the Senate Resources and Environment Committee.

Department of Water Resources Director Karl Dreher and Adjudication Chief David Tuthill both addressed that committee on January 15, and both said the SRBA is moving ahead and needs no significant course corrections at the moment.

"We're not requesting any [legislative] changes this year," Tuthill said. He said "the new judge (Roger Burdick] appears to be interested in carrying on the approach taken by Judge [Barry] Wood."

Legislator questions were fewer and less critically-tinged than in some past years.

Several, including Noh and Sen. Clint Stennett, D-Ketchum, asked what may happen to the hydropower water rights held by Idaho Power Company, when the adjudication reaches that area.

Tuthill said the department's review of those rights, which are located in the main stem of the Snake River (in what are designated basins 01 to 03) is not expected to occur until 2003 or 2004. ☒

AND IN 2002 (2/2002) Two measures proposed by the Idaho Department of Water Resources to speed along work in the Snake River Basin Adjudication have been approved by the Idaho Legislature.

● House Bill 415 reduces the period for filing responses to objections in the SRBA from 120 days to 60 days.

● House Bill 416 clarifies the amount of time in certain notices between filing a report with the director of the Department of Water Resources and the hearing, at which time the unobjected parts of the report will be decreed; and to clarify twhen IDWR files certain statements with district court. ☒

2008 SESSION (5/2008) Apart from two key northern adjudication bills which passed and were signed into law in March, most substantial water rights legislation had a tough time clearing passage before the Idaho Legislature adjourned for the year on April 2. Some that did pass:

● The first to become effective is **Senate Bill 1354**, which would "defer participation in the northern Idaho water adjudication of individual domestic water users and request the commencement order be issued only if the court determines it is possible to defer the adjudication of domestic and stock water users. In other Idaho water adjudications the court was able to defer domestic water users and they were not mandated to participate. This would make the treatment of northern Idaho citizens equal to the treatment afforded other Idahoans in the adjudication of water rights." Fiscal impact was estimated at $1.9 million.

● **Senate Bill 1418**, which would delete the Kootenai River Basin from the north Idaho adjudication, and clarify that the Clark Fork and Pend Oreille basins do not include Basin 98.

The statement of purpose said that "Given the absence of current water conflicts within this basin and the complexity of addressing international issues within this basin, there is no compelling reason to proceed immediately with the adjudication of the water rights within administrative basin 98."

● **Senate Bill 1348**, on non-forfeiture of rights in suspended mining operations. This measure, backed by the Idaho Mining Association, has been signed into law. Its statement of purpose said that "At times mining operations have not continued to put their water rights to beneficial use because mining activities have been reduced or discontinued due to low mineral prices. This bill exempts such water rights from forfeiture as long as the water right owner has maintained the property and the mineral rights for potential future mineral development." ☒

Paying for the SRBA

The Adjudication costs money. Plenty of money.

The original idea was that filing fees would pay for most or all of it, at least on the court site (and possibly at the Department of Water Resources as well). But more money than that has been needed.

WILL FEDS PAY? (5/10/1993) The U. S. Supreme Court on May 3 ruled in *United States v. Idaho, ex. rel. director, Idaho Department of Water Resources* (No. 92-190) against the State of Idaho's attempt to collect standard SRBA fees from federal government agencies participating in the adjudication.

However, state officials spent much of last week reviewing their options and considering other possibilities for collecting funds for federal agencies – or avoiding spending money on federal involvement in the case.

The case was argued on March 29. The decision came faster than many involved in the case had expected.

The decision was written by Chief Justice Rehnquist. Justices White, Blackmun, O'Connor, Scalia, Kennedy, Souter and Thomas joined in it, while Stevens offered a brief concurring opinion.

Like much of the argument surrounding the case, much of the decision focused on the McCarran Amendment, which "allows a State to join the United States as a defendant in a comprehensive water right adjudication...

"This case arises from Idaho's joinder of the United States in a suit for the adjudication of water rights in the Snake River. Under Idaho Code 42-1414 (1990) all water right claimants, including the United States, must pay 'filing fees' when they submit their notices of claims." These fees help pay for adjudication costs; federal officials and others have estimated federal fees could amount to $10 million or more.

The Court decided "that the McCarran Amendment does not waive the United States' sovereign immunity from fees of this kind."

The Court referred to the Idaho Legislature's approach to "financing the costs of adjudication water rights" by not allowing the Director of the Department of Water Resources to accept a water claim unless it is accompanied by "a filing fee based upon the fee schedule." Those funds are used to pay adjudication expenses.

When the United States tried to submit claims, the director refused them, citing the law. The United States then asked state district to require the director to accept the claims without payment. But District Judge Daniel Hurlbutt sided with the state, saying "The ordinary, contemporary and common meaning of the language of McCarran is that Congress waived all rights to assert any facet of sovereign immunity in a general adjudication of all water rights . . . which is being conducted in accordance with state law."

The Idaho Supreme Court upheld Hurlbutt. The U.S. Supreme Court agreed that "fees" and "costs" are different things. But the decision continued: "Before Idaho altered its system for recovering its expenses in conducting comprehensive water right adjudications in 1985 and 1986, Idaho courts, at the time of entry of final judgement, used to proportionately tax the 'costs' of the adjudication against all parties to the suit, and not simply against the losing parties. Idaho Code 42-1401 (1948). When Idaho revised this system, many of the items formerly taxed as 'costs' to the parties at the conclusion of the adjudication were denominated as 'fees,' and required to be paid into the court at the outset. This suggests that although the general distinction between fees and costs may be accurate, in the context of this proceeding the line is blurred, indeed."

The Court concluded, "While we therefore accept the proposition that the critical language of the second sentence of the McCarran Amendment submits the United States generally to state adjective law, as well as to state substantive law of water rights, we do not believe it subjects the United states to the payment of the sort of fees that Idaho sought to exact here. The cases mentioned above dealing with waivers of sovereign immunity as to monetary exactions from the United States in litigation show that we have been particularly alert to require a specific waiver of sovereign immunity before the United States may be held liable for them. We hold that the language of the second sentence making 'the State laws' applicable to the United States in comprehensive water right adjudications is not sufficiently specific to meet this requirement.

"The judgement of the Supreme Court of Idaho is therefore reversed, and the case remanded for further proceedings not inconsistent with this opinion."

State attorneys gave some consideration of whether the last two paragraphs afford any room for finding some other mechanism for imposing costs by the state. But they appeared, at week's end, to have more or less abandoned that approach. That initially seems to put the state in a quandary. Idaho legislators would rebel at digging up $10 million or more to pay, in essence, for federal participation in the SRBA.

And Idaho water right holders likewise would loudly object to paying the federal government (twice, to some lines of thought) to oppose their own water rights. Some possibilities and options:

• Because state law severely limits involvement in the case by anyone who doesn't pay fees, there was some talk in the Department of Water Resources last year that an adverse decision might shut out federal involvement in the case entirely. But such a course now seems unlikely, since the vast number of federal claims and objections already filed at the SRBA Court shows how incomplete an adjudication without federal involvement would be; some observers say it would be nearly worthless.

• A wide range of services commonly provided to parties involved in the adjudication, either at the Department of Water Resources or the SRBA Court, might simply be denied federal agencies (forcing them to pay for their provision on their own).

• The Idaho congressional delegation may be asked to back special legislation forcing the federal agencies to pay the Idaho SRBA fees; Congress could do this apart from the Supreme Court ruling. ☒

REPLACING FEDERAL FUNDS (6/7/1993) Who will pay the $10 million-plus that the state had hoped federal agencies would kick in toward meeting the bills on the Snake River basin Adjudication?

State officials are still quiet about how, exactly, they plan to address that question. But the issue will be taken this week to the top policy-making levels in Idaho government.

Thus far, attorneys in the Attorney General's office have discussed options. Early this week, Department of Water Resources Director Keith Higginson is expected to meet with Gov. Cecil Andrus to discuss some of those options.

• The difficulty is not immediate: SRBA funding as matters stand is on track for about two years, until about July 1995. However, the expected workload after that point, as massive numbers of water rights decisions are evaluated, is expected to push the budget far beyond current levels.

• Little has been done thus far in the congressional arena, publicly at least; Idaho's congressional delegation has said virtually nothing about the federal role in payment of adjudication costs. Some state pressure on the delegation to push for congressional payment of appropriation payments, seems likely. (The Supreme Court decision did not preclude a specific congressional appropriation.) State officials will cite a tight state budget; but members of Congress will cite even greater problems with the federal budget, and the difficulty of selling the federal payments as something other than a special-interest measure for the state of Idaho.

• The Idaho Legislature could be asked to provide the funding. Political opposition to that, however, could be tremendous. Many legislators would perceive themselves as being asked to use in-state tax money to pay for federal challenges to the water rights of their constituents, an extraordinarily difficult idea to defend in much of the state.

• Federal agencies could be forced to provide many services which the court ordinarily provides to filed participants in a case. But this probably would not make up even the larger share of the lost funding. ☒

FEDS: COMPLY! (8/2/1993) Was an order from the United States Supreme Court insufficient?

On July 19, Department of Justice attorney Peter Monson filed a request with the SRBA Court for the entry of an order in compliance with the decision of the U.S. Supreme Court specifically noting that federal agencies need not pay filing fees to participate in the SRBA. Monson's language notes that the high court having ruled that the United States has not waived in the McCarran Amendment, 43 U.S.C. 666, its sovereign immunity from monetary exactions in this case, the Director of the Idaho Department of Water Resources shall accept, process and file the United States' notice of water right claims without payment of filing fees.

About a week later, Idaho Deputy Attorney General Clive Strong offered a rewrite, suggesting that Monson's language actually went beyond the Supreme Court's, at one point saying it inaccurately expands the scope of the ruling.

Strong said Monson also went too far in referring to monetary exactions instead of the specific costs noted in the opinion. Strong's version says the McCarran Amendment does not waive the United States' sovereign immunity from I.C. 42-1414 [the SRBA court fee statute] ... ☒

SIMPSON SEEKS PAYMENT (3/2001) Idaho 2nd District Representative Mike Simpson in February reintroduced legislation aimed at requiring federal agencies to pay filing and other standard fees in water adjudication cases.

The "Water Adjudication Fee Fairness Act" addresses federal filing fees for water rights. Simpson introduced the same legislation in the 106th Congress. Currently, private citizens, companies and the state of Idaho all pay filing fees for reserving water rights in court, but federal agencies do not. Federal agencies have filed more than 40,000 claims in the Snake River Basin Adjudication court.

The bill is intended to help states that are caught in expensive water rights cases with the federal government. The Idaho Department of Water Resources estimates the State of Idaho has lost $113 million in unpaid federal claims.

"The federal government doesn't pay a dime when it files for water rights. The state of Idaho and other groups do," Simpson said. "This legislation is designed to ensure that private citizens, businesses and the state are on equal footing with the federal government when filing for water rights." ☒

PAYING FOR MEDIATION (7/2001) How much should the parties in the Hells Canyon and Wild and Scenic Rivers mediation sessions pay for the service? That was a topic of some discussion at the June 19 status conference, when federal and private parties proposed two different approaches. The federal view called for splitting the mediation costs evenly three ways, between the federal government, the state of Idaho, and the private parties.

The state and private parties proposal is that, since the federal agencies generally are on one side of the case and the private and state parties on the other, that the costs be split 50-50 between the two sides.

"We can't get off square one until we know how we're going to pay the person who is going to get us off square one," Judge Burdick said. He asked both sides to deliver briefs on their proposed plans within three weeks. ☒

SRBA FEES UP (7/2006) Beginning July 1, 2006, the fees to file a water right claim in the Snake River Basin Adjudication will increase across the board. The Legislature approved the increase during the 2006 session. It is the first time that filing fees have been increased since the SRBA process began nearly 20 years ago.

The increased fees will apply to those filing water right claims in the North Idaho Adjudication process set to begin next year.

Examples of the increased fees:

• Single family domestic and stockwater use, less than 13,000 gallons per day in total based on a permit, license, decree or statutory claim - ***50***

• All other previously unrecorded single family domestic, and stockwater use, less than 13,000 gallons per day in total - ***100***

• 100 acres irrigation, domestic and stockwater - ***300***

• Fish propagation, 14.2 cfs - ***384***

• Multiple family domestic, 1.6 cfs, irrigation of yards and gardens, 14 acres - ***448***

On July 1, 2006 the new fee structure for filing water right claims will be posted on the IDWR website: www.idwr.idaho.gov/water/srba/forms.htm - *Idaho Department of Water Resources*

BUDGET SLICES ADJUDICATION (3/2009) The state's and nation's ongoing economic crisis has impacted Idaho's water adjudications, along with so much else. A four percent budget recission measure (House Bill 61) cleared the Idaho House on a 68-1 vote, and it included a cut of $539,300 in the Idaho Department of Water Resources.

As of the end of February, budget activity—and much of the activity of the legislature generally—had slowed to a halt, partly because of rapidly-shifting economic conditions, and partly because of ongoing analysis of the just-passed federal stimulus package and its impact on Idaho.

On February 10, IDWR Director David Tuthill told the budget-writing Joint Finance-Appropriations Committee that the adjudications, Snake River and North Idaho, will continue on, but that cuts will slow them down.

He said that cuts in the department already have included 11 adjudication workers.

The northern Idaho adjudication now is estimated to be completed in 2018, a couple of years later than its original target date. Tuthill told the committee that his agency has received about 100 water right claims in the Panhandle, so far. Overall, however, he said that the northern adjudication process is continuing acceptably.

The Spokane *Spokesman-Review* quoted Senator James Hammond, R-Post Falls, as saying the delay is "probably OK, because there was so much apprehension. As more people get their rights adjudicated, other people will see that it's not as invasive as expected, that it's really good protection for a low cost." ☒

PRIVATE ATTORNEY GENERAL? (5/10/1993) A new twist to the way of adjudication in the SRBA was proposed last week by attorney Patrick Brown, his firm of Hepworth, Nungester & Lezamiz and the Hagerman Water Rights Owners, when they suggested use of a private attorney general structure. Private attorneys general, which have been used on occasion in other types of legal cases, are merited in this one, Brown said, because many water rights under adjudication will have statewide impact far beyond that of individuals who would have to pay for litigation costs.

Brown noted that the Idaho Supreme Court held, in a legislative reapportionment case (*Hellar v. Cenarrusa*), that "it is appropriate that the people of Idaho pay for services rendered in their behalf if there is a proper legal basis for their doing so." The bases, the Court indicated, centered around "the strength of the societal important of the public policy indicated by the litigation," the "necessity for private enforcement," the burden on the private arty and the number of people who could benefit from the result.

Brown did acknowledge that, "in the other cases [involving the private attorney general concept] the request to award attorneys fees came after the litigation was concluded. Here, the objectors request relief at the outset." But he maintained legal precedent for this, too, was ample.

In an affidavit, John Hepworth, senior partner in the firm, said that meetings with the Hagerman group had convinced him of its "inability to pay the fees that would be involved in the complex issues involved." Neither, he said, would his firm. No response been forthcoming yet from the state. It can be expected to object strongly. ☒

OK TO PRIVATE AG (10/25/1993) In his October 15 clarification of acceptance of a second Basin Wide Issue "the role of the director and Department of Water Resources in the SRBA" Judge Hurlbutt unleashed a decision that may have a tremendous impact on how private parties approach the SRBA, and on how it is paid for.

Specifically: the judge for the first time approved use of the private attorney general doctrine which allows an attorney for a private interest to be paid by the state for raising an issue of general public importance. ☒

APPEALING AWARDED COSTS (11/8/1993) The state of Idaho will appeal Judge Daniel Hurlbutt's $16,963 award – nearly all of the amount requested for attorney's fees under the Private Attorney General Doctrine. At stake: development of many new legal which possibly could be paid for in a similar manner.

Also at stake: an issue of whether Judge Hurlbutt's rulings on the private attorney general doctrine have been inconsistent.

This decision apparently is in addition to another approval of funds to be paid by the state to the Hepworth firm, in the case of designation of Basin Wide Issue 2. For the moment, quite a few people are holding their breath.

If the state does not prevail, the Department of Water Resources would have to come up with the money from some source other than the adjudication account (also called the 0337 account). What source that would be, is not clear.

The Private Attorney General Doctrine, outlined by the Idaho Supreme Court, holds in general than when a private party has to spent substantial amounts of money litigating a case with an outcome that in the public interest, and which no public entity would have brought, that public funds should help defray legal costs.

The award to the Twin Falls law firm Hepworth, Nungester & Lezamiz came following their successful argument that the Department of Water Resources had not, despite a statutory obligation, delivered water to several of their clients.

That case involved Alvin Musser, Tim Musser and Howard Morris, who found that water reaching their crops had fallen below their water right levels. Their requests for more water, filed with IDWR Director Keith Higginson, were rejected. But in court proceedings, Judge Hurlbutt found the director had not advanced any meritorious defense.

Hurlbutt also said the defenses against the Musser and Morris were "without a reasonable basis in fact or in law, and in some cases was frivolous and without foundation as well."

Hurlbutt's criticism of the director and the department was not soft or subtle. In one case, he noted, "IDWR's defense that no appellate case explains the director's duty to deliver water under the doctrine of prior appropriation also fails. The director does not need an appellate judicial interpretation of I.C. 42-602 in order to perform the duty clearly state by the legislature. Neither does he need a legal treatise… The director acted [by denying the Mussers' and Morris' request] in complete absence of any legal standards to governor his decision and as a consequence of not being prepared to lawfully perform his clear statutory obligation. The suggestion that he cannot perform his statutory duties absent judicial imprimatur is an abrogation of his duty rather than a defense."

The Hepworth firm asked for $17,099. Hurlbutt rejected only two small pieces of that request: $32 of discretionary costs for travel and telephone charges, and $136 of work (that being half of the total) on a secondary case filed at the same time as the Musser/Morris case.

Apart from arguing that it had in fact mounted a reasonable defense, the IDWR objected to most of the charges specifically.

The ruling stunned several state offices, and on October 25 Attorney General Larry EchoHawk personally signed a motion for permission to appeal the decision, to the Supreme Court, on an expedited basis. EchoHawk noted that Hurlbutt ruled prospective application of the doctrine is not justiciable, and, therefore, is not addressed here. The doctrine could be applies, Hurlbutt said then, only when a qualified issue, and a clear alignment of parties, came to fruition. No parties have been aligned in the current case.

EchoHawk also argued that by awarding attorney fees on a prospective basis and without regard to the ultimate resolution of the issues presented, "this Court has undertaken an unprecedented expansion of the private attorney general doctrine." Hurlbutt held that in fact the Mussers and Morris had prevailed in their claim. ☒

THE 0337 FUND (11/22/1993) The law passed by the Idaho Legislature setting up the basic SRBA fund says that it should be used for purposes of the adjudication. But what does that mean?

This seems to be yet another question likely headed for a court settlement, after a state Board of Examiners decision running directly counter to Judge Daniel Hurlbutt's ruling that an award of $16,963 for attorney's fees under the Private Attorney General doctrine, be allocated from the 0337 fund (the adjudication account).

The Board, in counterpoint, decided that the money should come from that account and only that account. The award to the Twin Falls law firm Hepworth, Nungester & Lezamiz came following their successful argument that the Department of Water Resources had not, despite a statutory obligation, delivered water to several of their clients.

At the November 9 Board meeting, Department of Water Resources Director Keith Higginson said that Hurlbutt's prohibition of that account for paying the fees "raises the issue of what other account should we take $17,000 from, to pay the award of attorneys fees."

The court has viewed the 0337 account, which is fed from water right filing fees, as intended for use basically for departmental investigation of water rights.

Board Secretary J.D. Williams, the state auditor, remarked that "there is a real question whether these funds as assessed by the court can be awarded from non-adjudicatory funds. That is why I wrote a special letter to Keith ... making it clear that the Board does not believe the Department is authorized as a matter of law to pay adjudication expenses from this account or other general fund accounts because as you read the adjudication statute, it is clear that all adjudication expenses are not to be paid with general fund, only funds generated through the fee process."

Clive Strong, the lead SRBA attorney for the state, told the board that the award of fees was being appealed to the Idaho Supreme Court, and asked for a decision from the Board as to whether the IDWR had authority to pay from the 0337 fund, "and use that as a basis for the motion for stay in the proceeding. I think this is an issue that is going to have to go to the Legislature and will ultimately have to go to the Supreme court as well to get some resolution or direction."

"In the absence of the ability and authority [to pay], the contempt of court is out there," Higginson noted.

Gov. Cecil Andrus, chairing the meeting, told Higginson that "neither you nor that judge have the authority to appropriate money. Only the legislature has that authority, so I guess the board can resolve this."

On motion by Attorney General Larry EchoHawk, all three board members (the others being Andrus and Secretary of State Pete Cenarrusa) voted not to pay out of the 0337 fund. ☒

A PRIVATE AG APPEAL (11/22/1993) The state of Idaho is appealing Judge Hurlbutt's prospective award for attorney's fees under the Private Attorney General Doctrine for pursuit of Basin Wide Issue 2 (to the Twin Falls firm Hepworth, Nungester & Lezamiz).

But the state has gotten no help from Hurlbutt, who has declined to give permission to appeal. The state asked the court to separate the issue of attorneys fees from the rest of the basin wide issue, to allow for faster appeal of it to the Supreme Court. The state suggested that it is preferable to determine the applicability of the private attorney general doctrine at this early stage.

That request was opposed by the Hepworth firm, which noted that Hurlbutt's ruling on the issue was not a final decision but rather opened the issue to court action. It has long been a fundamental rule of Idaho appellate practice that piecemeal appellate review is undesirable, and is to be avoided in the absence of compelling circumstances.

Hurlbutt's order does not stop the state from appealing, but does diminish the likelihood the Supreme Court will agree to consider it any time soon. ☒

MORE MUSSER FEES (7/11/1994) The Idaho Supreme Court settled another SRBA attorney fees question (on top of the conservation groups' request) in the other direction June 24, when it ordered fees be paid in the case of *Musser v. Higginson.*

Over the objections of the state agency, the high court awarded them costs and attorneys fees of $11,165. ☒

PRIVATE AG DISMISSED (10/1997) The Idaho Supreme Court also on September 10 reversed an SRBA Court award of "private attorney general" legal fees by the state to the Hepworth Lezamiz Hohnhorst firm (representing the Hagerman Water Right Owners) originally awarded several years ago.

It also had the effect of narrowing what some had thought to be the scope of "private attorney general doctrine" (in which private legal costs are reimbursed by the state). In the process, the Supreme Court indicated it was simply clarifying what had been the rule all along. ☒

Conflict of interest

CLERKS AND ATTORNEYS (5/24/93) It was an evident shot across the bow at Patrick Brown, the Twin Falls attorney who has been visible in developing motions on staying the adjudication in Basin 36, on the private attorney general doctrine, on records management and other issues . . .

On May 17 the Department of Justice filed a motion for clarification, by Judge Hurlbutt, of the practice of former SRBA Court clerks in the Adjudication. "This court will undoubtedly have other clerks that will end their clerkship and seek employment with firms that represent litigants in the SRBA." Brown, of Hepworth, Nungester & Lezamiz, was a clerk for Hurlbutt last year.

Earlier this year, Hurlbutt asked state Bar Counsel Michael Oths about the role of judge's clerks. Oths suggested in a March letter that, absent consent of all involved parties, a clerk should not "represent or oppose parties who had a contested claim heard by the judge while that clerk was employed." The federal attorneys asked Hurlbutt to clarify whether that meant his clerks were essentially barred from working in the Adjudication, or only in certain parts of it, or whether some other view was appropriate.

There was no word from the judge on when a response will be forthcoming. ☒

COURT PERSONNEL AND THE SRBA (1/31/94) What should be the allowed role of a person who works for the SRBA court, then becomes an attorney active in the case?

The federal government first asked that question last year in connection with Patrick Brown, an attorney with the Twin Falls firm of Hepworth, Nungester & Lezamiz and formerly a clerk at the SRBA court. Since then another former SRBA court clerk, Susan Hamlin, has joined the legal staff of the Idaho Department of Water Resources, and has been active in the SRBA.

On January 14, Judge Daniel Hurlbutt rejected the United States' request that he clarify "rules of practice for law clerks in the SRBA." Hurlbutt said that "a prerequisite to rendering a judgment or decision is that there be a justiciable case or controversy before the court … Having reviewed the motion, this court does not find a justiciable controversy. The United States' request for rules governing the legal practice of former attorneys is a request for an advisory opinion."

Besides that, he said, rules governing practice of law are set by the Idaho Supreme Court, and "this court has no independent authority to adopt further rules or amend the rules of practice promulgated by the Idaho Supreme Court."

However, a report from state attorney Clive Strong and federal attorney Peter Monson, which primarily concerned the status of the steering committee, included a section on "participation of judicial personnel." It noted that because the SRBA will run so long, "the Court will employ many non-clerical judicial personnel before this action is completed. Following their employment by the Court those judicial personnel may wish to obtain employment that will involve representation of parties in the SRBA." They suggested that current and former non-clerical judicial personnel draft a report describing all specific SRBA actions they worked on, and later barred from participation "regarding any subcase, motion, consolidated action or issues of fact and law, involving the same facts and parties or parties, with which the person had substantial involvement." ☒

WOOD CHALLENGED IN CONFLICT OF INTEREST (3/2000) SRBA Presiding Judge Barry Wood in February was challenged on whether he should be presiding judge in certain Nez Perce tribal water right claims – and possibly by implication (though not explicitly), in the entire adjudication.

By the end of a February 22 hearing on the matter, however, the challenge had opened the door to a host of other possibilities as well, from challenges to some or all of former Judge Daniel Hurlbutt's decisions over a 12-year span, to removal of some or all of the SRBA from state to federal court.

The specter of conflict of interest was connected during the month not only with Wood but with a number of other people involved in the case – from former Judge Hurlbutt to Idaho Supreme Court Chief Justice Linda Copple Trout.

Judge Wood agreed to a preliminary schedule on developing a procedure – offered by U.S. Department of Justice attorney Peter Monson – for determining resolution of conflict of interest issues in the future.

But he did not immediately rule on the issues of disqualification and setting aside the Nez Perce ruling.

Where matters would go from there is unclear.

An information-gathering procedure is one possibility, tribal attorney Steve Moore suggested – and that could include depositions from people including Wood, Trout, Wood's relatives, the Idaho Judicial Council members and others.

Some of the objectors argued that the SRBA court, for several reasons, lacks jurisdiction to rule on the case, so any ruling on it by Wood could be challenged. A ruling by the judge to disqualify himself might have to be squared with the Idaho Supreme Court order handing him the case.

Where the question would go after Wood acts is also unclear. Ordinarily, it might simply be appealed to the Idaho Supreme Court. But it also could go to the Idaho Judicial Council – which is chaired by the Supreme Court Chief Justice, Trout. Either eventuality could be interesting in itself, since Wood said – and Trout has confirmed – that the district judge discussed his interest in water rights with the chief. And, Wood said, Trout said she saw no problem in that area.

This dispute marks a rare occasion in the SRBA when federal attorneys raised, in seriousness, the prospect of a federal court adjudication.

The immediate trigger to the complaint: A water right in which Judge Wood has an interest, and other rights in which family members have interests.

Critics of the action said that the motivating trigger was a decision by Wood last November denying the tribe in-stream water rights in areas off the Nez Perce reservation.

In a February 18 reply brief, the Nez Perce Tribe offered this warning: "The State of Idaho and its judiciary are thus presented with an unfortunate and unseemly circumstance that requires immediate remedial action by this [SRBA] Court. No less than the integrity of the Idaho judicial system is at stake, not to mention important rights secured to litigants by the United States and Idaho constitutions. Moreover, if, as suggested by the Objectors' Responses, the State of Idaho is truly unable to find a disinterested judge, i.e., a judge who does not own irrigated farmland and whose immediate family members do not claim significant rights to water for agricultural irrigation, then the justification for state court jurisdiction under the McCarran Amendment is defeated and a federal forum must be made available to the Tribe and the United States."

Tribal and federal attorneys said that they first became aware that Wood might have a stake in the SRBA late last year. Tribal attorneys said that "it was not until November 18, 1999, eight days after Judge Wood issued his opinion and judgment in the federal/tribal in-stream flow case, that the Tribe, by using the[Idaho Department of Water Resources] database, could have discovered that Judge Wood was a claimant in the case asserting a substantial consumption right … It was on this date the IDWR entered the change of claimant information substituting the name of Judge Wood for that of his predecessor in title."

The tribal request for disqualification and set-aside of the in-stream flow decision was filed February 4. On February 11, Wood offered his view of the matter in a lengthy disclosure statement.

He said that in 1994 he acquired (through lease with option to buy) about 13 acres of land in Gooding County; terms of his judgeship required he live in Gooding County or Jerome County. About four years later obtained fee title to it. It "was a portion of a much larger parcel of land, most of which is irrigated farmland; both parcels were owned by my predecessor in interest. Fee title on this much larger piece of land was acquired by Jim and Julie Wolfe in November 1998. …

"Based upon my belief acquired from records (not personal knowledge) my predecessors in title, I believe in 1988, filed two water right claims in the SRBA relative to the entire parcel. One [37-11243] was a domestic and stockwater right which well is physically located on what is now the Wood parcel. The other was an irrigation well for irrigation of the entire parcel (less the homestead on the Wood parcel). When I acquired fee title to the Wood parcel on November 16, 1998, I also acquired legal title to the domestic water well, which has been assigned claim No. 37-11243 by IDWR in the SRBA. As part of this process, IDWR's Change of Ownership form for this right was submitted. While the original water right back in 1988 was for domestic and stock, I presently have no stock, save and except my pet cat, 'Wilder.'"

The other right is an irrigation water right (A37-07252B) also located on the Wolfe property, and rights to it are split, with the bulk of that right going to Wolfe.

The domestic and stockwater right was not objected to and is ready for partial decree, Wood said. The split irrigation right is scheduled for Department of Water Resources review in 2003.

He also disclosed water rights held by his brother and sister.

While the objectors suggested that Wood's personal stake in the SRBA was small, the tribal and federal attorneys put it this way in their February 4 filing:

"If the Tribe's claims were upheld in the SRBA, the shareholders of the Big Wood Canal Company and the American Falls Recreation District Number 2, including Judge Wood, might be denied access to water. Similar, the water interests of his brother and father are on rivers and stream systems which are tributary to the mainstem Snake River, and likewise could be diminished or affected by a judicial recognition of the Tribe's in-stream flow claims in sufficient quantities to shut off all or many upstream surface and groundwater appropriators."

(That statement in itself may be the most sweeping and far-reaching comment yet by federal or tribal officials about what may be at stake in the Nez Perce claims – a confirmation of what some objectors have contended.)

Beyond all that, Wood had this to say:

"I am a citizen of the United States of America, which entity is an interested party in the SRBA. I also pay taxes to the United States of America. I am a resident of the State of Idaho and I am employed as a District Judge by the State of Idaho, which entity is an interested party in the SRBA. I also pay taxes to the State of Idaho. I am a consumptive user of water; specifically I drink water every day and I use water in my daily household routine. I eat food daily which has been grown in Idaho with water. I use electricity which is generated by the use of water, i.e., hydroelectric power user and I receive and pay monthly power bills to Idaho Power Company, which entity is an interested party. Prior to my being assigned as the Presiding Judge of the SRBA, I owned a nominal number of shares of stock in Idaho Power Company. This fact was disclosed to the Chief Justice as well. Upon being permanently appointed the Presiding Judge, I promptly disposed of this stock. I engage in recreational pursuits involving water, specifically fishing and drift boating. I have filed no objections or responses to any claims filed in the SRBA and to my knowledge and belief, no one within the third degree of consanguinity or affinity to me has filed any such objection and/or response in the SRBA."

Other conflicts?

In researching the case, Deputy Attorney General Steve Strack uncovered in a February 16 filing information about other players in the SRBA:

• A Department of Water Resources printout "describing a domestic and stockwater right claim held by Linda Copple Trout [number 63-25315, by Linda Copple and Kim J. Trout of Kuna], chief justice of the Idaho Supreme Court. This printout was the result of my public records request to IDWR to perform a search of water right claims held by justices of the Idaho Supreme Court."

Strack said that he has not tried to research possible water right holdings by relatives of the justices.

• Records showing that the Hurlbutt Family Trust (which is associated with former Judge Hurlbutt) owned five shares in the Twin Falls Canal Company. That record was obtained by Twin Falls attorney John Rosholt at Strack's request. Rosholt said that he had been unaware of the Hurlbutt Trust's ownership, but noted that it was a tiny slice of a canal company roster of many thousands of shares.

Similar inquiry in any water interests by the special masters or their families could also be coming. ☒

WOOD: THERE'S NO CONFLICT (4/2000) SRBA Presiding Judge Barry Wood on March 23 turned back a challenge to his handling at least one SRBA subcase, saying that he does not have a meaningful conflict of interest in the case.

Wood wrote in his March decision that "there is no direct conflict between the Tribe's water right claims and the claims of Judge Wood or his family members. Any perceived conflict is indirect, speculative, and *de minimis* in the overall scope of the SRBA. Virtually every judge in the State of Idaho has some interest or affiliation in the SRBA based on the reasoning supporting the Tribe's motion. Therefore, in exercising its discretion, this Court denies the Tribe's motion to disqualify. As a consequence, the Tribe's requested remedy of setting aside all decisions rendered in this consolidated subcase is denied." ☒

CONFLICT: SUPREME COURT (6/2000) The Nez Perce Tribe on May 1 filed its conflict of interest complaint in the SRBA, requesting that SRBA Presiding Judge Barry Wood be removed from a key subcase involving the tribe. The filing by Heidi Gudgell representing the Nez Perce and Steven Moore of the Native American Rights Fund noted "this motion is made on the grounds and for the reasons that the March 23 order may not otherwise be appealable, involves a controlling question of law as to which there are substantial grounds for difference of opinion, and an immediate appeal will materially advance the orderly resolution of this litigation."

They went on:

• "In the March 23 order, Judge Wood concluded, in effect, that the SRBA is too large and complex to require literal adherence to the judicial canons contained in the Idaho Code of Judicial Conduct. The Tribe contends that the size and complexity of the SRBA, as well [as] fundamental due process concerns, require nothing less than strict compliance with the Code of Judicial Conduct in all proceedings in the SRBA. … The [Supreme] Court, should, therefore, grant the Tribe's motion [for appeal] and decide immediately whether, and to what extent, the Code of Judicial Conduct applies to judges, and special masters presiding over SRBA proceedings."

• "Given the fact that Judge Wood was sitting as a district court judge in the 5th Judicial District at the time he was appointed by [Chief] Justice [Linda Copple] Trout concerning the appointment to the SRBA, the requirements of Canon 3C1 should actually have compelled Judge Wood to refuse the appointment at the outset or disclose his interests, and those of his family, to the SRBA parties."

They noted that Wood "apparently was concerned enough about his personal water rights claims in the SRBA to disclose at least some of them to Chief Justice Trout before his appointment to the SRBA." Wood said that he informed her of his personal water right holding, and that she did not consider it a problem.

The counter-argument to the tribe appeared at the Supreme Court on May 8, in a brief by Deputy Attorney General Steven Strack.

He said that, for one thing, the appeal should be pursued through routes other than those taken. "It seeks review of a post-judgment order. Idaho appellate rule 11 allows appeals as a matter of right from 'any order made after a final judgement.' Thus, the appeal should be pursued under Idaho Appellate Rule 11."

As to the substance, Strack noted that conflicts in the SRBA "historically have been evaluated from the perspective of individual subcases, and neither Judge Wood nor any of his family members are parties to Consolidated Subcase 03-10022 [the Nez Perce Tribe off-reservation issue in question]."

And, possibly more notably, was this point that hadn't surfaced visibly before: "Clearly, the tribe's motion to disqualify the presiding judge was predicated in its assertion that its claims require 'virtually the entire flow of the Snake River,' an assertion intended to demonstrate a direct conflict between the Tribe's claims and those of the judge and his family. But, up until the filing of the motion for disqualification, the Tribe had repeatedly assured the SRBA District Court that their upstream flow claims would have 'very little impact upon the irrigators and other water users,' and that 'water development and fisheries have existed for many years in this state [and] they can continue to exist even with the guarantee of a decreed water right in the name of the tribe.' It further informed the court that 'there is simply no basis for the speculative assertion that somehow water in Southern Idaho will all have to be left in the river.' Thus, up until the filing of its motion to disqualify Judge Wood, it was the Tribe's express position that other water uses would 'continue to exist' if the Tribe's in-stream flow claims were decreed." ☒

WOOD ORDERS MASTERS DISCLOSURE (8/2000) Judge Barry Wood on July 14 ordered the three special masters in the SRBA to disclose any potential conflicts of interests they may have in the case.

Specifically, he ordered:

"The SRBA special masters shall, within 30 days of this Order, file a disclosure with the Court which discloses their water right interests in the SRBA, and those of their family members within the third degree of consanguinity or affinity. Further, all SRBA judicial officers shall keep themselves reasonably informed of their water right interests, and those of their family members within the third degree of consanguinity or affinity, and shall file supplemental/amended disclosures as necessary to reflect any future changes in such interests. Parties to the SRBA will be provided notice of these disclosures through the docket sheet."

Wood said that "At the outset, it is important to clear up any misperceptions that may have arisen regarding the application of the existing rules and procedures by stating that Idaho Rule of Civil Procedure 40(d)(2) and Cannons 3 C and D fully apply in the SRBA. This Court is not aware that it has ever suggested otherwise."

But he also renewed some conclusions he has issued previously in the conflict issue:

"That being said, the Court reiterates, as discussed at length in the March 23, 2000 *Order Re: Disqualification*, that for purposes of evaluating judicial disqualification under the foregoing rules, each subcase within the SRBA is now, and has always been, treated as a distinct piece of litigation (although at times multiple subcases with one or more identical issues may be consolidated and heard together). In other words, a judicial officer having a water right claim, and hence being a party to the overall SRBA, is alone insufficient to create grounds for judicial disqualification. There must be some significant connection between the judicial officer's interests in a water right claim and the subject matter of a particular subcase to create a disqualifying conflict." ☒

MASTERS DISCLOSE (9/2000) The three special masters in the SRBA in August filed disclosures outlining water right interests of themselves and family members in the Snake River Basin.

• **Terrence Dolan** – Dolan said August 3 that he does not claim any water rights in Idaho. He said that he owns and occupies a residence in Twin Falls, and receives his water from that city's water system. He said that he has no relatives in Idaho.

• **Brigette Bilyeu** – Bilyeu said August 7 that she and her husband Jeff Duggan live in a house in unincorporated Twin Falls County, and that they do not claim any water rights but do have shares in the Twin Falls Canal Company, "which provides water for the small acreage around our home." She said their domestic water is provided by a well not claimed in the SRBA.

Bilyeu has a large family in southern Idaho, and reported about water claims concerning 21 relatives. She said that her father Charles "Chick" Bilyeu (a former state senator) and mother Diane Bilyeu (the Bannock County assessor) do have a partial degree (29-11692) in the SRBA for a domestic well which provides water to their home; the partial decree has been issued, and no objections to it were reported. She said the same was true of an aunt and uncle, who had two SRBA partial degrees (29-11933 and 11934). Most other relatives, she said, were municipal water users who had no direct involvement in the SRBA.

She said that one uncle, H. Pierce Bilyeu, was along with another person an objector in a number of subcases, but those objections were dismissed in June 1997. And she said that some relatives, including her parents, use some water from the Fort Hall Project, but are not claimants of that water.

• **Thomas Cushman** – Cushman said on August 4 that he and his wife live in a house in unincorporated Jerome County, and obtain domestic water from a well which has not been claimed in the SRBA. He said they also own a residential rental house at Pierce, which is connected to that city's water system. He added that "we also are equity members of the Jerome Country Club, which claims water right 36-04271, within the SRBA. This right was decreed by partial decree prior to my appointment to the SRBA or to our purchase of the membership." Cushman said that his relatives living in the Snake River Basin do not claim water rights in the SRBA. ☒

The SRBA Court's jurisdiction

SRBA JURISDICTION (6/21/1993) The Idaho Supreme Court ruled June 16 that a district court which ordered delivery of water to a water use had no authority to do so, since water rights cases should be decided by the SRBA Court, and reversed the court's decision.

"We conclude that the trial court lacked jurisdiction in this case, because the case required the trial court to determine the right to the use of water, which may only be addressed as part of the Snake River Basin Adjudication (SRBA)," the Court said.

The case had been appealed from Seventh District Judge James C. Herndon, who had decided in favor of Young Harvey Walker. Reversed on the ground the trial court did not have subject matter jurisdiction. Racine, Olson, Nye, Cooper & Budge, of Pocatello, Idaho, represented Walker (attorney Randall C. Budge argued the case before the Court); Roger Ling of Ling, Nielson and Robinson, of Rupert, represented the Big Lost Irrigation District. ☒

The Special Masters

The position of special master is unusual in the Idaho judiciary, though not in water courts around the country. The three master positions in the SRBA are intended to help with handling the large workload and bring each disputed case (at least) to hearing. They could be considered "sub-judges": they do not have authority to render a final decision, but they do make recommendations on subcases which ordinarily are signed off by the presiding judge.

THE FIRST TWO MASTERS (6/21/1993) The first two special masters in the SRBA has been named and will begin work next month. Discussions with a candidate for a third position are ongoing but that position is expected to be filled shortly as well.

The first two masters are Boise attorney Brigette Bilyeu and Thermopolis, Wyo., attorney Terry Dolan.

Bilyeu will begin work July 12, Dolan on July 1. Now employed with the Boise law firm Elam Burke & Boyd, she has a background in general litigation rather than in water law; Judge Hurlbutt has said that he views the SRBA as more analogous to a normal civil case than to traditional water law settlements. Bilyeu has practiced law for five years and is a graduate of the University of Idaho School of Law.

She was drawn to the SRBA, she said, because "it's such an important case. And I was impressed with the way the whole system is set up. I'm impressed by the way the court is run."

Bilyeu has had extensive contact through her family with Idaho government and policymaking. Her father is state Sen. Charles "Chick" Bilyeu, D-Pocatello, who has served in that chamber since 1970. Her mother is Diane Bilyeu, who served one term in the Senate, ran for the U.S. House in 1980 and has been assessor of Bannock County since 1985.

Terry Dolan has been a special master in a water rights adjudication for a number of years: the "general adjudication of all rights to use matter in the Big Horn River system" in north-central Wyoming, under Wyoming Judge Gary Hartman at World (which is about 35 miles from Thermopolis). That adjudication also has been a long-running case: it was originally filed in 1977. Dolan has been a member of the Wyoming bar for 10 years. ☒

THIRD MASTER (7/6/1993) The third of the first special masters is Richard Simms of Simms & Stein, P.A., in Santa Fe, New Mexico. The firm handles only water law cases, and Simms has worked in water law about 20 years.

A graduate of the University of New Mexico law school, he was counsel for the New Mexico state engineer's office (working there with Steve Reynolds) and in other capacities, each time in water-related areas, before entering private practice. He has been involved with the several ongoing adjudications in New Mexico, and has some specialty in federal reserved water rights and interstate water litigation. He has taken several cases to the United States Supreme Court.

These are the first master to be hired, and the only ones scheduled to begin work at this point. But they are not expected to be the last. The roster of masters eventually is expected to reach 10 or more. ☒

➲ *A common prediction at the time, but ultimately unfounded: The number of special masters in the SRBA has remained at 10 ever since.*

MASTERS EX PARTE (11/22/1993) Federal attorneys have raised questions about a meeting between state attorneys and officials of the SRBA court, including the newly-appointed Special Masters, and about whether at least one of them may be biased against the federal government. The Department of justice even asked Judge Hurlbutt to delay formal appointment of the masters until the issues is resolved. Hurlbutt responded that there is no reasonable issue and the appointments stand.

All this grew out of issues concerning administration of water right issues in Basin 57 (mainly in Owyhee County); the subject was mentioned briefly at the June and August status conferences. In August, lead state attorney Clive Strong said a generally agreed-on proposal had been developed, and Judge Hurlbutt agreed to hear about it. He asked the masters (Terrance Dolan, Brigette Bilyeu and Richard Simms) and court counsel Carolyn Minder to meet with the state attorneys (Strong, Lynne Krogh-Hampe and Dan Steckel). They met, twice, on October 5. Krogh-Hampe and Steckel later mentioned the meeting to federal attorneys.

In a federal brief on the matter, attorney Peter Monson said "the United States is shocked … This *ex parte* briefing casts a cloud of impropriety over this entire adjudication that cannot be removed short of supplementing the record with sworn testimony concerning the substance and extent of the *ex parte* communications."

On November 12, Hurlbutt met with Monson and Strong, and said that based on Simms report, nothing substantive had been discussed, and the attorneys should not be deposed. But he also said policies about *ex parte* meetings, and communications with the court in general, should be reviewed, and he appointed Monson and Strong to head a committee on that subject. ☒

CHALLENGE TO SIMMS (12/13/1993) Federal attorneys filed on November 26 an unusual motion to disqualify newly-appointed Master Richard Simms "from participating in any SRBA proceedings involving the claims and objections of the United States." In their brief, they charge conflicts of interest and bias may limit Simms' impartiality. No court response to the request has been made yet. Simms is at work on a statement to be issued in response.

An affidavit from Thomas DuPriest, of Clarence M. Kelley & Associates, in Kansas City, suggested that, as of October 25, Simms was still an active partner in Simms & Stein, a New Mexico partnership specializing in water rights. Leif Johnson, the federal attorney filing the report, said that Simms has represented clients with interests opposed to the federal government. He said that he was still a counsel of record in Wyoming in the Big Horn River Adjudication, and has filed motions in opposition to federal stands.

Johnson said that Simms also has written a number of law articles critical of federal water claims, including claims involved in the SRBA.

"These statements and his continuing adversarial relationship with the United States give rise to the real concern that the United States cannot possibly receive full and fair treatment from Master Simms … ☒

SIMMS RESIGNS (12/27/1993) One of the first three special masters in the Snake River Basin Adjudication, Richard Simms, has resigned. SRBA Judge Daniel Hurlbutt accepted the resignation and said that no immediate replacement will be made. A hearing on the request to disqualify was briefly scheduled for December 21 but was cancelled when Simms resigned on December 17.

But his resignation letter said that he was "not resigning because I believe that the accusation that I could not impartially preside over the claims and objections of the United States is correct … I am resigning for two reasons. First, my experience in litigating for and against the United States has taught me that the United States is tenacious. In this regard, I am persuaded that if I were to remain as a Special Master the integrity of my work product would be subjected to continuing attack, assuming I were to make recommendations contrary to a given claim or objection of the United States. The potential of such a collateral attack would in turn undermine the integrity of the court.

"Second, I am resigning for personal reasons. I have never enjoyed the rancor which frequently accompanies litigation. Being made the subject of such behavior is something I cannot accept."

He said that he was still a counsel of record in Wyoming in the Big Horn River Adjudication, and has filed motions in opposition to federal stands.

In his 55-page response December 16, which he was said initiated and prepared by him and not reviewed with Hurlbutt, Simms said he had never heard of DuPriest, that Simms & Stein was not a partnership but a corporation, and that he had sold his stock in it and since September 15 has been "of counsel," informally associated with it.

Only the federal government challenged Simms; no other parties became involved. ☒

SIMMS ADMITTED TO SRBA (2/28/1994) Former Special Master Richard Simms has been admitted to the SRBA *pro hac vice*, in association with the Twin Falls law firm of Hepworth, Nungester & Lezamiz — but not without opposition. That came from the federal government, which had raised questions about his appointment last year. ☒

A NEW THIRD MASTER (8/14/1995) More than a year and a half after the last special master resigned, a new one has been appointed to fill his place: Fritz Haemmerle, currently the prosecuting attorney for Blaine County. His appointment, made on July 24 and announced a couple of days later, will become effective this fall. Court personnel said that he may begin work October 1, but other start dates also are possible.

Haemmerle, a long-time professional acquaintance of SRBA District Judge Daniel Hurlbutt, was appointed to the prosecuting attorney position in 1992 and was elected to the position (unopposed) late that year. He was appointed and elected to the prosecuting attorney position as a Democrat. ☒

HAEMMERLE LEAVES SRBA (9/1999) Special Master Fritz Haemmerle left the Snake River Basin Adjudication on August 31, after about four years in the position. He had told Presiding Judge Barry Wood in a February 16 letter that he would leave at that time, to join the Roark Law Firm in Hailey.

No replacement has been named as yet.

This position among the special masters is the only one to see turnover since the first three were named in 1993. The other two original masters, Brigette Bilyeu and Terry Dolan, still are in place. ☒

THIRD THIRD MASTER (10/1999) Thomas R. Cushman, a former magistrate judge and a former state legislator, is the new special master in the Snake River Basin Adjudication, replacing Fritz Haemmerle.

Cushman joined the court on September 1. He lives in Jerome.

"Like most things in life, it was fortuitous and accidental," he said. His wife had been offered a job as a school principal in Jerome; Cushman said that he had asked his wife to follow his career around the state on several occasions, and now it was his turn. Once the decision to move was made, and he saw the opening for special master was available, he decided to apply.

The new master has a varied background in the law.

Cushman served in the Marine Corps for six years, and was a flight instructor at Pensacola in Florida. He attended law school in that state as well, but moved to Idaho afterward; his wife is an Idaho native.

He entered private practice and, living in Horseshoe Bend, became the Boise County prosecutor. He served in the Idaho House in 1983, then was appointed a magistrate for Gooding County. He served there for three terms, for a year and a half as a district judge *pro tem* while one of the judges in the Fifth District was on administrative leave.

SRBA Presiding Judge Barry Wood presumably knows his work well; since 1994 he has been the district judge primarily responsible for Gooding County; and up to then Wood had been a magistrate in nearby Lincoln County. In 1995 Cushman moved north to Pierce when his wife was offered an administrative school position; there he started a private practice in Pierce, and served as a public defender in Clearwater County.

Cushman has not been a water lawyer; most Idaho water lawyers have been involved in some way with the SRBA and could not have taken the master's position because of conflicts. He is taking over some, though not all, of the cases Haemmerle had worked on. ☒

CUSHMAN DEPARTS (7/2004) Special Master Thomas Cushman, who has been one of the three special masters in the SRBA since September 1999, has resigned – to retire – as of July 1.

The job description (two have been posted on the SRBA Court's web site) provides some information about job duration and location:

"The remainder of the director's reports for water right claims will be filed with the Court at the end of 2005. Following the expiration of the objection and response period, the SRBA will continue until all contested claims have been decreed. This is estimated to take between 3-5 years to complete. Winding down will be based on the rate of progress and continued funding and will be conducted through attrition and seniority.

Cushman has worked in part out of an office in Boise, partly because some of the basins he was assigned were located in southwestern Idaho. ☒

FOURTH IN THIRD: BOOTH (9/2004) Gooding attorney Ted Booth was named in August by SRBA Judge John Melanson as the new special master in the SRBA. Booth is scheduled to start work at the SRBA on October 1, though there's a possibility he may start earlier.

During the last year, Booth has been an attorney in private practice with Tom Arkoosh in Gooding. Previously, he was a law clerk for 5th District Judge Barry Wood, himself a former SRBA presiding judge.

Cushman kept an office in Boise and did much of his work based there. Booth will be based at the Twin Falls headquarters; Melanson indicated he wanted to bring the SRBA Court operations back under one roof. ☒

BOOTH'S ASSIGNMENTS (11/2004) Gooding attorney Ted Booth became the new special master in the SRBA in October, and was assigned a chunk of work in the massive case. He will retain at least some of that work, in effect wearing two hats, functioning both as a special master and then offering review of initial decisions in his capacity as presiding judge. But much of the workload Cushman would have had still will go to Booth.

SRBA Court Counsel Eric Wildman noted that the 27 remaining basins which have not yet been "reported" by the Idaho Department of Water Resources were split between the three masters, based in large part on the size and complexity of the workload. Booth's share will be located mainly in the southwest and northern basins. ☒

BOOTH'S DISCLOSURE (5/2005) Special Master Theodore Booth in April amended his disclosure of personal water-related interests, originally filed last October. Since then, he said, he has moved, and his water-related interests have changed. They remain small, and are limited to domestic residential uses.

He said in his filing, "I own and occupy a single residence in Twin Falls County. The domestic water is supplied by a domestic well. I have filed a claim in the SRBA for a domestic water right, claim number 47-17214. In addition, lawn and garden irrigation water is supplied by a homeowners association, which holds shares in the Twin Falls Canal Company." He said that he knew of no water rights interest by any close family members. ☒

Steering committee/information sessions

From the early days of the SRBA, participants recognized a need for informal channels of communication between the attorneys, the Department of Water Resources, the court, and others. The presiding judge holds regular monthly "status conferences." These have functioned as a standard session for hearings, motions and other actions. Usually, they are scheduled for 1:30 p.m. on the third Tuesday of the month.

Beyond that, for several years a group called the "steering committee" met in the mornings prior to the monthly status conferences. The group was informal and amorphous, including anyone participating in the SRBA who showed up. These meetings usually were run by Idaho Department of Water Resources personnel, and covered subjects of general interest in the SRBA and progress on the case.

Since 1995 these sessions were replaced by morning "information meetings" held at the SRBA Court where IDWR personnel offer presentations on case progress and issues of general concern. Court personnel, almost always including the presiding judge, attend these meetings. The sessions are open to the public.

5 | Basin Wide Issues

In general

The normal rule in courts is that specific cases, not legal principles, are on trial. The SRBA is an unusual proceeding, however, and fairly early on Judge Hurlbutt concluded that certain broad issues – "basin-wide issues" – would have to be settled before there was much point in issuing decrees. (There was considerable prospect that a late-discovered underlying issue might overturn a whole mass of decreed rights.) So, beginning in 1993, a string of basin-wide issues were presented to and decided by SRBA court.

So far there have been 14 basin-wides, the bulk of them set by the late 90s but a few since. Basin-Wide 14 is much more recent than the others, dating only to 2008.

Initial Judge Daniel Hurlbutt said in July 1993 that "We're right on that line where it's flat too late to file basin wide issues. Future designations are going to be looked at very carefully."

They may have been looked at carefully, but there were more of them.

Basin Wide 1 (presumption)

PRESUMED EXPANSION? (5/10/1993) The tricky task of interpreting the "presumption statute" (I.C. 42-1416a) in Idaho water law has hit the crucible of the SRBA Court. The issue has sprouted from the motion filed recently by Twin Falls attorney William Hollifield on behalf of clients in the Lost River area, in one of the SRBA test basins.

Hollifield objected to the Department of Water Resources' plan for administering water in the area, which had drawn the ire of a number of area residents. Others were strongly in favor of it, and a trial on the matter planned for May 4 was expected to draw several hundred people.

On the preceding Friday, however, a pre-trial conference led to resolution of many of the issues at stake, and the full trial was averted (as was the prospect of a Courthouse jammed with angry water users). One major issue remained, however, and at the more lightly-attended hearing May 4 Judge Hurlbutt said it could have tremendous basin-wide consequences. He also said a large trial on it may be scheduled at some point in the months ahead.

The issue centered on the first two clauses of Idaho Code 42-1416a, and the two presumptions they contain. The most common understanding (there are alternate versions) of the first is that the owner of a decreed water right can expand his or her irrigated acreage (though not water flow) under their original priority date. The second presumption says that in the case of valid unadjudicated rights, where beneficial use rights and licenses are not decreed, an expansion in use but not in acreage can be claimed in the adjudication even if its in violation of the mandatory permit statute, and a water right priority date can be obtained as of the time of the expansion.

Deputy Attorney General Peter Anderson, after hearing the general nature of the challenge, noted that "we don't know which rights he's challenging." But Hurlbutt, while acknowledging that "We need one live, breathing right to explicate the issue," also told Anderson, "You know the impact as well as I do. It's going to be substantial."

Three Lost River water right holders sitting at attorney's tables, including Mitchell Sorensen, told Hurlbutt they were concerned about the prospect of an individual water right holder being stuck with paying the cost for litigating a major point in water law for the benefit of the whole state adjudication.

Hurlbutt told them he too was concerned about that possibility, but offered no clear solution to the problem. "The question is, does this present a real big problem?" Hurlbutt said. The answer is, it could. "The issue will come up, and it will come up attached to somebody's water right."

Resolution will not come quickly; cannot, in fact, because the exact issues under dispute haven't yet been fully defined. Deputy Attorney General Clive Strong took an initial crack at it, suggesting "The question that's coming into play is, how do we define the boundaries of a water right?" The issue, some attorneys indicated, could come to: To what extend is a water right defined by the volume of water diverted, and to what extent by the exact uses to which the water is put? And if the latter definition is used, how can the court determine the original uses of the water [right]? ☒

ISSUE DECLARED (7/19/93) On July 13, Judge Hurlbutt formally designated the first basin-wide issue in the Adjudication: the constitutionality of the presumption statute. ☒

ACTIVISTS (9/27/1993) Thus far, Judge Hurlbutt placed a number of attorneys on the participants' list, and others have asked to participate. In most cases, this has generated no interest or opposition. But on September 3 he noted a request by Laird Lucas, an attorney for the Land and Water Fund of the Rockies (which is representing four Northwest conservation groups), to participate in the basin-wide issue. The Fund has been rebuffed on several previous attempts to intervene in the SRBA, but Lucas said this is a strong case. In contrast to earlier requests, he said, he will not be asking to intervene on grounds of public trust doctrine, but on grounds of local public interest. ☒

WILL IT FOLD? (10/25/93) At press time, only one side was represented in the forthcoming debate over the constitutionality of the Presumption Statute. But early strong indications are that the statute will in fact be overturned by the SRBA Court and the Idaho Supreme Court.

One of the most notable points in the early briefs recommending overturning the statute is their heavy use of writings by Department of Water Resources attorneys Phil Rassier and Lynn Krogh-Hampe.

A focal point may be the issue of vagueness: What is the presumption statute?

In an article for the *Idaho Law Review*, Rassier wrote that the key code section in the presumption statute can be interpreted in at least five ways: that it provides an exception to mandatory permit requirements; that it resolves ambiguities involving older water decrees; that it serves as a defense to forfeiture; that it creates a presumption all water has been put to beneficial use; or that it allows a presumption that one who has conserved water can claim the water as saved.

Twin Falls attorney William Hollifield, representing the Big Lost River Water Users Association, was responsible for bringing the questions that led to designation of the presumption statute as the first Basin Wide Issue.

Challenging its constitutionality in his brief, he wrote it is so vague persons of common intelligence must guess at its meaning and clearly differ as to its application. "The terms and phrases contained in the statute are so vague and ambiguous that the statute violates due process of law and thus is unconstitutional. 'Previously adjudicated,' 'validly applied,' 'all water,' 'on lands being irrigated,' 'expansion of use,' 'valid unadjudicated right,' 'current water rights,' and 'substantially correct' are all terms which are ambiguous and undefined which allow Section 42-1416 to be interpreted many different ways. It does not provide any guidelines to prevent arbitrary and discriminatory enforcement."

Boise attorney Jeff Fereday said the original intent of the statute was clear. "In 1985, when the Legislature was considering the legislation it ultimately adopted to mandate the SRBA, certain agricultural interests grew fearful that their current water uses would be curtailed. Specifically, they feared that illegal expansions and unnoticed forfeitures would be brought to the attention of the court. Consequently, they lobbied the Legislature for special protection from such judicial scrutiny. The legislature responded by enacting the current statute."

This suggests that, for the first time in the SRBA, identifiable and substantial political and economic groups are likely to find themselves on opposing sides, much as they did during the Swan Falls debates which led to the formation of the SRBA. It also suggests the question of protection for irrigation or other interests is likely to return to the Legislature in 1994.

In his brief, the first direct participation in the SRBA by the conservation groups, Boise attorney Laird Lucas wrote that "The statutes at issue . . . represent a remarkable legislative attempt to rewrite history with respect to past water usage, to substitute 'presumptions' for reality, and to approve past illegalities on a wholesale basis without regard to fundamental precepts of water law, including the constitutional principle of 'first in time, first in right.' ... [It is] arbitrary, irrational, discriminatory, unrelated to legitimate legislative goals, or which are overly vague and uncertain." ☒

BASINWIDE TRIAL (12/27/93) Trial in the SRBA, of the "presumption statute" on December 14, has resulted in a string of sharp questions from Judge Hurlbutt but not yet a formal decision.

Twin Falls attorney William Hollifield, who filed the motions that resulted in designation of the "presumption statutes" as a basin-wide issue, led the charge for the statute's critics. He argued, as others did, that the statute should be held "void for vagueness," that it can be read in a number of ways by a reasonable person; he noted that a state filing even acknowledged that the statute is ambiguous.

Hurlbutt asked what he should do if one than one interpretation of the statute, each of which would be constitutional, could be drawn. Should he flip a coin, he asked, or "do we have an adjudication dartboard?"

Boise attorney Jeffrey Fereday picked up on that, noting that a number of possible interpretations run afoul of the Idaho Constitution. A "blatant expansion" of water use, he said, would run into the Constitution's first in time, first in right dictum.

Federal attorney Jack Haugrud went further, saying that "read on their face, these presumptions have no meaning. The court cannot ascertain by any reasonable test that the Legislature meant one thing rather than another … [and] the court must not guess at the meaning."

The most passionate argument for the statutes came from veteran Rexburg attorney and former state senator Ray Rigby, who noted that "presumptions are not new in the law," and said this trial was basically organized around a series of hypotheticals rather than a specific instance of the law's application, which might provide a clearer and more concrete result. "Practicality is an issue we haven't talked too much about," he said. And he suggested practical difficulties would arise if rejecting the statutes means water right users have to prove exactly how they used their water through many undocumented decades.

"And I fear it's going to be and you're going to put a lot of people to a tremendous amount of expense to accomplish that," he told the judge.

But Hurlbutt rained blistering questions on most of the attorneys supporting the statute, especially Deputy Attorney General David Barber, whose office was constitutionally required to defend the statute. Barber, like others, argued that if the statute can be found constitutional, it must be, that the presumption is of constitutionality and the burden was on the opponents to defeat it. (Hurlbutt did not dispute that.) But the judge shot back, noting that the attorneys supporting constitutionality had offered varying interpretations — and the difficulty of choosing one. Asked to back the state's interpretation over others, Hurlbutt said, "Forgive me if I'm inextricably and totally lost with the logic of that assertion." When Barber indicated some frustration in trying to explain, Hurlbutt said, "You're frustrated because this seems to me to defy logic." If four or five reasonable and even constitutional interpretations exist, "then we have a vagueness problem, don't we?" ☒

STATUTE TOSSED (2/14/1994) The "Presumption Statutes," legislation drafted integral to the SRBA intended to protect water rights of certain irrigators, have been thrown out by Judge Daniel Hurlbutt, who said they're unclear, "void for vagueness." He did not rule on other contentions raised by challengers to the statutes. That leaves open the question of whether, if the Idaho Legislature were able to simply clarify its intent and re-enact similar provisions, those would be constitutional.

The February 4 decision on what had been designated Basin Wide Issue 1 led to a hearing a few days later in the Senate Resources and Environment Committee, chaired by Sen. Laird Noh of Kimberly.

Deputy Attorney General David Barber, who had participated in helping defend the statute, said that it was generated by a group of Upper Valley irrigators had been "deficient" in their water right decrees, and were concerned the adjudication might remove their long-standing water rights.

The presumption state has been applied to water right considerations throughout the Snake River Basin. Barber said that thousands of rights will be impacted by the decision, but exactly how many, and how significant the impacts, won't be known for a while. Judge Hurlbutt followed his February 4 basinwide issue decisions with a February 7 order requiring the Department of Water Resources to identify any water rights on its director's reports which may be affected by the presumption statute.

Barber did estimate that in one of the "test basin" areas, in the Lost River area in Butte and Custer counties, the impact may reach 20% of water rights because many of the decrees there were older and may have spotty documentation.

In that area, SRBA Water resources administrator David Shaw said, direct impact of the ruling will comes as early as May 1, when the local irrigation season starts. Among other considerations, he said, the Department will need to figure out soon what to tell the local water master.

Another committee member, Sen. John Peavey, said "it looks to me like the people who relied on the presumption statute have lost a chance to go to the Department of Water Resources to document their usage. ... They've been damaged."

"I'm not going to disagree with that," Barber replied.

Asked whether the Legislature has a way to correct the situation, Barber said, "initially, it seems like there should be. On the other hand ... the major focus of the challenge to the statutes was not vagueness."

Hurlbutt said that he had to presume the statute was constitutional unless it failed to meet basic tests; but he said he was unable to find a "core meaning." So, he said, he was "left to choose an interpretation without any legislative guidance, either from the clear, plain meaning of the statute or from articulated standards ..." ☒

Basin Wide 2 (role of the Department of Water Resources)

THE ROLE OF THE DEPARTMENT (8/2/1993) As the SRBA Court prepares to open debate on the first basin-wide issue, it is beginning to see fallout from the second proposal to declare basin-wide issues. That second proposal included about a dozen main issues, and more than four dozen sub-issues, many related to the rule of the Department of Water Resources and procedures it uses as the Adjudication unfolds. It was filed by attorney Patrick Brown of Hepworth, Nungester & Lezamiz.

The first response to it came a couple of weeks later from Rupert attorney Roger Ling of Ling, Nielsen & Robinson (representing A & B Irrigation District, Falls Irrigation District, Burley Irrigation District and Aberdeen Springfield Canal Co.) and it was resoundingly critical. In many of the issues concerning the IDWR's rule, Ling said, although the questions are interesting, the moving party has not shown that there is an issue as to answer of each question. A review of the questions under this category would indicate that the answer is self-evident or immaterial.

Brown had questioned whether the IDWR would publish rules in certain cases involving investigations which may be quasi-judicial; Ling suggested that it is difficult to understand how the lack of published rules will have an impact on the subcase. ☒

MORE RESPONSES (8/30/1993) The replies are in on the proposal by Hepworth Nungester & Lezamiz for about a dozen main issues (more than 50 sub-issues) which it is proposing as basin-wide issues; for consolidation of some subcases; and for designation of one of its attorneys as lead counsel. They filed as counsel for the Hagerman Water Rights Owners.

The responses were all negative. Clive Strong of the Idaho Attorney General's office noted the court has standards for what is allowed for a basin wide issues. Underlying this standard are two further requirements, he said. "First, for an issue to be of basin-wide significance, the issue must be disputed and directly affect the parties to the dispute. This is a restatement of the requirement that there be a case or controversy. Thus, before the court designates a basin-wide issue, the proponent of the issue must demonstrate the issue's relationship to an actual subcase, as well as state proponents' position on the issue. Second, even though the issue may be disputed by a number of parties, it must be genuine, as opposed to a frivolous issue, to justify its designation as a basin-wide issue … Many of IDWR's objections to HWRO's proposed basin wide issues are based upon these two considerations. HWRO's motion fails to demonstrate how the proposed issues relate to the subcases identified. Thus, it is not possible, based upon the present state of the record, to determine in most instances whether there is an issue to b litigated. The parties are left to consider these issues in the abstract … Issues should not be designated as basin wide issues until a true controversy is identified."

Strong also said the statute assigned a unique role to the director, which is neither that of a plaintiff nor defendant but rather of a petitioner. In the absence of a 'special statutory authorization' to participate in the proceeding, the director could not participate, because he is not a real party in interest. ☒

BASIN WIDE 2 (10/11/1993) In an order October 1, Judge Daniel Hurlbutt declared the second basin-wide issue in the SRBA to be:

What is the role of the director, i.e., the Idaho Department of Water Resources, as a party in this statutory adjudication requiring the judicial determination of each claimant's right to the use of water in the Snake River Basin?

Hurlbutt's order suggested that a declaratory judgment will follow a decision. But he did not include in his order a legal rationale for the designation. The order grew out of a proposal for a basin wide issue (a large-scale matter of general importance to the SRBA) offered by the Twin Falls firm of Hepworth, Nungester & Lezamiz, which among others represents a Hagerman Water Right Owners group. That group proposed 13 main issues, and more than 50 sub-issues, all relating to the Department of Water Resources and its role in the adjudication. A number of the questions were very specific, such as how specific reports are prepared and should be considered in the adjudication. None framed the basin-wide issue in the same terms Hurlbutt did.

The proposed basin-wide issue was soon attacked, in nearly all of its parts, by almost all of the other law firms active in the SRBA. Many said in varying ways, as Rupert attorney Roger Ling did in his opening brief, that "the moving party has not shown there is an issue as to the answer of each question. A review of the questions under this category would indicate that the answer is self-evident or immaterial."

The issue of the director's role in the SRBA has, however, arisen in sometimes heated terms, and recently.

For a time, it placed the judge and Attorney General Larry EchoHawk, and his staff, at odds, over the subcase *Rim View Trout Co. v. State of Idaho Department of Fish and Game*. That case concerns water rights at Niagara Creek and a series of objections involving Rim View, the Idaho Department of Fish and Game and Idaho Power, which has nearby power production facilities. The Department of Water Resources became involved as a manager of water rights.

At a September 17 hearing, attorneys said that a settlement had been reached among attorneys for the main parties; some final agreements were still needed. An October 25 trial date remained tentatively in force, however, and the judge ordered that the state designate just one attorney to represent the state of Idaho's interests. When Strong said that he planned to designate attorneys for both the Department of Fish and Game (to advocate its claim) and the Department of Water Resources (to present its recommendation) Hurlbutt said he was ruling today the state of Idaho on its proprietary claim will speak once and consistently. It can do it through Department of Water Resources; it can do it through Fish and Game. I will not allow the state in any way, shape or form to argue any other than one position in this case. Period. He also ordered Strong to tell the court how he planned to comply, by October 4. Strong said that he was directed by the attorney general to respectfully disagree with that position.

Asking Hurlbutt to reconsider, EchoHawk personally signed an October 1 memorandum the ruling improperly prohibits the state of Idaho from both advocating vigorously for state-owned water rights as well as fulfilling the statutory responsibilities of IDWR to recommend in a neutral fashion the nature and extent of every state-law-based water right in the SRBA and appear as a party on objections filed. State law, he argued, requires the state to appear in the SRBA in two different ways, as a regulatory agency (Water Resources) and as a holder of water rights (Fish and Game).

Water Resources, he said, is not an adversary to other state agencies, but the basis for IDWR's involvement would be destroyed if IDWR were required to compromise its recommendations to satisfy the advocacy positions of other executive agencies. He also noted that in the Swan Falls case, resolution of which led to the Adjudication, three separate state agencies appeared and took separate positions through separate attorneys.

LEGISLATURE INVOLVED? (2/13/1995) On February 8, the Legislature took the unusual step of seeking to intervene in the appeal of Issues 2 and 3. In a brief filed by Idaho Falls attorney Timothy Hopkins, of Hopkins, Roden, Crockett, Hansen & Hoopes, lawmakers were said to seek the action "to protect its unique and substantial interests as the legislative branch of the government of the State of Idaho with the duty and the power to enact appropriate laws for the adjudication of water rights," including those involved in the SRBA.

"The controlling question on this petition is whether any interests of the Legislature may be affected by the outcome of this appeal," Hopkins wrote. He said "many courts have recognized that a legislature has a real interest in defending the constitutionality and enforceability of its enactments, that private litigants generally do not adequately represent that interest, and that the intervention of a legislative body promptly after the filing of an appeal from a court decision holding a statute unconstitutional is timely."

WHAT'S ON APPEAL? (3/13/1995) First round briefing in appeals of basin wide issues 2 and 3 is in at the Supreme Court.

But the unusual joint appeal of the SRBA Court decisions – appeals filed jointly on March 3 by the state of Idaho, through Clive Strong, deputy attorney general, and the Idaho Ground Water Appropriators (IGWA), through attorney Jeffrey Fereday – presents the court with two separate lists of Strong listed four major issues for the Court to consider:

• "The district court erred when it inquired into the legislature's motives for enacting the 1994 statutes." Hurlbutt said that the statutes were enacted essentially to reverse decisions in the SRBA he had made.

• "The district court erred in holding that certain provisions of the 1994 amendments were unconstitutional because the legislature could not affect ongoing litigation without violating the 'separation of powers' envisioned by the Idaho State Constitution."

• "The district court erred in prohibiting separate state agencies with proprietary claims from appearing in the SRBA to assert those claims and by ordering the Idaho Department of Water Resources to both represent those claims and make recommendations to the district court." Hurlbutt had ordered the executive branch to "speak with one voice" and resolve differences internally before coming to his court.

• "The district court erred in holding that the final decree cannot contain provisions fully defining a water right including how to administer that right in conjunction with all other decreed rights." ☒

SUPREME COURT: MOST LAWS UPHELD (6/26/1995) The Idaho Supreme Court decided on June 23 that the Idaho Legislature had authority to make most of the changes – though not all of those it actually made – in the Snake River Basin Adjudication, in its 1994 legislation.

The ruling overturned most, though not all, of the December 7 decision by Hurlbutt, in Basin Wide Issues 2 and 3. Those issues cover the role of the director (and the Department) of Water Resources in the SRBA, and the general constitutionality of the 1994 legislation. In all, the SRBA court decision was "affirmed in part, reversed in part, and the case remanded to the district court for further proceedings consistent with this opinion."

The decision gave state attorneys and their supporters most of what they had wanted, and stood in some contrast to the pounding several of them took at oral argument in the case on April 12.

State attorneys, Governor Phil Batt and others quickly hailed the ruling as (in the words of a press release from the Attorney General's office) having "cleared the way for the Snake River Basin Adjudication to move forward. In a day marked by a spirit of cooperation among the branches of state government, Gov. Phil Batt, Attorney General Alan Lance and Department of Water Resources Director Karl Dreher all lauded the Supreme Court's decision interpreting the Idaho Constitution in a way that will allow Idaho water rights to be settled in a more efficient and timely manner."

Dreher said that he has "been worked to help formulate renewed cooperation with the Court and the Legislature. This helps clear the way for processing the more than 170,000 claims in an efficient manner."

The decision generally turned on the Idaho Legislature's authority to "regulate by law, when necessary, the methods of proceeding in the exercise of their powers in all courts below the Supreme Court."

The decision did not hit head-on the question of to what extent the Legislature can alter the direction of an ongoing legal action, but took a broader view – turning mainly on whether particular legislation was "necessary" to the conduct of the SRBA – in turning thumbs up and down.

In the decision written by Chief Justice Charles McDevitt, the Court said that it "has consistently recognized that Article V, Section 13 of the Idaho Constitution empowers the Legislature of this state to enact procedural rules when such rules are necessary because of changing times or circumstances or the absence of a rule from this Court. Whether legislative action in this context is necessary within the meaning of Article V, Section 13 is a constitutional determination to be passed upon by this Court."

And that it did, ruling on one specific element of the legislation, and the Hurlbutt decision, after another. The Supreme Court upheld portions of the 1994 legislation which directed that the IDWR director's reports constitute prima facie evidence, that awards of attorney fees and costs against the state be banned (though it did allow for a major exception) and that the director of the IDWR be removed as a party in the adjudication.

In the case of director's reports forming prima facie evidence, for example, the court noted that court rules specifically say that court rules specifically contemplate the possibility of legislative presumptions concerning evidence, and allow for that. In this case, the Court ruled, "Unless that evidentiary presumption is overcome by the evidence or the application of that presumption is clearly erroneous on its face, the facts set forth in the Director's report are established." The effect appears to give a stronger weight to the Director's Report than had existed previously.

But the Supreme Court also said that other elements of the legislation were not "necessary" and therefore could not stand: designation of the director as an "expert," requirement that unobjected-to portions of the director's reports be decreed as reported. (The latter, the Court said, was unacceptable interference of the Legislature in a properly judicial function.)

Hurlbutt's ruling held that the legislation was bound together in such a way that because much of it was linked to provisions he deemed unconstitutional, that all of it (excepting only the "amnesty statutes" addressed separately from this decision) was unconstitutional. The Supreme Court said this was wrong: the Legislature had specifically said that if any part of the law was thrown out, that the remainder could stand.

But the Court also rejected an argument (as Hurlbutt also appeared to) that the 1986 legislation setting up key elements of the SRBA might be internally flawed. Appellants had suggested that if virtually any of Hurlbutt's reasoning were upheld, that the 1986 legislation might be constitutionally unsound as well. But the Court ruled flatly that those earlier laws were sound, that "when the SRBA was authorized by statute in 1986, no reasonable method of initiating the proceeding, providing notice to potential claimants, examining the Snake River Basin or preparing a report of that system … was provided by the existing Rules of Civil Procedure." ☒

Basin Wide 3 (the Legislature's authority in the SRBA)

THE ISSUE ITSELF (8/22/1994) The first response to the question posed by Judge Daniel Hurlbutt in Basin Wide Issue 3 suggested that he change the question. The basic issues tackled should remain similar to those outlined by the judge, under this proposal, but the approach used to grapple with them should change. In essence, the parties should not answer a question formulated by the judge, but rather develop questions of their own arising from specific controversies.

That proposal, in turn, came under fire from the federal government, which advised Hurlbutt to stuck to his guns.

The proposal for an amended basin wide issue came from James Tucker, attorney with Rosholt, Robertson & Tucker, representing Idaho Power Company, North Side Canal Company and the Twin Falls Canal Company.

In general, Tucker said that "remains of the opinion that raising issues, to the extent possible, by motion practice is the preferable alternative." The other alternative, he said, was "generic basin-wide designation" – which is essentially what Basin Wide Issue No. 3 is.

Tucker, like Hurlbutt, framed the overarching question as relating to "the authority of the legislature to expand or reduce the Court's jurisdiction in the SRBA after jurisdiction attaches to the parties and subject matter of the action …" Hurlbutt's point was much the same.

Hurlbutt's basin-wide issue explicitly asked, "Can the legislature expand or reduce the court's jurisdiction in the SRBA after jurisdiction attaches to the parties and subject matter of the action following issuance of the commencement Order and filing of the notices of claims. Specifically, can the following legislative changes to the court's jurisdiction be made during the pendency of the SRBA: changes in party status, pleadings and relief to the decreed; modification of the Idaho Rules of Civil Procedure with respect to the award of costs and attorney fees and the use of mandatory settlement conferences; modification of the Idaho Rules of Evidence with respect to the designation of expert witnesses, the rules governing expert witness testimony, the admissibility of evidence and the legal weight to be attributed to evidence; and expansion of the court's jurisdiction to decree provisions controlling the administration of water rights by the Director of the Idaho Department of Water Resources."

And, he said, resolution of those questions "requires determining whether the SRBA is a court or administrative proceeding."

Tucker (who was a member of the steering committee) included in his proposal to the court a piece of a letter he sent to Committee chairman Robert Bakes on June 17, which concerned "the development of a process or procedure for raising issues before the Court. The committee struggled with this concept for some time, discussing the merits of allowing parties to the SRBA to identify and raise issues in the context of specific motions … Various committee members expressed the opinion that this type of process might be preferable to a generic listing or designation of basin-wide issues by the Court because it would allow the parties to frame the issues through motion practice and focus on the attention of litigants and the Court on the precise issues that required resolution."

But the federal government, in a memorandum by U.S. attorney Peter Monson of the Department of Justice, took issue. "While the United States can foresee some benefits arising from the procedures suggested by the Companies [Tucker], on balance we believe that it will lead to more motions being filed thus causing additional delay and confusion," Monson said.

CRITICS (12/19/1994) The most common line was: "it's long on passion and conviction and short on analysis." While process was the subject at the December 20 court status conference, the substance of the December 7 ruling on Basin Wide Issue 3 was the topic at the last meeting of the legislative interim committee on the SRBA.

Witnesses repeated the "passion/conviction/analysis" refrain frequently at the December 14 meeting. Lawmakers and others left the session without an evident specific plan of action, but a strong sense that something further – on the legislature's part – would be done.

The lawmakers heard what amounted to an erudite seminar on why the Idaho Supreme Court should overturn the Hurlbutt decision. Many points made there are likely to wind up in appellate briefs. Two key points by speakers stood out and were emphasized by several speakers:

• Hurlbutt's conception of the relationship of the branches of Idaho government was wrong, and the Idaho Legislature has considerable power to affect the course of a lawsuit even after it has started process through a court.

• Hurlbutt was wrong that the 1994 amendments would jeopardize the state's standing under the McCarran Amendment (which requires the federal government to subject itself to a general state adjudication).

Separation of powers – University of Idaho law professor Dennis Colson, author of the book *The Ties that Bind* on the Idaho constitution, said that the Idaho Constitution does not refer to a "separation" of powers, but to a "division." That, he said, suggests a more blended approach where the branches share some responsibility.

"The text of the document expressly allows the Legislature to regulate the methods of proceedings," he said – the way the 1994 legislation did. Colson noted that the Idaho Supreme Court has taken different views through the years about judicial autonomy in governing itself, and that since 1975 the Supreme Court has tended to give more weight to judicial rules rather than to legislation when the two are in conflict. But he suggested that is in part due to misreading of a 1941 state law.

If the decision is upheld, he said, that would "tend to suggest that the legislature has not power" in the area of judicial rulemaking.

And Deputy Attorney General Michael Gilmore (who has not been actively involved in the SRBA but was asked to participate) said that "in my view, this decision of the court concerning separation of powers is quite literally unprecedented."

He said that in many cases through Idaho history, jurisdiction has been changed by legislative action. One example, he said, was the 1983 case *Garden City v. Boise*, which concerned a zoning dispute. While it was pending, Gilmore said, the legislature removed jurisdiction over the issue involved from a district court and gave it to a county commission.

He also noted that the legislature has the power to pass retroactive laws. And, counter to one of Hurlbutt's key points, Gilmore that state agencies could sue each other and take different sides in a single case, and in fact have done so "in dozens if not scores of cases." ☒

➲ *The Idaho Supreme Court considered Basin Wide Issues 2 and 3 together in its decision. (See the section on Basin Wide 2.)*

Basin Wide 4 (amnesty statutes)

FAMILIAR LINES ON AMNESTY (1/23/1995) Some familiar perspectives arose in the flurry of briefs filed on the constitutionality of the 1994 "amnesty" statutes passed by the Idaho Legislature.

The lines were drawn similarly, in fact, to those in mid-1994, when the similarly-intended "presumption statutes" were faced with constitutional challenge. Those were ultimately thrown out by both the SRBA and the Idaho Supreme Court; but that was done because the states were considered too vaguely written to be clearly understood. "Vagueness" was again an issue raised in the first (and in some cases second) round of briefing on Basin Wide Issue 4 (concerning constitutionality of the 1994 measure).

The statutes generally all were intended to protect water users who, years ago, expanded their use of water (often using the same amount of water but over a larger land area) under a very senior water right, provided that no other water right holders' interests were harmed in the process. Presumably, adjudication would result in restricting or eliminating many of those water uses, upending the farm economy in some places.

"While the amnesty statutes are less vague than the repealed presumption and accomplished transfer statutes," the United States said in a brief signed by Michael Gheleta, "significant uncertainties still exist regarding interpretation of certain key provisions of the amnesty statutes" – enough, he said, to warrant throwing out these laws too under grounds of "void for vagueness." He said that the statutes did not say what is an "enlargement" of use, or what is an "injury" to another party. More significantly, Gheleta argued, the new statutes (in contrast to those thrown out a year ago) fail to indicate what should be the priority date of a water right granted "amnesty."

The "conservation groups" (four organizations filing under the aegis of the Land and Water Fund of the Rockies) said that a whole range of issues were raised but not settled by the amnesty statues. "Especially where the legislature seeks to create an amnesty for past illegalities, as here," attorney Laird Lucas said, "the courts should not be left guessing at how broadly the statutes reach or how they are to be implemented."

(In a January 17 hearing, Lucas was denied permission to intervene in Basin Wide 4, but was allowed to file an *amicus* brief with the court.)

Attorney Jeffrey Fereday, representing the Idaho Ground Water Appropriators, took a middle ground. He said that one of the "amnesty" statutes, 42-1426, is clearly unconstitutional because it "violates the priority provisions of Article 15, section 3 of the Idaho Constitution, the Idaho Constitution's prohibition against retroactive legislation that upsets vested rights, and the prohibitions on takings in the Idaho and United States Constitutions." ☒

UPHOLDING THE STATUTES (3/27/1995) A year and a half after throwing out the old "presumption" statutes for being unconstitutionally vague, Judge Daniel Hurlbutt upheld their successor statutes – which he said were clear and did not violate any part of the constitution. Hurlbutt's reading of the statutes, however, do put a heavy burden on those water users who want to try to take advantage of them.

Hurlbutt had himself raised the question of the constitutionality of the statutes. On the same day he made his still-disputed ruling on the constitutionality of the 1994 statutes generally, he singled out the amnesty statutes – 42-1425, 1426 and 1427, also passed in 1994 – for special and further consideration. These statutes were essentially a rewrite, intended to be clearer than the amnesty statutes tossed out.

"The amnesty statutes do not suffer the same infirmities as their predecessors," Hurlbutt said: "Here a core meaning can be determined …":

• For 42-1425: "That it allows a party holding a valid decreed, licensed or constitutionally appropriated water right to claim an accomplished change to that right in the SRBA. The claimed change can be only as to place of use, purpose of use, point of diversion, nature of use or period of use and must have been completed prior to November 19, 1987. The claimant must prove by a preponderance of the evidence that the change in the use did not injure any other water right which was in existence as of the date of the change. Finally, the change cannot constitute an 'enlargement' of the original lawful use."

• For 42-1426: "That it requires a party claiming entitlement to an 'enlarged' use to bear the ultimate burden of persuasion to provide by a preponderance of the evidence a) the absence of injury to any water right existing on the date of completion of the 'enlargement;' b) that the 'enlargement' in use did not reduce the quantity of water available to any other water users on the date of completion of the 'enlargement;' c) the enlargement cannot exceed the rate of diversion provided by Idaho code 42-202; and d) the absence of any injury to any water right existing as of July 1, 1994, whether the water user is a party to the SRBA or not."

• For 42-1427 (the "ambiguous decree statute"): "prohibits it from being used to assert a claim to any expanded, enlarged or changed use of a water right ... The operation of [the statute] is interpreted as allowing any aggrieved water user to present evidence to show that the right, as claimed or recommended, is in reality a 'change,' 'expansion' or 'enlargement' of use that does not fall within the coverage of this statute. Any claimed, undefined element of water right under [this statute] cannot change or exceed the previously decreed or recorded element of the decreed or licensed right. The ambiguous decree statute cannot be used to claim an expansion of use beyond the beneficial use existing at the time the right was originally memorialized in a decree or license."

One key point likely to arouse interest is Hurlbutt's definition of "enlargement" of use, which (as he noted) is central to the way the statutes are put to use. An enlargement cannot include any increase in actual water used, the judge ruled, and that way "avoids violation of the prior appropriation doctrine [found in the Idaho Constitution].... Assuming the no-injury and no-enlargement burdens are met, the changed right can be given its original priority date. Legal issues as to what constitutes injury shall be decided on an as-applied basis."

In the case of 42-1426, enlargements of use would be given priority dates as of the date of the enlargement.

Along with his definitions of the statutes, Hurlbutt outlined a plan of action to incorporate the sense of this statutes into the SRBA procedures. That need not be a great amount of effort, Hurlbutt indicated, since much of the investigation and many of the claims that would apply under the three amnesty statutes also applied under the "presumption statutes" which were in effect when many of the claims and investigations were filed and undertaken.

APPEALS (5/8/1995) Judge Hurlbutt on April 26 rejected a request by a number of water user groups to reconsider his ruling on Basin Wide Issue 4, which upheld a specific interpretation of the 1994 "amnesty statutes" for water users.

But the same day he did approve requested made earlier in the month by four key SRBA parties (Pioneer Irrigation district, A&B Irrigation District, the Fremont-Madison Irrigation District and Mitigation Group, and a group of Upper Snake River Valley irrigators) asked Judge Hurlbutt to reconsider his Basin Wide Decision 4, or allow for a speedy (interlocutory) appeal.

The appellants argued that the amnesty statutes did not ban increases in the amount of water diverted as long as the rate of diversion isn't increase and as long as no other water users are harmed. Hurlbutt said that the statutes do bar any increase in the volume of water diverted.

An alternative response filed April 11 by Jeffrey Fereday for the Idaho Ground Water Appropriators contended that "the Court correctly perceived that in virtually all cases, except where there are no hydrologically connected juniors, any material increase in annual volume diverted necessarily results in more consumptive use and less water available to others, i.e., injury. Such users should not be entitled to the benefit of a statute which the Court properly construed to be aimed at avoiding injury."

LIVING WITH BASIN WIDE 4 (5/22/1995) This time, Judge Hurlbutt may not have thrown out a statute as unconstitutional – but he interpreted it in a way that upset plenty of people and raising questions about where the SRBA goes from here.

Hurlbutt on April 26 rejected a request by a number of water user groups to reconsider his ruling but did approve requests made earlier in the month by four key SRBA parties (Pioneer Irrigation district, A&B Irrigation District, the Fremont-Madison Irrigation District and Mitigation Group, and a group of Upper Snake River Valley irrigators) who asked him to allow for a speedy (interlocutory) appeal.

On May 12, however, he issued a supplemental order partially reversing that decision, though not with intent to block appeal. "The court does believe that Basin Wide Issue 4 should be heard as soon as possible by the Idaho Supreme Court," Hurlbutt wrote – but said that he had made a few mistakes in drafting his Basin Wide 4 order. "The court inadvertently failed to include the Rule 54(b) certification with its … order." He said that he made a correction.

That the order will be appealed is clear; one such request for appeal was filed May 14 by Ray Rigby for the Fremont-Madison Irrigation Group and Mitigation Group.

Meantime, Basin Wide 4 is in effect, and many attorneys have asked questions about proceeding under its impact.

Lynn Krogh, an attorney for the Idaho Department of Water Resources, said that agency has some concern about amending claims, and noted that "we need to know what priority date the claimant is claiming."

Critics of the ruling indicated portions of the Basin Wide 4 ruling was ambiguous in the procedures it outlined. Hurlbutt said that "if the state of Idaho or claimants require this court's guidance or direction with regard to every procedure to be followed, appropriate motion may be made for the implementation of the statutes." ☒

NO SETTLEMENT (9/14/1995) The Idaho Supreme Court, wending its way through a resolution of the Basin Wide Issue 4 case, has proposed to the parties involved that they sit down and try to resolve their differences at a settlement conference. The parties weren't buying.

On August 22, after some appeals documents had been rejected but one from Pioneer Irrigation District (on August 7) was accepted, and before others would make its way to the Court, Clerk Fred Lyons sent to 13 attorneys in the SRBA, all representing key clients in the case, a form letter noting that "the Court offers voluntary settlement conferences for civil cases on appeal. We invite you and your client to submit this case for an appellate settlement conference."

Rupert attorney Roger Ling said August 28, "Although we firmly believe that voluntary settlement conferences can provide significant benefits to the parties involved in a civil appeal to either the Supreme Court or Court of Appeals, we do not believe that it would lead to any significant resolution of the issues involved in the above appeals, commonly referred to as Basin Wide Issue No. 4. There are no factual disputes involved in these appeals. The issues involve the constitutionality of statutes and the legal construction of said statutes, as written. It is therefore our view that an opinion must be issued by the appellate court on the issues to provide the guidance needed in proceeding with the Snake River Basin Adjudication." ☒

AMNESTY YES, INTERPRETATION ... (11/1996) The Idaho Supreme Court upheld the constitutionality of the "amnesty statutes" passed by the Idaho Legislature in 1994. In upholding an earlier ruling on the subject by SRBA Judge Daniel Hurlbutt, the Court aligned with conventional wisdom on the matter. It set up considerable controversy, however, in also upholding Hurlbutt's interpretation of those statutes – his determination of what they mean. The high panel also, in its Memorandum Decision, set out procedures to be used by the parties obtaining water rights.

The high court noted "the district court viewed the absence of [the definition of "expanded use"] as raising an issue as to whether the statute was constitutionally void for vagueness on its face. In resolving this issue, the district court applied a 'core meaning' analysis to determine whether a person of reasonable intelligence can discern meaning of the term 'enlargement' as used in the amnesty statutes... In an effort to discern the meaning of enlargement, the district court referred to ... section 42-1416B for guidance. That statute defines 'expanded use' as follows: 'Expanded use' means an increase in the number of acres irrigated, or other additional use, under a valid ground water right without any increase in the rate of diversion or volume of water diverted."

The Supreme Court concluded, though, that "does not proscribe enlargements that include an increase in the volume of water diverted, so long as the enlargement does not exceed the rate of diversion originally authorized or injure water rights existing on the date of the enlarged use. The Court cannot engraft a condition that does not exist in the legislation. The question is whether that legislation as written is constitutional. As explained in the following section, the provision for enlargements in section 42-1426 is constitutional because of the mitigation provisions." ☒

HOW MANY CLAIMS? (12/1997) At the November information meeting, Hurlbutt noted, "Isn't it our experience that there have been very few amnesty claims?" The answer from Adjudication Administrator David Tuthill was: yes. Originally, the Department of Water Resources had thought as much as three to five percent of irrigated acreage might be involved, but upon investigation the numbers are turning out to be far smaller. ☒

Basin Wide 5 (general provisions)

Of all the basin wide issues, none has been as complex, lasted as long or taken as many turns (or as many appeals) as Basin Wide 5, which concerns the question of what descriptive details should be legally associated with a specific water right. If that sounds ministerial, this section may show it isn't.

CONJUNCTIVE MANAGEMENT GOES PUBLIC (8/2/1993) Planning for Department of Water Resources rules on conjunctive management is about to go public as department officials discuss how to go about one of the state's first examples of negotiated rulemaking. The rules will mesh department policies for handling surface and groundwater rights. Department officials intend to have rule language ready by March 4, 1994.

A general public comment period opened July 6, when Director Keith Higginson signed the rulemaking plan; public comment will be open until November 5.

And in between? "What we plan to do between now and then is also look at public information meetings and additional news releases to get the information out," said one IDWR official. The object between now and November 5 is to seek some kind of consensus. But Department officials acknowledge that won't be easy, and hearings are likely to be contentious. The new rulemaking comes at the same time as conjunctive management is thrashed out is the Adjudication. Higginson is among the state officials who flatly acknowledge that ground and surface waters are interrelated in the Snake River Plain.

The principle issue involved at this time relates to the extent to which existing ground water development from the Snake Plain aquifer can and should be related to maintain, or attempt to maintain, spring and other surface water. ☒

CHALLENGING THE RULES (1/23/1995) The Twin Falls firm Rosholt, Robertson & Tucker has filed a challenge to the legality of — and asked for an order invalidating — the extensive set of rules adopted last year by the Department of Water Resources on conjunctive (ground and surface together) water management.

Filing for Twin Falls Canal Company, the firm said that the rules as written run counter to "the priorities of the rights of the water users" and the prior appropriation doctrine. Other parts of the rules "misinterpret and misapply the 'futile call' doctrine, thereby ignoring the cumulative impacts of groundwater development and the hydrologic reality of the impact of groundwater extraction on surface rights …" ☒

CONJUNCTIVE RULES IN SRBA (3/13/95) Judge Hurlbutt ruled on March 1 that he will decide in a challenge to the state's new rules on conjunctive (ground and surface water together) management, overruling a state objection to his participation.

The state replied on January 27 that the rules aren't "uniquely applicable to water rights in the SRBA," but apply outside the basin as well, and the SRBA Court therefore is the wrong place to consider the question. Also, state attorneys said, the SRBA Court was set up specially by statute to perform one type of task, and lacked authority to hear administrative appeals.

But Hurlbutt said that when the Idaho Supreme Court outlined the SRBA Court's jurisdiction in *Walker v. Big Lost Irrigation District* in 1993, it set up a structure that clearly included such challenges.

"The resolution of the Canal Companies' action for declaratory relief constitutes a private adjudication as that term is used in *Walker*," Hurlbutt wrote. "The Canal Companies only have standing to challenge the regulations where they can demonstrate ownership of a water right or water rights.

"Further, the nature of the challenge clearly implicates a determination of priority date, point of diversion, quantity and a potential reduction of quantity by a review of conveyance loss. Therefore, a challenge to these administrative rules as a declaratory judgment action can only be resolved by a judicial determination of one or more of the elements of the Canal Companies' water rights." And he admonished the state: "The state's motion to dismiss represents a continued attempt to use jurisdiction as both a sword and a shield for the purpose of the State's litigation advantage. It is simply an attempt at forum shopping." ☒

GENERAL PROVISIONS STRUCK (5/8/1995) A large mass of water right-defining provisions were struck down May 3 by Judge Hurlbutt, as a violation of due process and "unfair, costly and a waste of time."

Attorneys in the Idaho Department of Water Resources and at the Attorney General's office have been reviewing the decision but have not decided whether to seek to overturn it.

The "general provisions" that were rejected by the court are not the basic elements of water right such as a priority date or point of diversion. Rather, they were elements included in the director's reports (from the Idaho Department of Water Resources) on water rights that, the department said in memorandum, "are specific right-defining provisions offered for inclusion in a final decree of water rights to enable IDWR to administer or enforce the courts decree. These so-called administrative provisions are not generally applicable to all water rights within the state or even necessarily all water rights within a particular basin. They may in fact only apply to discrete water and water rights, sometimes only to a single water right and generally are not amenable to general rulemaking under the Administrative Procedures Act."

Many of the provisions, however, do apply to large groups of water rights. The IDWR referenced them in the directors report as "general provisions" so as to avoid repeating them at length over and over for specific rights.

Hurlbutt, however, said that because the state has acknowledged that the "general provisions" do not apply in the same way to all rights, "it is fundamentally unfair to require a claimant to guess how, if or whether the possibility exists that the plead 'general provisions' might be applicable to his or her recommendation and compel filing of an objection to preserve the issue …

"Claimants deserve and the law requires that notice of the director's recommendation be given for each claimant. Due process requires nothing less. Further, claimants cannot be compelled to litigate over matters which do not directly affect the *prima facie* elements of their water rights."

Because the provisions were included in the reports mainly for administrative purposes, Hurlbutt ruled that their inclusion now, ahead of litigation, is premature.

Separately, Hurlbutt also struck down any general provisions references in director's reports for United States or tribal claims. There, he said that including general provisions was not only premature but also "violative of McCarran." Hurlbutt said that "the congressional waiver found in McCarran to include administration only operates after a general stream determination under subsection 1 of McCarran has been made."

Hurlbutt said that two of the most-used court forms, for objections and responses to objections to water right claims, would have to be changed to reflect the ruling. However, he said that no one who has filed a water right claim or objection needs to amend or change their claim or objection; the existing forms will be read by the court as if the general provisions aspects were not there at all. ☒

REACTIONS (6/19/1995) Appeals and requests for stay have been among the first round of reactions to Judge Hurlbutt's May 3 order striking "general provisions" in many water rights documents.

On May 10, Idaho state attorney Matthew McKeown asked for a stay of the order or for "permissive appeal" to the Idaho Supreme Court.

That was followed on May 18 by a request for stay by Idaho Power Company. Attorney James Tucker noted that the firm was the primary objector in a number of subcases where "the only issues in such cases being the Company's objections to the General Provisions in the Basin 36 Director's Report. ... While the Company's objections to the General Provisions are generally premised on the view that the SRBA decree should not be vehicle for the expansion of the administrative powers or duties of the IDWR or its director, the inclusion of some form of general or administrative provisions in the decree may be necessary and advisable to facilitate the enforcement of the decree by the IDWR or the watermaster."

He added: "depending on the scope and content of the Supreme Court's decision on the 'administrative provisions' issue, the Company may desire to approach this [SRBA] Court, after that decision is rendered, asking the Court to reconsider its May 4, 1995 Order and allow the references Subcases to go forward ..."

On May 16, attorney Roger Ling asked for a stay or permission to appeal.

Judge Hurlbutt rejected the requests on May 23, saying the provisions were stricken "because of recent judicial admissions made by the State of Idaho to the Idaho Supreme Court acknowledging that the 'general provisions' included in the director's reports are not general at all and rather consist of 'specific right-defining' provisions." ☒

A NEW BASIN WIDE? (9/25/1995) A large group of parties in the Snake River Basin Adjudication, including the state and several dozen private interests, have proposed a question of how to deal with general provisions in the SRBA as the next basin wide issue, what would be numbered 5.

They boiled this issue down into one question: "Do the general provisions included in the Director's Report for Republican Areas 1, 2 and 3 [the test basins] define, or clarify an element of the rights, or assist in the efficient administration of the recommended rights?"

The attorneys involved in developing the motion include Clive Strong, chief of the Natural Resources Division in the Attorney General's office; Ray Rigby, for the Fremont-Madison Irrigation District and Mitigation Group; Josephine Beeman for the Water Resource Coalition; Roger Ling for the A&B Irrigation District and the Big Lost River Irrigation District; Jeffrey Fereday for the Idaho Ground Water Appropriators; and William Ringert for the Nampa & Meridian Irrigation District.

Earlier this year, SRBA Judge Daniel Hurlbutt issued an order striking all general provisions in the directors reports. Several attorneys protested, saying that the provisions were in some cases unnecessary but in others needed to properly outline and define water rights. On September 11, Hurlbutt agreed to vacate his earlier order and reconsider the matter.

The attorneys in the new filing note that while some provisions really are "general" and apply to all water rights, others are very specific in their application. They note, for example, that in the director's report for area 2, "General Provision 10 applies to water from Reynolds Creek water system ... General Provision 11 applies to all water rights in Basin 57 shown with domestic use as a purpose of use ... 13-17 apply to all water rights in Basin 57 shown with irrigation as a purpose of use." ☒

THE BLIZZARD (4/1996) Stacks of new paperwork – pleadings and more – are piling up in SRBA-related law offices in the wake of impending action on Basin Wide Issue 5 and its children (5A and 5B), where the fate of a number of "special provisions" will be decided.

It shows indicators of becoming a complex and major turning point in the SRBA. One case in point: the court's reaction to a proposal to settle a piece of the basin wide issue away from the court.

That came through an agreement among unlikely partners.

On March 4, several parties filed a stipulation and settlement on the Reynolds Creek portion of Basin Wide Issue 5A in Owyhee County. This was an area where several conservation groups had been granted the ability to intervene; they used it here to oppose some elements of general provision 2 on grounds that allowing use of "excess water" could violate Idaho water law. But their attorney, Laird Lucas, said that the groups were not trying to oppose any specific water rights in the area or adjudication of them based on historic and beneficial use. So the groups agreed to a settlement on that issue with Jerry Hoagland, a Reynolds Creek water right owner, and his attorney. David Shaw of the Department of Water Resources signed off on it as well.

But on March 7, Special Master Fritz Haemmerle declined to accept it. He said in his decision "the question of legal necessity must be made by the court. The court will consider the Reynolds Creek provisions proposed by the director and the revised provision as proposed by all parties."

Department of Water Resources Adjudication Administrator David Shaw addressed the "necessity" issue in one report to the court. He said on March 13, concerning two provisions in Basin 34 (the Lost River area): "because these practices are not described by the statutory elements in the description of individual water rights and are not otherwise defined by existing law." General provisions 2a and 2b provide that upper and lower parts of the Big Lost River will be administered as separate sources; otherwise they would be administered together, whereas the area has been traditionally administered as separate sources.

An expert at last: In a string of orders related to Basin Wide 5, the Department of Water Resources and its personnel have been formally designated for the first time as special experts for the SRBA Court.

And the Department has already started issuing its expert opinions.

On March 4 Judge Hurlbutt named the Department as a special expert and required the director (or a subordinate) by March 11 to submit a report "presenting his opinion on why it is necessary for this court to include general provisions on irrigation use to enable him to lawfully administer water rights as decreed. This expert opinion shall be served on all parties participating in Basin Wide Issue 5."

Just a week later, on March 11, Adjudication division administrator David Shaw offered a detailed reply (later expanded in a second report). On "Why is it necessary for the court to include general provision 1 in the basin 36 report and general provision 3 in the basin 36 report as to conjunctive management ...?" ☒

THE BASIN WIDE QUESTIONS (9/1996) A variety of parties filed on August 26 seeking appeal of Basin Wide Issue 5, relating to general provisions. The most wide-ranging set of questions developed in the appeal came from the Idaho Attorney General's office. Those issues included:

• "Does Idaho Code 42-1411(3) and 1412 (6)require that a general provision apply to 'all water rights in the test basins'?

• "Did the SRBA District Court apply the wrong legal standard to the review of the proposal general provisions?

• "Does Idaho Code 42-1412(6) require the district court to determine every element of a water right set forth in Idaho Code ... even if some of the elements are not necessary to define or administer a water right?

• "Did the SRBA Court err in determining as a matter of law the irrigation season of use?

• "Does an irrigation purpose of use include incidental stockwater use?

• "Did the SRBA district Court err in refusing to allow a factual hearing to establish the necessity of the proposed general provisions for the definition and administration of water rights in the SRBA?

• "May general provisions be used to further define a water right based upon historical and custom practices of the area?" ☒

APPEALING 5B (4/1997) Critics of Judge Daniel Hurlbutt's recent ruling on Basin Wide Issue 5B, concerning general provisions, did not wait long to push on to the Idaho Supreme Court. Hurlbutt on February 27 granted a request asking the high court give expedited consideration to the issue.

The first motion for appeal, along with a memorandum outlining some of the issues, was filed March 13 by Deputy Attorney General Cheri Copsey.

Specifically, she noted the issues on appeal as including: "The binding effect of previous decrees; the legal standard for inclusion of general provisions; whether general provisions can be used to further define a water right based upon the historic and customary practices of the area."

Beyond that, she said, and beyond issues already on appeal to the high court (several are awaiting determination there), are "(1) whether, based on historic practices, the Idaho Department of Water Resources has the authority to change elements of water rights decreed by the SRBA district court; and (2) whether uncontroverted evidence, that physically interconnected water rights have been administered historically as separate sources in reliance on a decree, established the propriety for continuing to recognize that historic practice in a general provision."

She continued: "The state's position is that where groups of physically interconnected water rights have been administered historically as separate sources, this historic practice defines an element of each of the water rights affected by those practices – the source. Therefore, where the Director's investigation confirmed this historic practice and no evidence is introduced to contradict the director's report recommending its retention in a general provision, the appropriateness of its inclusion is established. The district court held that as a matter of law it has no authority to include this or similar provisions addressing the historic practices, that this would require it to improperly administer water in derogation of the Director's authority, and that these matters were already covered by rule." ☒

SPECIAL PROVISIONS AT SUPREME COURT (10/1997) The "special provisions" argument that has raged in SRBA Court got a hearing at the Supreme Court level September 8; a decision will be forthcoming.

The immediate case concerned special provisions in Basin 34 (the Lost River area) which in part governed the reading of the relationship between ground and surface water and the Big and Little Lost Rivers. In general, Judge Daniel Hurlbutt had held that some subjects should not be included in "general provisions" because they did not apply to all water rights.

The issue came up when Justice Cathy Silak asked why those elements could not be included in each individual water right decree.

Deputy Attorney General Cheri Copsey, arguing for the state of Idaho, said that they could. But she pointed out that as a matter of practice water rights are administered by many local water masters, and establishing common rules that work broadly across large numbers of rights make them much easier to manage.

"It makes no sense to do so [list the provision by individual decree]", she said. "The decree is something that has to work in real life."

Justice Byron Johnson, noting that Judge Hurlbutt had been reluctant to include in general provisions matters he thought more purely administrative, asked whether some of those provisions were basically administrative.

Copsey replied that water right decrees routinely mix descriptive with administrative, since they are to be used in practice, not merely referenced.

Attorney Roger Ling of Rupert noted that the people in the Lost River area have relied on these provisions (including such matters as rotation and season of use) for more than 60 years, and they are concerned about the possibility of challenges to long-standing practices. That could occur, he suggested, if the provisions are left to state administrative fiat (and the outside lobbying that goes with it) as opposed to being locked in place through court decrees. "These general provisions are part of the general custom of the Big Lost River," he said.

Twin Falls attorney Patrick Brown suggested that the real issue should be not what is descriptive (or the "element of a water right") as opposed to administrative, but rather: what belongs in a water right?

"The problem with Judge Hurlbutt's decision, the threat, is that he says anything that not an element of the right is 'administrative.' And his decision talks about administrative flexibility. Administrative flexibility is fine. What is not fine is omitting the conditions under which the right came into existence." ☒

SUPREME COURT: MIXED RESPONSE (11/1997) The Idaho Supreme Court continued its stream of SBBA decision on October 3 with a ruling that supported much of Adjudication Judge Daniel Hurlbutt's ruling that a series of "general provisions" should be struck from consideration in the SRBA.

The decision, written by now-former Justice Charles McDevitt, did reverse Hurlbutt in at least one significant area (firefighting provisions).

And it kept alive several key issues concerning conjunctive management of ground and surface water, ordering several relevant provisions to be re-argued in SRBA court.

The decision generally won acceptance by the whole court, but all four other justices signed separate dissents and concurrences on specific portions of it.

The Idaho Supreme Court, in its decision, did come with a definition and an explanation: "A general provision is a provision that is included in a water right decree regarding the administration of water rights that applies generally to water rights, is not an element of the water right, or is necessary for the efficient administration of the water rights decreed. Administering a water right is not a static business. While some administrative provisions would clearly apply to a certain type of water right in certain circumstances other administrative provisions clearly would not apply to a certain type of water right and every circumstance."

Firefighting: Judge Hurlbutt held that some of the provisions that allow for water use for firefighting are not truly general; the Supreme Court held otherwise. "The proposed provision regarding firefighting generally applies to all water rights," the court said. "The proposed provision provides that firefighting purposes is an alternate use for which any water right may be used, and firefighting is recognized as a lawful use of water with or without a water right."

Irrigation season: Some water rights had been earmarked for early and late irrigation seasons. Judge Hurlbutt struck such references, and the Supreme Court agreed with him. "We agree with the SRBA district court and the Director [of the Department of Water Resources] that due to year to year changes in climatic conditions and variability in each area's soil type, the period of use for irrigation water rights should not be defined as a fixed period of use. The period of use for irrigation is the irrigation season. The irrigation season is determined by the irrigator based upon when water is available, needed, and can be put to beneficial use for that purpose. No irrigator has the right to waste water. The Director has the administrative duty and authority to annually determine the beginning and ending of an irrigation season and to prevent wasteful use of water by irrigators. The period of the year when water is used for irrigation purposes shall be determined annually by irrigators subject to the authority of the Director and any reasonable rules and regulations the Director may adopt."

Conjunctive management: The high court ordered re-argument on the general provision concerning interconnection and conjunctive management of surface and ground water rights. It did not address that subject. ☒

A PROVISION REMANDED (2/1998) The Idaho Supreme Court on January 6 remanded one aspect of the general provisions debate back to SRBA court, from whence it had been appealed. But it did attach instructions.

In the case designated *State of Idaho and Big Lost River Irrigation District v . G. David Nelson, San Felipe Ranch; Mitchell D. Sorensen; Francis L. Smith; Wiley F. Smith; and United States* (and opinion No. 1 for 1998 for the Idaho Supreme Court) the court held that – contrary to the views expressed by SRBA Presiding Judge Daniel Hurlbutt – general provisions need not apply to every water right, but could be imposed wherever necessary for clear administration of the right.

The court sent the case back to Hurlbutt for further review as to whether the general provisions in question are needed for administration.

Basin Wide Issue 5B is a companion to the cases on 5 and 5A, heard by the Idaho Supreme Court last term. It arose out of issues concerning water rights in the Big Lost River Basin (Basin 34, the first test basin) in Custer and Butte counties.

The area was long governed by the "Utah Construction" decree, but since other water rights in the area had not been adjudicated, they were not subject to the decree or administration by a watermaster. The SRBA Court in 1992 issued an order for interim administration of the water rights there in accord with the Department of Water Resources Director's Report. The Director's Report contained the provisions at issue in BWI 5B:

Provision 2a says that during certain water level conditions all water is to be administered as a single system, but at other times the natural flow rights with a point of diversion above Mackay Reservoir would be administered separately from those diverted below.

Provision 2b provides certain streams are to be administered separately from the Big Lost surface water.

Provision 2c requires water from the "Back Channel", which separates from the main channel, should be administered as part of the natural channel of the Big Lost River.

Provision 4 mandates a "rotation for credit" practice – a procedure already long in use in the area – and requires a minimum amount of water remain in Mackay Dam and Reservoir. "Rotation for credit" means that water stored in the Mackay Reservoir is to be allocated first to the junior natural flow water right holders, and only later to the senior right holders. That would mean junior right holders get most of the stored water so all users in the Big Lost receive adequate supply for the irrigation season.

In saying that general provisions need not cover every water right, the Supreme Court did say they should be included in a decree if needed to define or administer water rights.

The court noted that "At the time of its decision, the district court did not have the benefit of this Court's statement in *A & B Irrigation Dist. v. Idaho Conservation League* that, 'a general provision is an administrative provision that generally applies to water rights but it need not apply to every water right.'"

Provisions 2 and 4 were returned to Hurlbutt for a factual determination whether they are necessary to define or efficiently administer water rights.

"Since these General Provisions regulated whether water is administered from a single or separate water source," the court held, "it is possible that these provisions define the source element or are necessary for the efficient administration of a water right. Considering this test was not employed by the SRBA Court, we remand this case for further factual findings as to whether these provisions are necessary for the efficient administration of a water right or to define a water right."

The Supreme Court was even more explicit in the case of one of those specific provisions. "The district found that without General Provision 4b, the administration of these water rights might be nearly impossible, yet the provision should not be included because I.C. Section 42-1411(3) precluded the inclusion of the provision because the provision did not apply to all water rights. As noted above, a provision is to be included in a decree if it is necessary to define or for the efficient administration of a water right, and it is not necessary that the provision apply to all water rights. Therefore, if the provision is necessary for the efficient administration of a water right, we hold that the provision should be included in the decree, and remand for further factual findings as to the necessity of this provision either to the definition or the administration of these water rights." ☒

SUPREME COURT: MORE PROVISIONS (5/1998) The Idaho Supreme Court on April 22 revisited an earlier decision on Basin Wide Issue 5 – the general provisions – and added some explication. It reversed Judge Hurlbutt on his decision against including irrigation season and conjunctive management general provisions in its eventual water right decrees.

In the new decision, the Court remanded one area to the SRBA Court: It ordered a factual determination on whether general provisions regarding interconnection and conjunctive management should be included in its decrees. In addition, the Court withdrew its previous holding that the period of use shall be the "irrigation season." The high court said each irrigator's water right must be decreed with a specific period of use, and ordered Hurlbutt to consider the factual question of the appropriate period of use for each irrigation water right. It also ordered Hurlbutt to reconsider whether general provisions regarding early and late season use are necessary to define or efficiently administer a water right.

This decision was not unanimous; Justice Byron Johnson dissented on several key points, holding that the SRBA Court rulings were correct. ☒

REYNOLDS CREEK AT SUPREME COURT (5/1998) The Idaho Supreme Court on April 6 reinstated a general provision – Provision 2 – which had been stricken by an SRBA special master and Judge Daniel Hurlbutt.

It did not specifically say, however, whether the *res judicata* or collateral estoppel principles mean an earlier adjudication decree (the Reynolds Creek Decree) must be included in the eventually-issued SRBA decree. It sent the matter back to SRBA Court for additional work.

The ruling marks a near-end to work on Basin Wide Issue 5A.

The decision, written by Justice Cathy Silak was of a piece with other recent Supreme Court decisions on general provisions, issued since the SRBA Court acted on this one. This appeal goes back to 1996. It grew out of a dispute at Reynolds Creek in Owyhee County (in Basin 57), where an earlier adjudication appeared to settle most water right questions. A general adjudication for Reynolds Creek began in 1978; a final decree was issued in March 1988, in which the district court set the respective rights of water users within Reynolds Creek and decreed rights to "excess water." When the Idaho Department of Water Resources issued a Director's Report on the water rights there, it included General Provision 2, to cover the question of using "excess flows" which had been a point of dispute between water users in the upper and lower reaches of the basin.

The Supreme Court explained: "The term 'excess' water refers to the fact that during spring runoff, the flow in Reynolds Creek is high, and the creek contains more water than can be used. However, later in the year, the flow becomes nearly nonexistent. General Provision 2 is identical to a stipulation entered into by the parties during the Reynolds Creek Adjudication … That stipulation was based on historic practices in the Reynolds Creek Basin regarding 'excess' water."

The Court also noted by way of definition: "'excess' water is defined as the amount of water flowing at the Upper Basin Tollgate weir in excess of 37 cubic feet per second (cfs.) and the amount of water flowing at the Outlet weir in excess of 57 cfs. If the flow at the Tollgate weir is less than 37 cfs., or the flow at the Outlet weir is less than 57 cfs., the Upper and Lower

Basins are administered as one basin. If the flow at the Outlet weir exceeds 57 cfs., the Upper Basin Users (Upper Users) are permitted to divert the 'excess' mounts, even though diverting those amounts will mean that the Upper Users are diverting more water than that permitted by their respective water rights. Further, the Upper Users are not permitted to store any excess water during the irrigation season."

The general provision was challenged by the Idaho Conservation League and other conservation groups, concerned about the allocation to water users of water not specifically used for beneficial purposes.

The Court's analysis of Hurlbutt's ruling partly agreed, partly disagreed.

Hurlbutt said Provision 2 is not a general provision because it doesn't apply to every right in the basin (a point the Supreme Court overturned several months ago). The Supreme Court agreed that the provision doesn't properly describe a right to divert "excess" water or high flows, and that it doesn't fall clearly into a list of the elements of a water right.

The Court also held that the water users in the Reynolds Creek Basin do not have a water right in the excess water.

But the Court did say general provisions covering administration of water rights is allowed by state law. Silak also wrote that while the provision doesn't prescribe a right to "excess" water, it does describe a procedure under which certain water right holders can use that "excess" water. For that reason, the justices said, the provision is useful and may be necessary for "the efficient administration of water rights." ☒

SPECIFICS (6/1998) The brace of decisions which included the irrigation season rulings also covered an overruling of Hurlbutt decisions that the general provisions applying to water right decrees should be thrown out because they do not all apply to all water rights.

Now, the judge has told IDWR officials, you're going to have to tell me specifically which provisions apply to which rights. That, he suggested, may involve reopening objection periods in a number of cases. And, he said, all of the SRBA players will have to figure out how to handle the provisions procedurally.

"So this is my predicted nightmare," he said. "It sounds to me like we're starting all over again in the test basins."

The Supreme Court said the general provisions could be imposed where necessary, but Hurlbutt said he is unclear what constitutes necessity – or how to bring closure to the case under those conditions. "You understand the case will never end under these circumstances," he said. "So I guess we do have a permanent water court."

The most sensitive area may be that of conjunctive management - of ground and surface water – and IDWR Administrator David Tuthill suggested including a "placeholder remark" in Basin 35 decrees until more details can be worked out. ☒

CONJUNCTION IN PROVISIONS (8/1998) Parties in the SRBA are moving closer to a revised "general provision" on conjunctive – groundwater and surface water – management in the case. At least, there are no lack of options.

A working group of attorneys and others met in Burley on June 10 and again on June 24 to review the conjunctive management general provisions in the SRBA. At the meeting, conducted by the Idaho Department of Water

Resources and attended by about 20 participants, participants developed 11 options for conjunctive management language for water right decrees.

That is in addition to the options previously developed by IDWR, and to a new one, "Option 14."

Despite all the varied ideas, Adjudication Administrator Tuthill said that "there is a great deal of common ground on a general provision for conjunctive management ... more common ground than disputed ground." He said that on July 13 the Department of Water Resources sent participants in the process a sheet outlining how the Department would expect to carry out conjunctive management provisions.

Under "Option 14", a three-part form would be sent to relevant water right holders:

"Water rights decreed in the SRBA from the following list of sources of water in Basin __ shall be administered separately from all other water rights in Basin __. [list sources]

"Water rights decreed in the SRBA from the following list of sources of water in Basin __ shall be administered separately from all other water rights in the Snake River Basin. [list sources]

"All other water rights within the basin are from connected sources of water in the Snake River Basin and shall be administered conjunctively in accordance with law."

Hurlbutt said that this approach is consistent with his rulings. ☒

IRRIGATION SEASON (12/1998) The Department of Water Resources has recommendations on accounting for specific irrigation seasons in water rights – as mandated by the Idaho Supreme Court. Judge Hurlbutt said that they appear to pass legal muster and may be put into effect. ☒

RESTRUCTURING BW 5 (9/1999) Judge Wood said at the August 25 SRBA information session that he's considering restructuring the splintered Basin Wide Issue 5 cases. Basin Wide Issue 5 was set up to consider the matter of "general provisions" in the SRBA – provisions which former Judge Hurlbutt at one point struck and which were mostly reinstated by the Idaho Supreme Court. Elements of BW5 were broken out during the appeals process; Basin Wide 5A covered mainly the Reynolds Creek provisions in Owyhee County (in Basin 57) and Basin Wide 5B covered mainly the Lost River area (in Basin 34). The main Basin Wide Issue 5 covers mainly irrigation and conjunctive management general provisions. All three are back in the SRBA Court, on remand from the Idaho Supreme Court.

Judge Wood said that, in considering when and how to reconsider them, he is considering renaming the cases as Basin Wide 5/34 (for BW5B) and Basin Wide 5/57 (for BW5A), to clarify the cases.

Rexburg attorney Gregory Moeller of Rigby Thatcher said, "It makes a lot of sense to me. That's how we have our files set up." ☒

QUESTIONING CONJUNCTIVE (9/1999) Department of Water Resources officials have suggested some changes in the increasingly complex procedure for handling conjunctive management remarks. Conjunctive management refers to the approach for managing underground as well as surface waters.

At an information meeting in Pocatello on August 25, IDWR Adjudication Chief David Tuthill said that when the agency developed its Director's Reports (recommendations on water rights) for basins 35, 51, 55, 61, 71 and 72, conjunctive management (groundwater provisions) were noted as "remarks" on each individual right. He noted that "format was chosen because it provided an easy method of providing notice of IDWR's conjunctive management recommendation in individual water right recommendations, in the absence of general provisions ..." The Department intends these remarks to be treated as general provisions, which would have impact across many water rights.

But the authority for these specific notations is unclear (two separate Idaho Code sections, 42-1411[2]k and 42-1411[3] have been cited). And IDWR Attorney Peter Anderson noted, "There is a risk of inconsistent partial decrees in each basin if the Court decrees some rights with the provision, and then modifies the provision for other water rights because of objections. Substantial work is required to remove this provision from partial decrees."

He said the department can, first of all, prepare partial decrees for the SRBA Court for unobjected-to rights, which do not include the general provision recommendation. In other cases, he proposed inserting new "savings language" in partial decrees.

The language in many decrees includes language like this, which was taken from a specific water recommendation in Basin 35:

"The following water rights from the following sources of water in Basin 35 shall be administered separately from all other water rights in Basin 35: [lists any applicable water rights and sources, but usually "none" – unless, Anderson said, there's a "preponderance of the evidence" showing that the water sources are in fact separate].

"The following water rights from the following sources of water in Basin 35 shall be administered separately from all other water rights in the Snake River Basin: [again, lists any applicable water rights and sources, but usually "none"].

"All water rights within Basin 35 are from connected sources of water in the Snake River Basin and shall be administered conjunctively."

The new language would say, "This partial decree is subject to those general provisions determined by the Court to be necessary for the definition of efficient administration of the water rights."

That way, the IDWR officials said, people would know when they get their water right decrees that those decrees are limited by some outside restrictions.

And Tuthill pointed out that in some cases (though not in most) the general provisions which apply to water rights are long and complex, and there would be little sense in trying to attach the full language to each water right document.

That approach wasn't satisfying to a number of people in the court, however.

Special Master Terry Dolan suggested that would mean people would be getting a water right permit that wasn't complete; it would only say, he noted, that it is subject to some other provisions, somewhere, which may be imposed at some time. That may make it easy for the department or court to amend in the future, but difficult for a water user to use.

And, he asked, what if the rules change from basin to basin? Will water users, he questioned, have to wait until the SRBA is complete before they know what their water rights really are? ⊠

BW5 REALIGNED (10/1999) Presiding Judge Barry Wood on August 31 issued an order realigning the remaining live issues under Basin Wide Issue 5. Wood said that the process had become confusing, and "Because the directions on remand require an evidentiary hearing specific to each hydrologic basin as it relates to the respective proposed general provisions for that Basin, this Court upon its own initiative realigns the issues by Basin and designates them henceforth as follows:

- " Basin-Wide Issue 5-34, all remaining issues in Basin 34 which are: Beginning and ending dates of irrigation period of use; Conjunctive management; Administration of surface rights; division of Big Lost River, separate stream, back channel, storage rights, flow below Mackay Dam, rotation with storage.
- "Basin-Wide Issue 5-36, all remaining issues in Basin 36 which are: Beginning and ending dates of the irrigation period of use; conjunctive management.
- "Basin Basin-Wide Issue 5-57, all remaining issues in Basin 57 which are: Beginning and ending dates of irrigation period of use; conjunctive management; which specific decrees should contain 'excess' water provisions."

He added, "In other words, it is the Court's intent to have all general provision issues now existing in Basin 34 to be designated as Basin-Wide Issue 5-34, all in Basin 36 to be designated as Basin-Wide Issue 5-36 and all in Basin 57 to be designated as Basin-Wide Issue 5-57."

The decision was organizational, not substantive; but the judge did add that "Because this Court has "realigned" the issues and designated those applicable to a particular basin, if on future appeal, any party wishes to utilize any portion of the record prior to realignment, the party will have to designate those portions on appeal." ☒

CONJUNCTIVE IN BASIN WIDE 5 (11/1999) An October 20 SRBA Court meeting in Arco for people in the Lost River Area (test basin 34) has led to a major change in the most persistently difficult of the basin wide issues.

Judge Barry Wood said that he will issue an order redesignating Basin Wide Issue 5, which has had to do with general provisions, as concerning conjunctive management. Basin Wide Issue 5/34, which Judge Wood earlier had designated as a basin wide issue, now will be designated as applying to general provisions 1 through 6, which have covered such matters as definitions for determining separate streams (an especially difficult issue in the Lost River area). ☒

HOW DETAILED THE CONJUNCTIVE? (12/1999) The difficult topic of conjunctive management – deemed by attorney John Rosholt in his presentation "probably the most important issue in the whole SRBA" – took another step toward resolution in November. Under consideration in November: The question of how detailed should be water right decrees in describing surface and ground water right relationships.

On November 2, Judge Barry Wood sent a letter to a number of parties in the SRBA including prospective language (developed by the Idaho Department of Water Resources) for issuing uncontested partial decrees pending resolution of conjunctive management considerations.

Immediate responses were all over the board. ☒

MOVING ON CONJUNCTIVE (1/2000) Final decisions on the law and facts of conjunctive management – the relationship between groundwater and surface water – are some distance in the future, but on December 3 Judge Barry Wood set out an interim plan for attack for coping with that situation while keeping partial decree issuance underway.

In two orders, Wood outlined his plan.

First, he decreed language that will appear in all partial decrees until conjunctive management is resolved: "This partial decree is subject to such general provisions necessary for the definition of the rights or for the efficient administration of the water rights as may be ultimately determined by the Court at a point in time no later than the entry of a final unified decree. I.C. 42-1412(6)."

He re-named the conjunctive management issue as "Basin-Wide Issue 5 on Remand – Conjunctive Management, Snake River Basin-Wide." And he said that "if there are factual issues unique to a particular sub-basin relative to the interconnection of sources of water, then those issues will be dealt with in that particular sub-basin (e.g. Basin 34)." ☒

ADR ON CONJUNCTIVE (7/2000) Judge Barry Wood on June 14 ordered a type of mediation, and named a mediator, in an attempt to resolve a number of conjunctive management – surface and ground water relationship – issues.

The mediator, however, later was withdrawn.

After reviewing suggestions from a number of parties, Wood said that non-binding mediation would be used, and named University of Idaho Professor Douglas Grant as mediator. However, on June 19 Grant sent the SRBA Court an e-mail asking to be withdrawn from the case. ☒

PARTICIPANTS WILL BE BOUND (4/2001) Several participants in a Lost River basin settlement conference who asked to withdraw their approval of the resulting stipulation will have to stand by it instead, Judge Roger Burdick ruled on March 15.

That decision is the latest turning point in the very long history of Basin Wide Issue 5, originally set up to determine the validity of a number of "general provisions" the Idaho Department of Water Resources had attached to a number of its water right recommendations.

The Lost River area (Basin 34) has been the scene of some of the most difficult conflicts. Former SRBA Judge Barry Wood decided in April 2000 that the Lost River issues would move forward on "dual tracks" – litigation and efforts by parties to settle as many issues as possible. He named Special Master Thomas Cushman to preside over those settlement efforts.

Language for several of the provisions had been agreed on earlier, and in February discussion focused on Provision 6, which concerns conditions under which the Big Lost River will be administered as separate systems above and below the Mackay Dam.

Although some parts of that provision left some participants uneasy, at first they all seemed willing to sign off on a stipulated agreement. An attendance sheet was sent around the room, and participants were asked to initial their names if they agreed. All but one, McCray, did; she asked for, and was given, two days to consider the matter. In the meantime, three other participants, Babcock, Anderson and Smith, changed their minds and said they would withdraw their approval. ☒

BURDICK OKS CONJUCTIVE DEAL (9/2001) SRBA Judge Roger Burdick on August 30 entered an order which could resolve much of the debate on conjunctive management, and ordered interested parties to respond to it by November 14.

He also renamed "conjunctive management" – which relates to the relationship between ground and surface water – as the "connected sources general provision." It remains numbered as Basin-Wide Issue 5.

That came as a result of a settlement agreement announced August 24 by parties negotiating on conjunctive management provisions; Burdick had imposed an August 28 deadline for them. Those parties submitted, and the Idaho Department of Water Resources agreed with, a proposed "Settlement Agreement and Stipulation for Entry of Agreed Findings of Fact, Conclusions of Law, and Partial Judgment on Basin-Wide Issue 5."

Burdick had also been proceeding on a second trial track in the event negotiations failed. After the agreement was sent to him, he cancelled evidentiary and pre-trial hearings.

The judge noted, "Although the agreement reached by the Parties represents potential settlement of Basin-Wide Issue 5, the Court is still charged with the duty of reviewing the contents of the agreement to ensure compliance with the law. The Court is not required to 'rubberstamp' either the recommendations contained in the director's report or any agreement reached by the Parties to the extent they are contrary to law. The Court's role however, is somewhat limited because a trial was not conducted on the merits and the Court is not required by statute to conduct an evidentiary hearing in order to accept a stipulation as final resolution." ☒

WOOD THROWS OUT A CONJUNCTIVE PROCESS (7/2006) 5th District Judge Barry Wood, a former water adjudication judge, held on June 2 that the state's system of conjunctive management—managing surface and groundwater as part of a single system—has the effect of unfairly disadvantaging some surface water users by not giving them full advantage of their water claim priority dates. He threw out several of the conjunctive management rules adopted by the Idaho Department of Water Resources.

The decision grows out of a January 2005 call on water by a number of Magic Valley senior water right holders, who argued they were denied water in that low-water year because groundwater users with later priority dates had used it first.

The state Department of Water Resources issued orders that groundwater users provide water or other compensation, but some of the surface water users said it wasn't enough, and sued the department to expand its remedies.

Wood's initial decision appeared to side with the surface water users. But he asked them, as a next step, to deliver to him their specific demands for compensation.

The significance of all this may be complicated somewhat by the weather. 2005 was a drought year in southern Idaho, the last of several, but 2006 so far has been a water-surplus year. That may put off some demands for immediate compensation, but the legal issue could have impact again the next time a low-water year hits. ☒

SUPREME COURT UPHOLDS CUNJUNCTIVE RULES (4/2007) In a long-awaited opinion in the case of *American Falls Reservoir District No. 2, et al. v. Idaho Dept. of Water Resources* – closely watched by the Idaho water community – the Idaho Supreme Court on March 5 upheld the Idaho Department of Water Resources rules on conjunctive management.

The decision reversed a ruling by Fifth District Judge Barry Wood, who had held the state's rules on conjunctive management (of ground and surface water) were unconstitutional. He had said that a number of "procedural components" in the rules were lacking, and found other defects as well.

The Supreme Court did, however, go out of its way to say that the lower court decision was well-crafted, and did accept a number of elements of the Wood decision, even if reversing it on the key point.

Governor C.L. "Butch" Otter remarked, "The court made it clear that we must be guided by the 'prior appropriation' doctrine in the Idaho Constitution and conjunctive management rules developed to preserve and protect our precious water. In the near future I will announce plans for a water summit that will put that guidance to work in charting our course forward."

The Supreme Court overruled Wood, holding that the Rules were not unconstitutional on their face based on a lack of procedural components. The Court observed that if there are circumstances under which the Rules may be constitutionally applied to provide adequate procedural safeguards, then the Rules withstand a facial challenge. The Court noted that Rule 20.02 specifically incorporates by reference the Idaho Constitution, statutes and case law; therefore, the rules need not specifically restate previously articulated procedural requirements, such as proper presumptions, burdens of proof and evidentiary standards.

The court also held that the rules were not facially unconstitutional in asking a senior water rights holder to provide information necessary to the director's determination of whether material injury had occurred, although that does not permit shifting the burden to the senior to re-prove or re-adjudicate the right he already has.

The court also determined the "reasonable carryover" provisions in the Rules are facially constitutional in permitting some discretion in the Director to determine whether the carryover water is reasonably necessary for future needs. Finally, the Court held the district court did not abuse its discretion in denying the City of Pocatello's motion to intervene in this case. ⊠

Basin Wide 6 (tribal in-stream flow)

TRIBAL IN-STREAM? (9/25/1995) Do reserved water rights doctrines, treaties and other such agreements give Idaho's Indian tribes a legal right to claim in-stream flows? That would be Basin Wide Issue No. 6, proposed September 20 by attorney Scott Campbell. Campbell, of the Boise firm Elam & Burke, represents organizations including the Pioneer Irrigation District, Settlers' Irrigation District, Payette River Water Users Association, Little Salmon River Water Users Association, Little Weiser Irrigation District, and the Lost Valley Irrigation Company.

Campbell proposed: "As a matter of law, are the Indian Tribes entitled to off-reservation in-stream flow water rights as described in their Notices of Claims?"

He outlined more specific questions concerning specifically claims of the Nez Perce Tribe, the Shoshone-Bannock Tribes and the Northwestern Band of the Shoshoni Nation.

"The proposed Basin-Wide Issues are broadly significant to the SRBA due to geographical scope of these off-reservation in-stream flow claims," Campbell said. "The claims are located in 16 main stem and tributary basins. These in-stream flow claims affect every other water claimant within these

16 basins who has filed a diversionary claim upstream from the in-stream flow claims. These in-stream flow claims also affect claimants upstream and outside these 16 basins."

And, he noted, "Once this court establishes the precise legal basis for the in-stream flow claims, the parties will be able to evaluate the relative strengths of their cases. This knowledge will prevent unrealistic expectations of parties and stimulate settlements." ☒

THREE BASIN-WIDES (10/25/1995) SRBA Court has set November 21 as the day to consider an unusual three requests – all at once – to designate new basin wide issues.

The proposals, which are suggested to be designated as Basin Wide Issues 6, 7 and 8, come from attorney Scott Campbell of Elam & Burke of Boise, attorneys for a large group of water user individuals and groups in Southwestern Idaho.

The three proposed issues all relate to in-stream flow claims by federal-related entities: 6 concerns tribal claims, 7 concerns Forest Service Claims, 8 concerns Fish & Wildlife agency and related claims. The proposed issues are sure to bring more energy and focus to discussion of how to proceed next in the arena of federal in-stream flow claims, already a subject of considerable interest.

There are no responses yet to any of the issues, other than Hurlbutt's agreement to set a hearing on them at the November status conference.

However, J.R. Simplot Co. attorney Terry Uhling asked the court to hold off designating the issues and hold an expedited hearing on whether they should be designated, and to consolidate a number of subcases in the SRBA before designating the issues. Hurlbutt agreed to take that up as well on November 21.

In Issue 6, Campbell is challenging directly the tribe's claims to in-stream flows, primarily off-reservation claims, saying that their legal basis for those claims is flawed. "The tribes cited several treaties and various other documents to support their in-stream flow claims. Pioneer argues that the tribes lack the legal authority to for these in-stream flow claims. The federal reserved water rights doctrine, treaties and other documents cited by the tribes do not provide an adequate legal basis for the in-stream flow rights as claimed by the tribes in their Notices of Claims." Campbell suggested the court use a civil practice rule, 56(c), as a basis for determining that legal adequacy.

Campbell structured his proposed issue question as five questions, one for each of the five groups of tribal claims – three separate groups of Nez Perce tribal claims, and claims for the Shoshone-Bannock Tribes in eastern Idaho and the Northwestern Band of the Shoshoni at Duck Valley. The former of the question in each case, though, was essentially the same: "Is there an adequate legal basis, via treaty or otherwise, for the off-reservation in-stream flow water rights in the … Tribe's notices of claims … in the Snake River Basin Adjudication? Is the … [tribe] entitled to any off-reservation in-stream flow water rights based on the legal authority cited by the [tribe]?"

The tribal rights issue is significant, Campbell said, because "due to the quantities claimed by the tribes, many claimants with state-based claims will be divested of their water rights or otherwise adversely impacted if the requested in-stream flow claims are decreed as described in the Notices of

Claims." He noted that all claims in 16 main and tributary basins are affected by the tribal claims. ☒

➲ *Tribal in-stream rights in effect were acknowledged later on as part of the Nez Perce Tribe water settlement package.*

Basin Wides 7 & 8 (Forest Service rights)

ISSUE 7 (10/23/1995) Campbell's second proposed basin-wide issue, concerning U.S. Forest Service claims, includes a direct challenge to the Service's withdrawal of most of its water right claims in the SRBA. Noting that "to date no definite ruling on the validity of the USFS Notice of Withdrawal has been issued," he said that the action was taken under a procedural rule that allows withdrawal only prior to certain actions by adverse parties and by filing a stipulation of dismissal signed by all parties who appeared in the action. Neither of those requirements, Campbell argued, has been met.

Presumably, those arguments, not a part of the court record, will be brought in near future and could – if Campbell's arguments are upheld – reverse the Forest Service's withdrawal of water right claims.

Campbell's Issue 7 focuses, however, on the underlying basis of any Forest Service claims, since the agency uses the same legal basis to support both the withdrawn and retained claims. His basic question is "As a matter of law, is the USFS entitled to any in-stream flow water claims under the legal authorities relied upon by the USFS in the Notices of Claims?" He goes on to challenge specifically nine areas of law or doctrine that the agency has used to defend its claims. ☒

ISSUE 8 (10/23/1995) Finally, Campbell is challenging a set of claims by the U.S. Fish and Wildlife Service, saying that "the FWS cited federal statutes and various other documents to support its in-stream flow claims. Pioneer argues that the FWS lacks the legal authority for the in-stream flow claims."

Campbell noted that all of the FWS claims (though not large in number) are in the main Snake River, and therefore "affect every other water claimant who has filed a diversionary claim on the Snake River or any tributary thereto upstream from the in-stream flow claims." ☒

Basin Wide 9 (Public Water Reserve 107)

BLM 107 RIGHTS (11/13/1995) Does the federal Bureau of Land Management have authority to designate land as a Public Water Reserve 107 reserve after repeal of the statutes on which the reserve authority is based?

That narrow question may not sound as if it has much to do with the Snake River Basin but veteran Lost River basin SRBA activists Mitchell Sorensen and Harvey Walker maintain that it does. And they asking that question be designated as Basin wide Issue 9. There's been no response to the request yet from other parties or from the court.

Sorensen and Walker, non-attorneys filing on their own behalf (*pro se*) said the issue has wide significance because the federal government originally had 887 notices of claim for water rights based in Public Water

Reserve 107 sections just in reporting area 1 (the Lost River area). About 365 of these were later withdrawn, but that leaves about 522 claims. In the SRBA overall, Sorensen and Walker said, "the United States actually filed over 10,000 claims based on Public Water Reserve 107."

Some of these waters designated as PWR 107 were designated before 1976, but apparently most of them were designated after that date. That is significant, they said, because the controlling federal law in the area, changed in 1976 with enactment of the Federal Land Policy and Management Act; after that time, they said, the BLM did not have authority to make the designation. ☒

PWR 107 (3/1996) Judge Hurlbutt said that he would take the question of whether to designate the issue under advisement. He suggested that he probably would designate an issue in this area, but he would consider carefully the options for phrasing and structuring it.

Public Water Reserve 107 was declared in 1926 by President Calvin Coolidge, withdrawing from normal public domain uses certain watered areas, including many lands used for stockwater in the West. Because it is a withdrawal more by description than by geographic notation, it has been called a "floating blanket" withdrawal, and many public lands are included under it. The cloud on federal water rights claimed under that reserve came from a change in federal law. The reserve was allowed by laws passed by Congress in 1910 and 1916. In 1976, however, those laws were superseded by the Federal Land Management and Policy Act (FLPMA). That has led to the question of whether the federal reserves are still in place, since the laws originally authorizing them have been wiped out.

Lost River area water user Mitchell Sorensen said that the issue has come to the fore because of the large number of federal water rights in his area, and the "aggressive rate" that Special Master Brigette Bilyeu has met trying to resolve water right questions in that area. Many of the water users there, he said, are financially unable to take on federal agencies in contesting the validity of the Reserve 107 rights.

Hofstetter also proposed a second question (which would be Basin Wide Issue 9A): "Does the BLM own the water rights associated with private livestock use of the public domain?"

The point involved was phrased another way in a February 14 brief by attorney Richard Simms: "The state law claims of the United States are not based on historical stockwatering uses of the BLM or any other agency of the nation's government. As far as we know, the United States has grazed no stock in Idaho." The BLM does lease large areas of land for use by private cattle owners. A number of those stockwater users have been active in trying to ensure that the SRBA proceedings do not result in their losing ability to water their cattle as they historically have.

Simms said he thinks the real issue in Basin Wide Issue 9 is whether the federal government can claim a water right based on the efforts of a private person trying to perfect their own water right.

Deputy Attorney General David Barber said state attorneys generally support Simms' position. He said that he had an internal memorandum from the BLM which could call into question the agency's own view of the validity of its water rights.

But Department of Justice attorney Daria Zane suggested that the issue be framed a little more narrowly: whether the Reserve 107 provisions are grounds for declaring a water right. (That approach presumably could leave open the possibility of securing a water right based on other criteria, whereas the Simms approach might shut down BLM claims early on.) ☒

BASIN WIDE (4/1996) While warning that he will not want to approve many more, Judge Hurlbutt on March 8 okayed another basin wide issue on the burner for a few months. Basin Wide Issue 9 is "Whether Public Water Reserve 107 is a valid basis for a federal reserved water right." ☒

STOCKWATER NECESSITY (1/1997) A large number of federal water right claims based on a federal land reservation law were held to be invalid in a December 9 SRBA Court ruling. The ruling most strongly affects the Bureau of Land Management, which had made the largest number of claims based on Public Water Reserve 107.

Judge Hurlbutt ruled that "implied reservations of water were never necessary to serve PWR 107 land withdrawals. The express purpose of a PWR 107 reservation was to prevent the monopolization of land. So long as the United States may reserve land surrounding water sources, the purpose of the reservation is served. The purpose of the reservation is not 'entirely defeated' without water. No federal purpose would be served by an implied reservation of water. Consequently, this court does not find an implied reservation."

The decision marks a win for two non-lawyer water right holders, Mitchell D. Sorensen and Young Harvey Walker, who brought the challenge to the law pro se (representing themselves).

Hurlbutt noted that the authority for the president to make the public land reservations came from two laws, the Pickett Act of 1910 and the Stock Raising Homestead Act of 1916. The first allowed the president to "temporarily withdraw from settlement, location, sale or entry any of the public lands of the United States including the District of Alaska and reserve the same for water-power sites, irrigation, classification of lands, or other public purposes." The second more specifically allowed the secretary of the Interior to "hold open for the general use of the public, important water holes, springs, and other bodies of water that are necessary for large surrounding tracts of country; so that a person can not monopolize or control a large territory by locating as a homestead the only available water supply for stock in that vicinity."

Hurlbutt said that in evaluating the meaning of the reservations, he had to read through the "plain language" of the laws and the Coolidge declaration.

He said that first, "Congress recognized that full settlement of Western lands would be prohibited where one homestead was strategically established to surround a water source of sufficient quantity to be used for the benefit of additional potential homesteads nearby. Such strategically placed homesteads would then be able to control the water source and prevent homesteading on large areas of land. This occurrence would be contrary to federal settlement policy which sought to maximize Western land use. PWR 107 was issued to prevent control of water sources by individual homesteaders and subsequent control of adjacent land. Its express purpose was to reserve the land immediately surrounding water sources to ensure that water would remain available for public use and appropriation. PWR 107 was not an express appropriation of water for use by the United States government." He noted too a court ruling in the 1980 case *United States v. City and County of Denver*, in which he said a court found that the public water reservation doesn't explicitly allow for reservation of water in public springs or water holes.

Hurlbutt noted court rulings that an implied reservation occurs when water is "needed to accomplish the purpose of the reservation."

He noted the federal contention that "without a water reservation, it is still possible for an individual to control the entirety of a water supply thereby defeating the purpose of the reservation. This court disagrees. The view that, but for a federal reservation, water on public land may be monopolized assumes no sovereign entity controls or regulates the appropriation of water from that source. This assumption fails because the United States Supreme Court has ruled that the state both controls and regulates the appropriation of all non-navigable water within its borders."

The state control over water was a key component in Hurlbutt's reasoning. He said that upholding the federal agencies "would effectively shift control over the appropriation of non-navigable waters from the state to the federal government. Accepting that PWR 107 impliedly reserved water in addition to expressly reserving land would constitute a complete reallocation of federal and state sovereignty with respect to the appropriation of non-navigable waters. It would be a feat of legal gymnastics to read the Pickett Act and the SRHA as a Congressional declaration for the federal takeover of state sovereignty over the appropriation of its non-navigable waters." ⊠

SEEKING MORE TIME (4/1997) The Bureau of Land Management (through the Department of Justice) has asked for another month to isolate the water right subcases where its claims are based on Public Water Reserve 107.

DOJ attorney Lee Leininger asked a new deadline of April 30 to submit to the court a list of PWR107 claims for determination of a stay.

On February 27, Judge Hurlbutt issued an order requiring that the United States submit to the special masters for the test basins within 30 days lists of subcases for which a stay is requested. He said that a stay is appropriate for those cases where PWR107 is the sole basis for a claimed water rights, or where PWR107 predates a state-based claim.

BLM is reviewing its claims. Leininger said "the process of completing the list, however, has been more complicated than expected. In a number of cases, a different water right number was assigned to dual claims based upon state and PWR107 federal reserved law. ... In addition, the United State is concurrently reviewing claims to sources of water that have a PWR107 claim and a state-based claim that post-dates PWR107. In appropriate cases, the adjudication of the state-based right that post-dates a PWR107 claims should also be stayed. This is because the final disposition of Basin Wide Issue 9 may also affect junior state-based claims." ⊠

AT SUPREME COURT (12/1997) The Idaho Supreme Court now has under advisement – and may decide soon – whether the Bureau of Land Management in fact has many of the stockwater rights widely assumed for many years to be federal.

Federal attorney Bill Lazarus said presidential reservation followed several decades of attempts by private parties to monopolize the use of public domain, and limited water on it, by acquiring access to the land around the often scarce water in the West. The reservation came after an Interior secretary wrote Coolidge that "it is believed important to retain title to and supervision of such streams and water holes on the unreserved public domain as have not already been appropriated." Lazarus said that the Colorado Supreme Court and other courts have recognized that "PWR 107 affected the federal reservation of water … Nonetheless, the district court below held that PWR 107 'withdraws from entry public lands which surround water resources' but did not also affect a federal reservation for the public water and springs."

And, he added, "We have to ask a question which has puzzled me from the start, which is: what exactly is the state's interest in keeping the federal government from having the federal reserved rights on the public domain lands? They are being used by the citizens of Idaho. Why do they care? Is it simply so the state can conduct an abandonment or forfeiture process? It would seem that it would be in the interest of the state that those complications would not arise."

Hurlbutt got support from Shawn Del Ysursa, an attorney at the J.R. Simplot Co., who argued that "the federal government through PWR 107 seeks to displace the state of Idaho in its role as primary water manager. This displacement should not be allowed to occur." She noted the traditional deference Congress has given to states in managing water.

But Justice Byron Johnson asked, "You don't mean to suggest the federal government can't reserve water rights?"

"Certainly not," Ysursa replied. "The United States can reserve water on the public domain where it specifically expresses an intent to do so in the statute or executive order, or if it impliedly intended to do so ..."

The reservation, she suggested, applied to the land around the water, not to the water itself. Lazarus pointed out that "Neither the district court nor the respondents address the fact that the reservation is after all entitled the Public Water Reserve not Public Land reserve. And the United States Supreme Court has made clear that a provision's title should be used as a guide to construction. Water is a defining element of this reservation."

To that point Ysursa replied, "A title is just a title. It is not a substitute for the text. The plain and ordinary language of the text indicates a reservation of land only. The title describes the land to be reserved."

Chief Justice Linda Copple Trout countered, however, that "clearly it does make reference to water, and there would be no purpose in reserving that land but for the water holes that are found on the land being reserved. So in terms of determining whether or not the reservation would be entirely defeated, it seems to me that if there were not a water hole on the land reserved it would be indeed entirely defeated. There would be no purpose in reserving the land in the first place. ... So even though clearly the reservation itself speaks to lands surrounding the water hole, it is difficult for me to see how that does not inferentially include water itself as part of the reservation, part of what is being protected."

And Lazarus argued that "Recognition of federal reserved rights in the springs and water holes in the public domain assures use of that water by those members of the public permitted to use the range lands at any given time. That was the purpose of PWR107 ... By contrast, use of that water by those with grazing privileges is not assured under the court's ruling, if the water use is dependent on state water rights and beneficial use."

Trout suggested, "it seems as though, were this court to adhere to Judge Hurlbutt's decision, a system of permitting which permits these people that are grazing on the land to use water for stockwater, that system is probably in jeopardy because now there would be claimants, as Mr. Lazarus suggests, who would try to perfect water rights through the state law and, hypothetically, let's say a party that has a lot of grazing rights might try to perfect a state water right, [and] thereafter gives up cattle grazing and sort of goes into the water sale business so that subsequent cattle ranchers would have to pay this individual for the stockwater. Why does that not occur, why is that not a possibility?"

Ysursa suggested the private right could not be sustained that way, because "Without beneficial use they have no water right."

Idaho Deputy Attorney General David Barber said that "from the very beginning it was always contemplated that this public water reserve would be completed or perfected by identification of a specific legal description. ... [Stockwater is treated in a distinctive fashion.] Isn't the system in jeopardy? Absolutely not.

"Let's assume we have the circumstance that you posed [about a former cattleman peddling water rights]. We have a cattleman who loses his permit, has a water right, and then proposes to hold up other people, saying that 'I've got the water for that spring, no one else can use it.' Let me explain to you what happens. One of the aspects of our prior appropriation doctrine is that you only have a right to what you can use. Here, the man doesn't have a right to it. Whether in fact that loss of a permit would be considered an immediate abandonment of the right or whether the forfeiture period of five years will occur, in any event at some point he's going to lose it. If the water is available in the spring, someone else that now has the permit puts his cattle on the range, there isn't a problem. If there's water in that trough, his cattle can drink out of it and he's created a water right for himself for that purpose." Johnson asked, "So the answer to my question is, absent a grazing lease, you can't appropriate the water."

Barber: "That's absolutely right. You can't."

Johnson asked: "As a practical matter, how does a private individual go about appropriating water that arises and remains in the public domain?"

Lazarus: "This is a matter of some controversy right now at a lower level within the SRBA. And at this point I could simply say that it is being contended by some that that is permissible. That is not a position to which we adhere. However, there are those who say that those who have the grazing privilege can perfect the water right for that water, creating a problem if that privilege is transferred to somebody else, and the prior person holds the water right and can essentially hold hostage the later permittee for the use of the water. It is precisely that sort of a monopolization of water that PWR 107 was intended to prevent by allowing the federal government to hold reservation of the water ..." ☒

FEDS HAVE PWR 107 RIGHTS (5/1998) The Idaho Supreme Court, reversing a decision of the SRBA Court, unanimously held on April 6 that Public Water Reserve 107 water right claims are a valid basis for a federal reserved water right, though only for the limited purpose of stock watering.

The case grew out of what was designated as Basin Wide Issue 9, brought initially by several parties contending that federal water right claims (primarily for stockwater purposes) under PWR 107 were invalid.

"We hold that PWR 107 is a valid basis for a federal reserved water right for the limited purpose of stockwatering," the opinion said. "In addition, we conclude that the United States has the right to administer such water rights on the public lands managed under the Taylor Grazing Act. Furthermore, we conclude that the passage of FLPMA does not affect the PWR 107 withdrawals."

The Supreme Court also agreed with an argument posed by the challengers that even if a right had existed at one time, it was wiped out by passage of the 1976 Federal Land Policy and Management Act, which set up current land law for the Bureau of Land Management (and reversing the old homestead law).

The Supreme Court held that "where a reservation of public land for a particular purpose does not expressly declare that water is needed as a primary use to accomplish the purpose of the reservation, or the exact purpose of the reservation is not clearly set forth in terms readily demonstrating the necessity for the use of water, the courts must consider the relevant acts, enabling legislation and history surrounding the particular reservation under review to determine if a federal reserved water right exists." In this case, "After considering the plain and ordinary words of the enabling statutes and executive order underlying PWR 107, we conclude that PWR 107 evidences an express intention by Congress that reserves a water right in the United States." ☒

STOCKWATER RIGHTS AGE (2/1999) The state of Idaho and the federal government agree that federal stockwater rights have a priority date extending back at least as far as 1934 under state law (also coinciding with when the Taylor Grazing Act was passed). But the federal government is asserting that its rights are actually older than that – that its implicit rights run back much further. On that point the state disagreed.

So for that matter do two of the special masters in the SRBA. Master Fritz Haemmerle, in a subcase decision, said that the federal rights did not precede 1934; but in another subcase, Master Terry Dolan said that they did.

Before his departure from the court, Judge Daniel Hurlbutt upheld Haemmerle's ruling, but did not act on Dolan's.

On January 19, the issue came to interim SRBA Judge Barry Wood, along with the question of whether this is one of those issues in the SRBA that can be appealed as a separate piece to the Idaho Supreme Court. Because of its unusual nature, not all of the SRBA has to be concluded before appeals to the Supreme Court can be undertaken; but there's some uncertainty about exactly what can and can't be appealed under rules of civil procedure.

State attorney Peter Ampe argued that this is one of those areas that shouldn't be certified for appeal until the whole SRBA is wrapped up. Ampe said that about 1,000 subcases are at issue. ☒

Basin Wide 10 (partial forfeiture)

PARTIAL FORFEITURE (5/1996) Judge Hurlbutt on April 26, when in Basin Wide Issue 10 he ruled that partial forfeitures of water rights is not allowed in Idaho. The question concerns water rights where the beneficial use is not fully exploited: whether, for example, a farmer who engages in water conservation, formerly using 100 acre feet of water and now using 50, would lose some of his water right as a consequence.

Hurlbutt said that he would not. He noted that the parties participating "are evenly split as to whether partial forfeiture is a recognized principle in

Idaho." He said that while the Idaho Supreme Court has addressed the question of whether multiple water rights can be forfeited entirely, "To this court's knowledge, this is the first opportunity for any court in Idaho to squarely address the issue of whether partial forfeiture exists in Idaho as a matter of law."

If it does exist, he said, it would have to be noted under the forfeiture law (42-222-2). But he said that while that statute makes reference to loss of "all rights to use of water" after a failure over a period of 5 years to apply it to the beneficial use, "It is clear that partial forfeiture is not provided for within this statute." ☒

OTHER VIEWS (1/1997) Briefs continue to pour in on the Idaho Supreme Court-level appeal of Basin Wide Issue 10, on the issue of partial forfeiture. A number of active parties in the SRBA, including the Hagerman Water Right Owners and the Nampa & Meridian Irrigation District, have argued that partial forfeiture can occur.

A November argument by the Idaho Ground Water Appropriators and Chemical Lime Company of Arizona, by Michael Creamer, Christopher Meyer and Jeffrey Fereday of Givens Pursley & Huntley, argues otherwise. The other parties, they say, "confirm a radical new vision of western water law. By asserting that water rights may be retained in whole, though used only in part, Respondents describe a water right confirmation and allocation system which rewards speculation, not use, and which promotes hoarding, not efficiency."

The attorneys concluded that "Idaho's forfeiture statute as originally conceived in 1903 simply codified the common law principle that a water right exists only by virtue of, and only to the extent of, its beneficial use. The statute's single departure from the common law was the imposition of a five-year automatic forfeiture point which obviated the need to prove the difficult element of intent which existed under common law abandonment. The obvious goal was to move water more quickly into the hands of those who had the actual need and willingness to put the water to use." ☒

SUPREME COURT OKS PARTIALS (10/1997) The Idaho Supreme Court on October 10 held that partial forfeiture of water rights is allowed under current Idaho law. Judge Hurlbutt held as early as 1993 that the Idaho Legislature could allow for partial forfeiture, but never had passed a statute specifically allowing it – and that the practice was disallowed until it did. Full forfeiture of a water right, he noted, specifically is allowed under Idaho law.

The primary backers of Hurlbutt's ruling, the Hagerman Water Right Owners, said partial forfeiture of water rights would encourage water users to waste water, rather than forfeit part of the use. (Under the full appropriation, a water user could use only a portion of their water right to retain all of it.)

Idaho Code section 42-222(2) says that "All rights to the use of water acquired under this chapter or otherwise shall be lost and forfeited by a failure for the term of five years to apply it to the beneficial use for which it was appropriated . . . ."

The Supreme Court (in a unanimous decision written by Justice Gerald Schroeder) noted that "The district court focused on the word 'all' in this section and reasoned that the plain and ordinary meaning of this provision is that 'partial forfeiture is not provided for in this statute.'" The Supreme Court said that "The district court determined that I.C. Section 42-222(2) unambiguously does not provide for partial forfeiture. This determination was incorrect." Among other things, it said, the statute is ambiguous: it "does not explicitly provide for partial forfeiture. In fact, the statute does not address any particular quantity of water at all that may be forfeited. The statute simply refers to 'it' and 'water.'"

The Court reached the point of saying "The use of the word 'all'... does not unambiguously close the door on the possibility of partial forfeiture." At that point, the Court fell back on the interpretation of the statute which has historically been used by the Idaho Department of Water Resources: that the statute does allow for partial forfeiture. "Case law and the record in this case show that the general public did indeed understand and depend upon the prior IDWR interpretation, policy and practice that partial forfeiture is a recognized concept in Idaho," the decision said.

Finally, the Court said that (and implicitly used as part of its rationale) the decision in favor of partial forfeiture serves two public policy goals.

"If this Court were to find that [the statute] does not authorize partial forfeiture of a water right, once the amount element of a water right is decreed, a water user could hold the water against all subsequent appropriators by using only a part of the water. Such a scheme is inconsistent with Idaho water law .... Contrary to the water users' claims, the Court's decision does not promote uneconomical use of water in order to avoid forfeiture. A water user is not entitled to waste water ... It follows that a water right holder cannot avoid a partial forfeiture by wasting that portion of his or her water right that cannot be put to beneficial use during any part of the statutory period. If a water user cannot apply a portion of a water right to beneficial use during any part of the statutory period, but must waste the water in order to divert the full amount of the water right, a forfeiture has taken place." ⊠

Basin Wide 12 (stockwater)

STOCKWATER (7/1996) Judge Daniel Hurlbutt on June 13 designated another basin wide issue – Number 12 – this one concerning stockwater rights and how they will be handled in the SRBA. The results of the issue could affect livestock operations throughout Idaho, especially those which are operated on federal lands.

Specific issues designated:

"What constitutes a *de minimis* stockwater right and may the annual consumptive use volume for such rights be described as *de minimis*? Is a statement of combined usage necessary for the definition or administration of a *de minimis* water right and, if so, where should it appear in the decree? Is it necessary to include the number of head of cattle allowed to describe or administer a *de minimis* water right and, if so, where should it appear in the decree? Should the quantity used in cubic feet per second for a *de minimis* water right be based on a 24-hour rate, a 2-hour rate or a set constant based on a 13,000 gallon-per-day rate? Does a water right with a stockwatering purpose of use include use for wildlife? Whether a single water right can be decreed with both a state and federal basis?" ⊠

Basin Wide 13 (meaning of Swan Falls)

THE MEANING OF SWAN FALLS (9/2004) The most recent basin wide issue was ordered on August 23 by SRBA Presiding Judge John Melanson.

Fittingly perhaps, it reaches back to the origins of the adjudication itself. The question to be resolved is, "To what extent, if any, should the Swan Falls Agreement be addressed in the SRBA or memorialized in a decree?"

Interested parties will have plenty of time to pull their thoughts together. Melanson also ordered that all activity on this issue be stayed until the Idaho Department of Water Resources issues its director's report on water right claims by Idaho Power Company in Basin 02 (in the lower reach in Idaho of the Snake River).

That determination is expected in December 2005, according to current schedules. That may make this decision the first action that specifically extends legal activity in the case into 2006.

Such claims by that company marked the origin of the adjudication. A stockholder dispute over whether the company was fully exerting its rights at the Swan Falls Dam on the Snake River (on the border between Ada and Owyhee counties) led to an Idaho Supreme Court decision that it was not, and a series of high-profile negotiations between the company, the state and other parties. The Snake River Basin Adjudication was established in 1987 pursuant to one of those agreements.

Melanson noted, "In general terms, the Swan Falls Agreement subordinated a certain flow of Idaho Power Company's hydropower rights to upstream consumptive uses in exchange for certain guaranteed minimum flows and the development of a comprehensive plan for managing the watershed."

A proposal to incorporate terms of the agreement came in a group of objections to 346 water right designations in Basin 37. That idea was raised in 2002 and bounced back and forth between actions by SRBA judges and attempts – ultimately failed – among the involved parties.

Then, this year, the issue seemed to catch fire. As Melanson wrote, "At a January 20, 2004, scheduling conference set by the Court, certain of the parties indicated that they planned to submit a joint Motion to designate the matter as a basin-wide issue, and move to stay the action pending the reporting of Idaho Power Co.'s rights in Basin 02. No Motion was filed by the parties, however, and the Court set a Status Conference to determine how best to proceed prior to the filing of further Director's Reports.

"On June 10, 2004 a Joint Motion for Designation of Basin-Wide Issue and for a Stay of the Proceedings was filed by the State of Idaho and Idaho Power. Faulkner Land & Livestock, North Snake Groundwater District and Idaho Ground Water Appropriators submitted a Notice of Joinder to the Joint Motion on June 14, 2004. On June 14, 2004 the City of Pocatello submitted its own Motion for Designation of Basin-Wide Issue and Stay of Proceedings. Also on June 14, 2004, Clear Springs Foods submitted a Notice of Opposition to the Joint Motion for Designation of Basin-Wide Issue and For a Stay of the Proceedings. On June 15, 2004 a hearing was held, and an Order Setting Expedited Oral Argument on Motion to Designate Basin-Wide Issue and Stay Proceedings was entered on June 18, 2004. The parties submitted briefs and oral argument was heard July 20, 2004."

The judge listed five issues that the parties cited as important in resolving the Swan Falls language matter:

• "That the Swan Falls Agreement needs to be addressed at some point in the SRBA to ensure that the Agreement is binding and is not subsumed by an SRBA final decree.

• "It was alluded to, without specifics, that issues exist regarding the scope and substance of the Swan Falls Agreement. Some of the parties discussed having a forum for addressing such issues.

• "The United States asserted that negotiations involving the Nez Perce instream flow claims rely on the minimum flows defined in the Swan Falls Agreement. The United States urged that any issues regarding those flows be resolved as soon as possible in keeping with the time tables imposed in the Nez Perce negotiations.

• "Lastly, Clear Springs opposed designating the matter as a basin-wide issue based on the argument that all of the basin-wide issues should have been raised and resolved in the three test basins. Clear Springs is concerned that a general provision resulting from a basin-wide issue in effect would "re-open" subcases that have been completed to more litigation." ☒

Basin Wide 14 (aesthetic, wildlife, recreational)

AWR USES (7/2008) A rarity at this stage of the Snake River Basin Adjudication: Designation of a new basin-wide issue, a legal question broad enough to affect many water users and claimants throughout the basin. Such designations have been discouraged in recent years since they could change the legal picture in many subcases which already have been presumably settled.

However, SRBA Judge John Melanson indicated that this one was of substantial enough significance that it must be dealt with, and that he would designate a basin-wide issue:

"Are aesthetic, wildlife and recreation [considered] beneficial uses of water if the water right is held by a private party?"

That may or may not be the final language; an alternative approach was developed by the state of Idaho.

A number of governmental organizations (including federal and Idaho state agencies) hold claims based on such beneficial uses, but those were not being challenged in the issue. The fact that a similar use was being suggested as proper for some parties but not for others has been, however, mentioned by some critics of the idea.

The origins of the issue go back to a series of claims and objections in Basin 37, in the Wood River Basin. There, a number of private landowners claimed water rights based on aesthetic, recreational or wildlife uses—uses difficult to quantify compared with irrigation or domestic uses. The private claims were filed on grounds not of public interest but for private enjoyment.

Albert Barker, an attorney for the neighbors who filed between 60 and 70 objections, remarked about the discussion that followed, "there has been a lot said about what the objections mean, and a lot of lawyers up here writing briefs ... and not one of them really got it right."

He said that nothing in Idaho state code or in Department of Water Resources rules appear to recognize aesthetic, recreational, and wildlife uses as a beneficial use of water (which is the basis for a water right claim in Idaho). He did note that, "we did not say that the public does not have the right to acquire water rights for scenic uses," and said that had been specifically upheld.

After the initial objections were filed critical of the ARW basis for use, Barker said, he and his clients backed off "for strategic reasons" and instead more narrowly challenged the claims on the basis of the quantity of water sought.

He indicated they would be seeking a consolidation of those cases, and if that happens—depending on the outcome—the basin wide issue might be moot, that no specific concrete parties would remain at odds and what would remain would be a legislative policy issue.

But other attorneys on various sides argued that the issue remains real regardless.

Jeff Fereday, an attorney representing several Boise-area interests, said that the argument that ARW-based claims are invalid is a direct legal assault on claims "held by hundreds of water users in this state. It raises a purely legal issue. There appears to be no dispute about that, that it would affect all of those rights …"

Scott Campbell, representing Sinclair Oil Corporation (owner of Sun Valley Inc.) filed the motion for a basin-wide issue on March 24. "In this case we have a very strange hybrid," he said.

Exactly how many claims around the state might be affected by the basin wide issue is unclear. But attorney Dana Hofstetter noted that at least one of her clients, with property at Indian Creek in southwest Idaho, might be. She said "the record reflects that this is a historic pond," used for many years for recreational and other purposes, although those water right holders also use some of the water for irrigation purposes as well. ☒

SETTLEMENT? (1/2009) Many although not all of the parties in the relatively new Basin Wide Issue 14 – which concerns the designation of recreational, aesthetic and wildlife uses of water as bona fide beneficial uses of water – apparently have signed off a settlement agreement which has made its way to SRBA Court.

Issue 14 was developed after parties in the SRBA asked for water rights for aesthetic, wildlife, or recreational purposes, a proposition that has generated widespread debate because of their prospectively far-flung natures.

SRBA Judge John Melanson said on December 16 at a monthly status conference that a motion for approval of a consent decree in the issue has been filed. He did not discuss the details or general approach of the proposal.

However, it was sufficiently advanced, he indicated, that he suggested, "a good way to proceed," would be issuance of a "show cause" order delivered by the court, which would give any parties objecting to the settlement an opportunity to be heard.

Melanson said he would prepare the order.

HYDROPOWER RIGHTS (3/2003) Should the water right holder protections noted in the Swan Falls settlement between Idaho Power Company and the state of Idaho nearly 20 years ago, be noted and maintained in the SRBA?

Almost everyone seems to agree that they should be. The question arises from concern that a new decree of Idaho Power water rights on the Snake River might, in effect, wipe out earlier agreements which have limited the utility's claims on water.

The upshot, as of late February: A committee will work on possible language to be inserted in Idaho Power water rights, intended to ensure earlier agreements are maintained.

The motion to propose the question as a basin wide issue came from Josephine Beeman, attorney for the North Snake Groundwater District, and drew immediate comment from a number of other attorneys – including spokesmen for Idaho Power Co., a participant in the Swan Falls negotiations.

If ultimately designated as a basin wide issue, it probably would be Number 13.

The SRBA grew out of a water right case involving Swan Falls Dam on the Snake River, at which Idaho Power had water rights. A 1982 Idaho Supreme Court decision on those rights – declaring they were much more extensive than many people in Idaho had expected – led to extensive negotiations. It led also – in March 1990, after the launching of the SRBA in 1987 – to a settlement concerning Idaho Power's water rights. The settlement included a consent judgment signed by then-4th District Judge Alan Schwartzmann. Its last substantive provision notes, "The Swan Falls Agreement, dated October 25, 1984, shall not be merged into nor integrated with this Judgment, but shall remain in full force and effect independent of this judgment." Not only Idaho Power but also other water users – at least those upstream of Swan Falls – are affected. (Beeman cited Idaho Department of Water Resources estimates of 57,421 water rights.)

The settlement documents on Swan Falls brought in "third party beneficiaries," not just Idaho Power. "This is the information that caught my eye – this is the designation of third party beneficiaries," she said.

Moreover, she suggested, because that 1990 decree is independent of the SRBA, a careful handling of these cases is needed to ensure that provisions and protections in the Swan Falls agreement aren't "erased" by SRBA actions.

Often in water law, she noted, when a decree exists and then a later decree is issued covering that same water right, then the earlier decree "is gone."

"This is really a preservation argument," Beeman said. "Whatever they [provisions in the 1990 decree] mean, we don't want them erased from the SRBA." She said she is not asking for an interpretation of the Swan Falls documents, only that their import not be disturbed.

Deputy Attorney General David Barber said that while he might suggest some differing specifics, he concurred that a basin wide issue should be declared. He said there's a major question in the Swan Falls territory, possibly "How should the benefits and burdens of the two agreements be designated in water rights? … We do support this broader designation I just described." But, he noted, "we're not supporting any particular version at this point in time."

He agreed with Beeman that mediation would be appropriate.

"Certainly the Swan Falls agreement has been the very fabric of water law in southern Idaho since 1984," said James Tucker, an attorney for Idaho Power. "But I don't know what the case or controversy is here … I fail to see the controversy here today that brings it to the forefront."

He said that Idaho Power has assumed that the Swan Falls decision would remain part of the basis of water rights provisions in the state.

He said he was concerned about mediation, noting that for 17 years there's been no real dispute about the meaning or intent of the Swan Falls agreement. Mediation, he said, could be "fraught with peril."

"There certainly are benefits to any number of water users from the Swan Falls agreement," he noted. He said there's more merit to a suggestion by SRBA Judge Roger Burdick that maybe the issue ought to be put on hold until the court considers the major Idaho Power water rights issues.

Burdick suggested, "It would get all the Idaho Powers issues in one bundle, at one time."

Burdick expressed some concern about the implications of the question – whether implicitly he would be asked to "freeze" legislative or other action, and whether separations of powers issues could arise.

"Nobody wants Swan Falls to go by the wayside," he said. He suggested there's been little ambiguity over a span of 18 years concerning the agreements.

Mediation efforts can be expensive, he noted.

The judge inquired about whether a small group could develop language which could be inserted into Idaho Power water rights, and whether that might resolve the issue. ⊠

IDAHO POWER SUBCASE RESOLUTION (8/2006) Snake River Basin Adjudication Presiding Judge John Melanson on July 23 took charge and set up a path for resolution of a string of key hydropower and other claims on the Snake River by Idaho Power Company. The case was named Consolidated Subcase 92-23. Proceedings except for discovery are stayed until December 5, but the judge scheduled a status conference for December 17.

It relates to 21 Idaho Power rights, most (13) in Basin 2, and Idaho Power's objections to parts of the Department of Water Resources recommendations for them.

Those objections led to an amended director's report in February proposing splitting the ownership of three important claims so that the state of Idaho would hold "legal title" and the state and Idaho Power would joint hold "equitable title." The state objected to that revised report. Idaho Power soon also had a statement of its position, "complaint and petition," as well. It said that it wanted:

- A declaration there was no "Trust Water" available when the Swan Falls Agreement was executed in 1984, and so no trust *res* and no valid trust established under the Swan Falls Settlement.
- A reformation of the Swan Falls Settlement based on mutual mistake of fact regarding the existence of Trust Water, eliminating any asserted trust while retaining provisions unrelated to the purported trust.
- A declaration that to the extent there is a valid trust, the trust *res* is water and not water rights, the State of Idaho does not hold legal title to

Idaho Power's water rights, and title to the water rights referenced in the Swan Falls Settlement is quieted in Idaho Power.

● A declaration that the state's claim of legal title to Idaho Power's water rights is barred by the doctrines of estoppel, waiver and laches.

● That Idaho Power's water rights for hydropower generation are not, through the Swan Falls Settlement or otherwise, subordinate to the use of water for ground water recharge. ☒

6 | Other Issues

Federal claims

FEDERAL ROLE (3/1/1993) State and court officials say they now anticipate the federal government will file about 50,000 claims by March 25, about 20,000 more than had been projected. That would put total anticipated water rights claims in the SRBA at about 150,000.

"Part of the reason this was put together by adjudication," Judge Daniel Hurlbutt said, "is, nobody really knew how many rights were out there." ☒

BLM OBJECTIONS (3/15/1993) "There's definitely some consternation" was the way one Arco businessman described the mood in the Lost River Valley after many residents received their copies of federal (primarily Bureau of Land Management and Forest Service) objections to their water right claims. So many objections arrived in late February and the few days of March that the Court staff, then state Department of Water Resources staff, were swamped trying to handle them. Some 1,469 public and private objections to the director's report filed in that period; the bulk were federal, and nearly all of those were Bureau of Land Management objections.

The BLM received complaining visits and phone calls from water right holders.

Most concerned Basin 34 (the Lost River basin), where the objections resulted in a number of local irrigators and water users meetings last week.

"There's an example of the fellow who came in, and the way he understood it we were after all his land and water," said Jeff Runkel of the BLM Boise office. Runkel said the agency had simply objected to the way the right was initiated at the point of diversion. "It's not a water grab," he said, in the words of some critics. Runkel made several points:

- His agency would rather deal with irrigation districts than with individual right holders; as it is, each individual holder has been served with notice of objection.
- BLM and Forest Service objections largely are concerned with water uses by traditional users of their administered lands, notably livestock grazing. Water uses for wildlife also played into the objections.
- The large number of objections resulted from the vast area involved; but the volume of water of direct interest to the agencies is small because their water users (such as animals) are light users.

FOREST SERVICE DROPS OUT (10/9/1995) In a move that took many players by surprise, the U.S. Forest Service on October 4 withdrew the majority of its claims in the Snake River Basin Adjudication.

The agency said it had signaled its intent months before, but offered little immediate comment on its rationale for withdrawal. Officials did say that they saw the move as a positive step toward resolving conflicting water claims in the SRBA.

The original claims, numbering more than 3,600, were mainly for stockwater and general drinking permits. About 70 claims of the USFS remain in the SRBA. The remaining claims are primarily in-stream flow claims, intended to help preserve general water quality and fish and wildlife habitat.

In its notices of withdrawing claims filed September 29, the Forest Service said that "many of these claims were claimed as federal reserved water rights and as a state law-based appropriative water rights. The federal reserved water right claims were abstracted in the supplemental Director's report for federal in-stream flow claims. The state law based in-stream flow claims were assigned separate water rights claim numbers by the IDWR. These claims have not yet been abstracted by the IDWR and no objection period is open. The United States' withdrawal applies to most, but not all, of the state law based in-stream flow claims."

It went on to say: "No objections have been filed to the great majority of these claims, however, very recently objections have been filed to some of these claims and once the United States identifies the claims to which objections have been filed, the United States will file separate motions concerning those claims. ..."

The withdrawal came only days before parties in the SRBA were required to file objections and challenges to federal and tribal claims. Many parties, especially including Idaho state government, had already developed massive volumes of responses to the federal claims.

WHO SIGNS? (5/1997) When a farmer negotiating with an attorney from the Department of Justice reaches an agreement in that discussion, the farmer, as water right claimant, clearly is able to sign off on the deal on his own behalf.

But who signs for the United States?

That question arose at an April 15 information meeting at the SRBA Courthouse. And the answer no doubt surprised some of the people present.

The basic answer is: someone pretty high up. Maybe at the cabinet level.

Attorney Randy Bramer said that "I'll be the first to admit that with the Department of Justice, the authority problem is a problem."

Attorneys Jack Haugrud and Lois Shiffer generally have authority over federal activities in the Idaho adjudication, he said, but the legal signoff authority may go higher.

So Judge Daniel Hurlbutt asked, "Is Janet Reno going to want to come down here and look at a 13,000 gallon water right?" Beyond that, he asked, will water right holders even be interested in direct negotiations with federal attorneys if they realize they have no direct authority to cut a deal?

The question remained unresolved.

The issue came up as Bramer was pitching for more time to discuss water rights objections related to federal claims with local residents. ☒

CHANGES IN USFS CLAIMS (5/1997) The U.S. Forest Service is asking to change its water right claims in the SRBA, again. And that's upsetting a number of other parties.

What the agency is asking to change, USFS attorneys said at the SRBA status conference April 15, is the amount of water claimed: "They've gone up; they've come down; the location has changed." The reason is that additional research in the last few years has shown that some of the original estimates were off, and the adjustments are being requested in the interest of precision and accuracy.

The request angered other parties, who recall how the agency dropped most of its original claims after other parties had gone to considerable time and expense to research and respond to them. Boise attorney Scott Campbell suggested that had the agency done its work properly in the first place, it wouldn't be making this request. He noted that the study methodology hasn't changed over the last few years.

And Deputy Attorney General Cheri Copsey said the Forest Service hasn't thoroughly explained why, exactly, the changes are needed – and the burden is on it to do so. "If you read everything they've written," she said, "it's fundamental to their process that they misunderstand the process." ☒

BACKING OUT A LITTLE MORE (7/1997) Still more federal water right claims may dropped in the SRBA, but now with a difference: the United States and Idaho are considering reimbursement for expenses by federal agencies. A June 20 letter from U.S. Department of Justice attorney Bruce D. Bernard to Clive Strong, chief of the Natural Resources Division (of the Idaho Attorney General's office) confirmed a conversation "concerning the United States' intent to withdraw certain claims in the SRBA.

"We have agreed to work out a stipulated motion to dismiss which would provide for the United States' reimbursement to the State for costs of work which the State can show was directed at the investigation of these claims and which the state will not be relying upon in its opposition to the United States' other claims."

The claims involved concern rights on:

Johnson Creek, John's Creek and Trapper Creek – all involving channel maintenance. Fish habitat for claims on those streams plus Valley Creek, Little Slate Creek, Trapper Creek. "Recreation" claims on the North Fork of the Boise River, the South Fork of the Boise River and 4th of July Creek on the Salmon River. ☒

FEDERAL RESERVED CLAIMS (1/1998) SRBA Judge Daniel Hurlbutt has approved federal water rights claims for Idaho wilderness areas and for the Hells Canyon National Recreation Area. But in the same decision, released December 18, he rejected 37 federal claims for national forest lands, on grounds that the law under which they were claimed did not support the claims.

The issue had drawn in a large range of parties, including the federal government, the state of Idaho, numerous irrigation companies, several cities, utilities, farm and mining interests and others. It had been the subject of several hearings and litigation for months.

The decision may be appealed to the Idaho Supreme Court, though action in that direction had not been taken as of press time.

Hurlbutt noted that in general states have control of water within their borders, but a federal reserved water right claim is a recognized exception. He said that "if there is no express reservation of water, an implied reserved water right may be granted if the following three criteria are satisfied:

"(1) an implied reservation of water exists only if necessary to fulfill the primary, not the secondary, purpose for which the reservation of land was created …

"(2) The water claimed must be the minimum amount necessary to achieve the purposes of the reservation, and "(3) Without the minimum amount of water claimed, the purposes of the reservation must entirely be defeated."

Wilderness areas: Based on the Wilderness Act of 1964, the federal government asked for rights to all water arising in the Frank Church-River of No Return Wilderness, Selway-Bitterroot Wilderness and the Gospel Hump Wilderness. Hurlbutt held that the Wilderness Act was a reservation of land. Objectors to the claims had pointed out that the land was really a re-designation, that it had originally been reserved as national forest land. But Hurlbutt said land can be "re-reserved."

He also settled another hotly disputed point: what was, if anything was, the primary purpose of the land. "The three wilderness areas were established for the primary purpose of wilderness preservation," he concluded. He noted that while wilderness previously had been allowed as a use of national forest land, the new designation "legislatively recognized certain designated areas where wilderness purposes would be elevated above all other preexisting purposes."

Various objectors argued that wilderness preservation was a secondary use of the land, saying that the Wilderness Act was simply "supplemental" to the main national forest law. They relied on a New Mexico Supreme Court decision which applied that theory to another federal resource law, the Multiple-Use Sustained-Yield Act (MUSYA). Hurlbutt said the comparison didn't hold, that MUSYA was drafted to work within the existing Forest Service system, while the Wilderness Act was separate and distinct, with its own primary purpose.

The judge found no explicit reservation of water. "The United States claims that it is entitled to a reservation of all water naturally flowing in the wilderness areas. The Objectors argue that this amount is not needed to fulfill the purposes of the reservation and that the United States has failed to prove the quantity that is sufficient to fulfill those purposes. The issue is whether the United States may reserve all unappropriated water flows without specific quantification of the reserved right."

Hurlbutt maintained that they could – and, in effect, had to, since the state could not appropriate the water for wilderness purposes.

After all, the judge said, "the stated purpose of the prior appropriation doctrine [the basis of Idaho water law] is to further domestic and economic development." That runs exactly counter to the reason for creating a wilderness area in the first place.

"State law appropriation of water for the beneficial uses allowed by the Idaho Constitution is not compatible with the legal definition of wilderness preservation. Appropriation of wilderness water would entirely defeat Congressional intent to preserve wilderness character."

He then reasoned that "appropriation of water within the wilderness areas would defeat Congress' primary purpose of preserving wilderness character. The amount of water minimally sufficient to fulfill Congressional intent is the total amount of unappropriated water within each area, such that none is ever available for future appropriation."

National Forests: Whatever water rights the federal government has in national forests, they won't be based on the Multiple-Use Sustained-Yield Act, Judge Hurlbutt implicitly said.

The main reason for that, he said, is that MUSYA simply re-aligned the uses of forest land, but didn't constitute a re-reservation of it.

He quoted a federal brief on the subject (in the case of the water rights for wilderness land) as saying: "MUSYA did not create a new reservation of land but only broadened the purposes for which the national forests were to be administered." Hurlbutt dryly said that he agreed – and the MUSYA claims were disallowed.

Hells Canyon: However, Hurlbutt did find a specific, explicit federal claim for water in the Hells Canyon National Recreation Area. As in the case of the wilderness lands, Hurlbutt here found a specific reservation of federal land for specific purposes (preserving the "natural beauty, and historical and archeological value" of the area). But, he suggested, debate over the purpose of the reservation wasn't needed in this case, since federal law did provide for a specific water right.

He said that the law specifically said it would reserve an area that "comprises the land and water" within the region. Noting that various objectors had brushed aside the reference to water, Hurlbutt said "This argument lacks merit. The 'boundaries' of an area are directly relevant to describe what Congress meant to reserve. Congress described the boundaries of the area to describe what it was reserving." ☒

SAWTOOTH RIGHTS (10/1998) Judge Hurlbutt on September 15 said a reserved water right exists for the Sawtooth Wilderness Area, with a priority date of August 22, 1972. And within that area, the judge said, "all unappropriated water ... is reserved for the United States."

Beyond that, he said, a federal request for a reserved water right for the Sawtooth National Recreation Area was granted, but "the United States is not entitled to a decreed federal reserved water right for the entire unappropriated flow of all natural water sources within the SNRA 'recreation area.' The quantity reserved raises genuine issues of material fact requiring a denial of the United States' Motion for Summary Judgment to all unappropriated flows in the 'recreation area of the SNRA."

As in several key matters now before the SRBA Court, a central issue relates to when a "reserved" water right – one which is implied from the language of a federal land reservation – can be properly claimed by the federal government. The basic rule is that a reserved right can be approved if it is based on a specific formal reservation of land and must be necessary to fulfill the primary purpose of the reservation – necessary to the point that without water the purpose would be completely defeated.

Hurlbutt held that both conditions exist in the Sawtooth's case.

The reservation, he said, came with the Sawtooth National Recreation Act, which in effect set up two reservations of land: one portion as wilderness, the other as a recreation area. The purpose of the first, he said, was to fulfill the terms of the Wilderness Act of 1964 (to preserve wilderness character); the purpose of the second is to "assure the preservation and protection of the natural, scenic, historic, pastoral and fish and wildlife values and to provide for the enhancement of the recreational values associated therewith" (quoting the SNRA Act).

Since wilderness is "predicated on the absence of humanity's influence," Hurlbutt wrote, "where water is naturally found in the wilderness area, the entire amount of that water is necessary to fulfill the primary purpose of wilderness preservation."

In the case of the recreation area, the amount of water reserved, Hurlbutt said, should be determined at trial. Federal attorneys had asked for reservation of the entire flow within the area, but Hurlbutt said there's no proof yet that all that water is needed to meet the purposes of the Recreation Area. The subcase is 65-20766. ☒

ORGANIC ACT (10/1998) Argument on summary judgment on federal claims under the Organic Act has been scheduled for October 7. But even prior to that, settlement negotiations between the federal government and other parties are underway. Department of Justice attorney Bruce Bernard said that resolution of the cross summary judgment motions now filed should focus the direction of the subcase.

In sum, he said, the state of Idaho contends the purpose of the Organic Act is limited to ensuring that water is available in the national forests for consumptive purposes allowed under state law. The U.S. Forest Service expands that view to include preservation of watersheds and other related purposes. If the state prevails, the case is over subject to appeal, he said; but if the federal agencies prevail, it leads to a motion for partial summary judgment.

He said that the parties are working on negotiations, but the subject matter is complex, involving many thousands of documents.

Judge Hurlbutt quipped: "Sure this wasn't the Starr report?"

"I've read portions of both, and I don't believe so, your honor," Bernard replied. ☒

ORGANIC ACT ALIVE (1/1999) It's not conclusively upheld but, in one of his last rulings in the SRBA, Judge Hurlbutt held on December 22 that the United State could proceed to trial to prove the factual necessity of a federal reserved water right for channel maintenance under the Organic Act. In ruling that, he denied a request by the state of Idaho and other parties that might have resulted in throwing out the claims entirely.

What's at stake? In Hurlbutt's description: "The United States seeks recognition that the Organic Act of 1897 … authorizing establishment of the national forests, implicitly reserved water to accomplish the purpose of 'securing favorable conditions of water flows.' The United States further maintains that 'securing favorable conditions of water flows' gives rise to an implied reservation of water for the improvement and protection of watersheds, including the stream channels that lie within them. The State of Idaho asserts that the United States' claim is contingent on whether 'Congress intended to preserve stream channels in their historic condition as a primary purpose of the Organic Act' and that the United States Supreme Court has essentially precluded in-stream federal reserve water rights under the Organic Act." ☒

ORGANIC AT SUPREME (11/1999) A sharply divided Idaho Supreme Court held on October 1 that the United States does have implied reserved water rights for wilderness areas in Idaho – and those rights include all the water that naturally flows through those areas.

On the same day, it turned down federal claims filed under the Multiple-Use Sustained Yield Act of 1960, saying that act was not specifically a reservation of land and therefore didn't carry an accompanying reservation of water.

Both decisions upheld rulings by former SRBA Judge Daniel Hurlbutt, made on December 18, 1997.

The wilderness decision led to a request for rehearing filed a couple of weeks later by the Idaho Attorney General's office.

The wilderness ruling resulted in uproar in several parts of the state, especially in parts of Custer and Lemhi Counties where some existing water uses could be in danger. Areas covered included the Frank Church River of No Return, Gospel Hump, and Selway-Bitterroot Wilderness Areas, and the Hells Canyon National Recreation Area. The legal reasoning behind the decision on the first three was different than for Hells Canyon.

Governor Dirk Kempthorne remarked that "In a precedent-setting case, where the lives and livelihoods of tens of thousands of Idahoans could be affected, a second look is critically necessary."

Former U.S. Sen. James McClure called the decision "incredible," and said it didn't reflect what members of Congress intended when they passed the wilderness legislation.

State Rep. Lenore Hardy Barrett, the one state legislator from the affected area, was strongly outspoken. "First they took our land, now they're taking our water," she said. In the Challis area, large numbers of residents were rapidly signing petitions asking the Idaho Supreme Court to reconsider its decision.

The Supreme Court's majority – in an opinion attributed to Justice Cathy Silak – noted that while in general water rights fall under state authority, "a claim by the United States to a federal reserved water right is an exception to the state's plenary authority over its water."

The court's decision (and much of the dissent) turned on interpretation of the 1976 U.S. Supreme Court decision in *Cappaert v. United States*. In that decision, the national court said that when the federal government reserves land for a specific purpose, "by implication, [it] reserves appurtenant water then unappropriated to the extent needed to accomplish the purpose of the reservation. In so doing the United States acquires a reserved right in unappropriated water which vests on the date of the reservation and is superior to the rights of future appropriators."

Those rights can be "express" – stated specifically in legislation – or "implied" – in which case, the reservation of land is assumed to carry with it water rights sufficient to match the purpose for the land reservation. (Or, put in a reverse fashion, enough water must be reserved so that that the purpose of the land reservation would be "entirely defeated" without it.)

The three wilderness rights were said to be "implied" rights, and the Hells Canyon right was said to be "express." The court said (as virtually everyone else in the case had) that there was no "express" water right reservation by Congress for the wilderness areas. The question of what impact outside water use would have on the "wilderness" use of the land led to one of the court's most-quoted sentences:

"A review of the Wilderness Act demonstrates that the prior appropriation doctrine is inconsistent with congressional intent to preserve the wilderness character of the Wilderness Areas."

It said that wilderness was the primary use of the land (in contrast to arguments by some of the appellants, who argued that simple preservation is a "secondary" purpose under the law).

A briefing paper prepared by Jeffrey Fereday and Christopher Meyer of Givens Pursley in Boise provided a roster of criticisms of the decision. It said "there is no threat to wilderness in Idaho from upstream water diversions. The upstream communities such as the towns of Salmon and Challis, and other water users consume only the tiniest fraction of water flowing through the wilderness. But while the decision is inconsequential in terms of wilderness protection, it is catastrophic for all upstream communities and water users. Even though their uses are so small as to have no measurable impact on the wilderness, that means every post-1978 water right [there] is now invalid. In other areas, water rights may be invalidated back to 1964. Moreover, it means that these communities can never grow – not by a single well." ☒

MORATORIUM (11/1999) On October 25, Department of Water Resources Director Karl Dreher signed an order halting development of water rights in the area affected by the Supreme Court's wilderness rights order.

The order applies to all consumptive water uses, the department said, including municipal, agricultural, and commercial; and all administrative processing of about 60 pending applications for permits to appropriate water. It also stops development of water rights under approximately 90 permits that previously had been issued.

Dreher's order said in part, "The claims filed by the United States in the SRBA for federal reserved water rights for all unappropriated water in the [three wilderness areas] did not limit the claimed amount to unappropriated water arising solely within the wilderness areas as of the date the wilderness areas were reserved, nor did the claims include subordination to existing permits to appropriate water having junior priority dates for private holdings within the wilderness areas." ☒

REVISITING THE WILDERNESS RULING (1/2000) The high court agreed November 30 to a rehearing of its highly controversial decision. ☒

WOOD: MOVE ON ORGANIC (2/2000) SRBA Presiding Judge Barry Wood sent an unmistakable message to parties in the Organic Acts consolidated subcase: He wants no more delays, and wants the case brought to trial soon.

"All of you need to start talking and sharing information," he said after a January 20 hearing in Boise. At that session, state of Idaho counsel said that repeated changes in the federal government's case have led to recurring delays in bringing resolution to the case.

Federal attorneys agreed with the idea of a closing date for adding new information which could be included in deciding the Organic Act case; a possible cutoff date (September 30 of this year) was even mentioned.

But the situation was not entirely resolved in January.

The Organic Act claims are among those which have been filed by the federal government in the SRBA as implicit under terms of federal lands law. The list includes:

• **Organic Act**. 12 claims filed, still under adjudication. There are 54 objectors and 19 specific objections; the state has been the lead objector in the case. Other parties, notably those grouped as the Coalition (and represented by lead attorney Jerry Rigby) have been active as well.

• **Multiple Use Sustained Yield Act of 1968** (MUSYA). 8 claims.

• **Wilderness Act**. 5 claims. These claims have been upheld by SRBA Court and, in a decision last fall, by the Idaho Supreme Court as well. A rehearing on that high court decision is scheduled for next month.

• **Wild and Scenic River Act**. 7 claims.

• **Sawtooth National Recreation Area**. 5 claims. These federal claims generally have been upheld.

• **Hells Canyon National Recreation Area**. 1 claim.

U.S. Forest Service attorney Bruce Bernard noted that "there's overlap" between the claims, notably in the area of the Organic Act. And he noted that the eventual legal fate of some of the other federal claims could have a direct impact on the Organic claims.

The Organic Act of 1897 covers several areas and reservations of federal rights on land as well as water; the application in the SRBA is for 12 non-consumptive in-stream flow claims.

They are supposed to be used for "securing favorable conditions of flow," in part for managing sediment in the streams. Bernard said the law puts the burden of proving the need for the flows on federal agencies.

Claims are not for a specific amount of water, but for a range of flows, varying from an initial discharge trigger level to a high-flow cap.

The federal government in 1993 filed the Organic claims, and a trial was at one point set for October 1998. The trial never happened, and the reasons for that – and some actions that occurred soon after – provided much of the grist for dispute at the January hearing.

Bernard said that the main areas of disagreement were whether the federal government was entitled to the stream flow right and, if it is, how much it should get. The latter question in particular has led to accumulation of large amounts of technical data and expert analysis. ☒

SUPREME COURT REHEARS (3/2000) The Idaho Supreme Court justices who heard for a second time arguments on federal water right claims in wilderness areas were told this time that the actual claims are much smaller than has been widely assumed.

U.S. Department of Justice attorney Sean Donohue argued that the federal claim actually did not – as the Idaho Supreme Court apparently has said it does – cover water in the Salmon River system before it enters the wilderness areas. If so, water rights in the Salmon, Challis and Stanley areas, which have been bracing for severe limits on water developments, would not be affected.

"The main Salmon itself, and tributaries that enter the main Salmon upstream of the boundary of the Frank Church [River of No Return Wilderness] are not covered by our wilderness right at all," Donohue said, "which is why we believe that some of the contentions that have been made about the impacts of these water right flows are incorrect."

Idaho Deputy Attorney General Clive Strong, one of the attorneys asking the Court to change its wilderness water ruling of last October, said that "what we have seen is a repeated series of concessions by the United States to avoid the illogical consequences of its claim. First, it says to the court, 'we're not claiming the main Salmon', but as shown in the state's reply brief, they've made that claim before the district court and all the way through the appeal, until it became disadvantageous. Now they're saying, 'we're only claiming the waters within the wilderness area.' What they're asking this court to do is based upon an implication of implied reserved water rights to allow flow and then at the same time apply exceptions."

The United States in 1993 claimed water rights for the wilderness areas. On December 18, 1997, SRBA Judge Daniel Hurlbutt granted summary judgment in favor of the United States, saying it was entitled to an implied reserved water right to all unappropriated water in the wilderness areas.

Many parties, including the state of Idaho, a number of cities including Challis and Salmon, and businesses including the Potlatch Corporation appealed to the Idaho Supreme Court. Their points on appeal were:

• "Whether the SRBA district court properly inferred from the Wilderness Act of 1964 Congressional intent to reserve all unappropriated flows within the Frank Church River of No Return, the Gospel-Hump, and the Selway-Bitterroot Wilderness Areas.

• "Whether the Hells Canyon National Recreation Area Act reserved all unappropriated flows of tributaries to the Snake River within the HCNRA."

All these arguments occurred on February 14. The next day, first-time arguments were placed before the Court on two other matters.

Sawtooth National Recreation Area: Many of the same legal principles carried over from the Wilderness Act debate to the Sawtooth NRA.

This case grew out of a 1997 filing by the federal government for a federal reserved water right to the unappropriated flow of the waters within the Sawtooth NRA. Hurlbutt ruled in September 1998 partly in favor, partly again, the claim. He said the federal government does have an implied federal reserved water right for the Sawtooth NRA, but water rights in non-wilderness parts of the Sawtooth NRA would have to await a specific amount claim (quantification).

The Supreme Court has been asked whether Hurlbutt wrongly inferred a federal reserved water right for the Sawtooth NRA and whether he erred in ruling that the federal government is entitled to all unappropriated flows within the Wilderness Area.

The issue of "reservation" of land came up again.

Idaho Deputy Attorney General Peter Ampe said the NRA was approved by Congress in large part because it feared key scenic areas, such as the Stanley Basin, would be overrun by subdivisions. Private landowners, many of them ranchers, long have held property within the NRA, Ampe said, and there was no intent or desire to kick them out or reduce their operations. The NRA act, he said, functioned almost like a large-scale zoning ordinance.

Wild & Scenic: The Court heard somewhat similar arguments on another environmental act as well.

This appeal from SRBA Court grew out of the 1968 Wild and Scenic Rivers Act. Basing its claim on language in that law, federal agencies asked for reserved water rights for the middle fork of the Salmon, the middle fork of the Clearwater, the Rapid River, and the main stem of the Salmon. Hurlbutt gave the federal agencies a right even stronger than they had requested, not a reserved but an *express* (explicit) reservation of water. He noted, however, a request for all unappropriated flows in the Rapid River and the main stem of the Salmon be awarded to the United States. Both aspects wound up in front of the Idaho Supreme Court.

Justice Silak drew a key distinction between this case and the others: in this case, the water was being sought only to remain in the river, not for any other use. Fereday urged, "don't be misled by the [argument for a] need for water." A water right, he said, is purely and simply the right to shut down the use of a junior right holder, and that is what the federal government is seeking here.

"I don't think at this point it would be fair to say anyone would be shut down," Silak replied. "This idea of shutting down is something that is hyperbolic."

Hecla attorney Thomas Root noted that no normal reserved water right could be had under the Wild and Scenic Rivers Act, because no reservation of land was specifically involved.

But Trout said she found significant comments made at the time of passage by then-Sen. Church that the enactment of the law did amount to a reservation of water for the purpose, since there was no way the federal government could comply with state water law and still ensure the water flow it sought. (Idaho water law allows water to be claimed in water rights only for "beneficial uses," which not scenic and related purposes.) ☒

DECISION 2 (4/2000) The Idaho Supreme Court unanimously held on March 9 that the federal government could not use the state's "constitutional appropriation" method to claim non-diversionary water rights for anything other than stock watering.

At issue is a means of obtaining a water right which was allowed until 1971, but not since. "The constitutional method of appropriation" allowed people to claim a water right not by filing for a permit (that being the other way of obtaining a right) but simply by diverting water and putting it to a beneficial. use.

That decision marked a reversal of former Snake River Basin Adjudication Judge Daniel Hurlbutt's holding. But the high court upheld him on a ruling barring participation in a key subcase in the matter by a number of irrigation and canal companies.

The case concerns water flowing from Smith Springs into Lake Walcott near Minidoka Dam (in Blaine County) at the Minidoka National Wildlife Refuge (subcase 36-15452). The water has been used by the refuge for many years, since its creation in 1915, but federal agencies never claimed (as they did in some other places) a reserved water right.

Instead, they said that since the United States had put the water to a beneficial use before 1971, it had a "constitutional" right to the water.

The federal claim said the water from Smith Springs is a source of fresh water to the bay, maintains the wetlands when the reservoir is drawn down, and keeps much of the bay open during winter, "thereby providing important habitat for over-wintering birds." The Supreme Court noted that "The United States acknowledged that there were '[n]o developed diversion works' at Smith Springs."

The director's report of the Idaho Department of Water Resources in November 1992 said the federal claim ought to be disallowed, on grounds that a diversion – not just a use – of water is needed to perfect a constitutional claim.

Federal agencies filed an objection to that report, and for a time they and the IDWR were the parties in that subcase. However, the IDWR was removed as a party from the SRBA entirely as a result of 1995 state legislation. No one else filed to enter that subcase, leaving the federal claim unobjected to (though the IDWR report remained evidence in the subcase). The federal government asked, in December 1995, for a summary judgment on the case.

Days later, in January 1996, several major water organizations in the area – the Twin Falls and North Side Canal Companies, and the A&B and Burley Irrigation Districts – filed paperwork in an attempt to enter the case, either to file a late response or to participate outright. Special Master Terry Dolan agreed to limited participation, but the following month recommended that summary judgement be granted in favor of the federal government.

In October that year, Hurlbutt said that a diversion was not required for a constitutional-type water right. He sent back to the special master portions of the case concerning the exact amount of the water flow; but meanwhile, the question of whether a diversion was needed was appealed upward to the Supreme Court.

The court noted "Idaho water law generally requires an actual diversion and beneficial use for the existence of a valid water right. ... Only two exceptions to the diversion requirement exist. No diversion from a natural watercourse or diversion device is needed to establish a valid appropriative water right for stock watering. In addition, State entities acting pursuant to statute may make non-diversionary appropriations for the beneficial use of Idaho citizens. Neither of these exceptions covers the United States' claim. Although the stock-watering exception applies to appropriations made under the constitutional method, it applies only to watering livestock and does not extend to beneficial use for wildlife habitat." ☒

REVERSAL (11/2000) The Idaho Supreme Court on October 27 partly reversed itself on an earlier key federal water rights decision, and held in general that Congress must explicitly state, or very clearly implicitly reserve, water for a federal reserved water right to exist for wilderness areas.

In a commentary to the Idaho Environmental Forum, Boise attorney Christopher Meyer of Givens Pursley said "The result was that [the Court] allowed federal reserved water rights only where it found an 'express' determination by Congress, which it found in the Wild and Scenic Rivers Act and in the Hells Canyon NRA. Today's cases hold, essentially, that Congress must speak expressly (or, in the case of one member of the majority, with a compellingly clear implication) before the Court will 'imply' the override of state water laws."

Dissenting Justice Cathy Silak delivered this commentary: "The practical effect of the majority's misapplication of Winters is the extinction of the doctrine of implied water rights."

That marks a major change in how the SRBA has treated a number of federal water rights. It marks a major change from last year's decision on wilderness water rights. That earlier decision was a 3-2 decision, as was this one. The changed vote: Chief Justice Linda Copple Trout.

In the main wilderness ruling, Trout offered some thoughts about her change of view on reserved water rights: "Having now had the opportunity to further examine the federal reserved rights doctrine as it has been asserted in cases involving federal acts other than the Wilderness Act, I have come to question the continued vitality of the doctrine. The federal reserved rights doctrine was originally developed as a means of determining legislative intent in the absence of any legislative history regarding the intent to reserve water. Because the doctrine is one of implication, the United States Supreme Court has traditionally applied it very narrowly.

"...I believe we are faced with a situation far different from any other case in which the United States Supreme Court has applied the federal reserved rights doctrine. Given the fact that the Wilderness Act of 1964 was passed almost 60 years after the *Winters* case [a key ruling on the subject of reserved water rights], and a year after *Arizona v. California*, which expressly expanded the doctrine to federal reservations other than Indian reservations, it must be assumed that Congress was aware of the federal reserved water rights doctrine at the time the Act was passed.

"Therefore, in this case, Congress was aware that conflicts had developed over the issue of water rights for federal reservations of land. Additionally, when Congress passed the Wild and Scenic Rivers Act just a few years later, it included an express reservation of the amount of water necessary to fulfill the purposes of that Act. Thus, it is reasonable to believe that, at the time the Wilderness Act was passed, Congress knew how to create a water right if it believed one was necessary. Where, as in this case, Congress has chosen for whatever reason, not to create an express water right despite its knowledge of a potential conflict, I believe it can no longer be inferred that such a right is necessary to fulfill the purposes of the reservation. Therefore, while I fully concur with the Court's opinion that water is not strictly necessary to accomplish the purposes of the reservation, I believe, under the circumstances of this case, such a result is also mandated by Congress's failure to include an express reservation of water in the text of the Act itself."

Dissenting Justice Jess Walters even said at the end of his dissent: "I suggest that the parties seek certiorari to the United States Supreme Court for clarification of the application of that doctrine to this case."

The Supreme Court on October 27 simultaneously released three decisions, on wilderness, the Sawtooth National Recreation Area and the Wild and Scenic Rivers Act. The Sawtooth decision was written by Trout, the other two by Justice Gerald Schroeder.

Wilderness. The wilderness case grows out of interpretations of the 1964 Wilderness Act, under which several wilderness areas were established in Idaho. In the SRBA, federal agencies filed claims in 1996 for reserved water rights in the Frank Church-River of No Return, the Selway-Bitterroot, and the Gospel-Hump wilderness areas.

The "reserved" refers to a doctrine that when Congress sets aside land for a specific purpose, it implicitly – even if not specifically – also sets aside enough water to carry out the purpose. That doctrine has been widely applied in water decisions.

Former SRBA Judge Daniel Hurlbutt ruled that the federal government "is entitled to an implied reserved water right to all unappropriated water within the Frank Church-River of No Return, the Gospel-Hump, and the Selway-Bitterroot wilderness areas based on the Wilderness Act," the Supreme Court later noted.

On October 1, 1999, a sharply divided Idaho Supreme Court held that the United States does have implied reserved water rights for wilderness areas in Idaho – and those rights include all the water that naturally flows through those areas.

That affected not only water within the wilderness areas, but also water flowing into it. That had the primary practical effect of subordinating all water rights in the Stanley, Challis and Salmon areas to federal wilderness rights – should the federal government choose to assert its right.

(On the same day, it turned down federal claims filed under the Multiple-Use Sustained Yield Act of 1960, saying that act was not specifically a reservation of land and therefore didn't carry an accompanying reservation of water. That decision has remained intact.)

Federal attorneys said later, at a rehearing before the Idaho Supreme Court, that they weren't claiming water from the main stem of the Salmon River, which flows through the wilderness.

In its new decision, after reviewing several much-touted cases it said were only slightly relevant, the Idaho Supreme Court contended:

"Analysis of the claim by the United States begins with the language of the Wilderness Act to determine if implied water rights must be recognized to avoid defeat of the purposes of the Act. There is nothing within the Act that compels that conclusion. Unlike the Presidential Proclamation in *Cappaert* which expressly reserved a pool to maintain a unique variety of fish, the Wilderness Act does not define purposes that necessitate a reservation of water. Similarly, the purpose in *Winters* and *State of Arizona v. State of California* was to provide habitable land to Indian tribes which required that there be enough water for irrigation. Each of the cases decided by the United States Supreme Court involved agreements or a statement by which a standard for quantification could be determined – enough water for human habitation or preservation of a rare fish. There is no standard by which quantification of the amount of water could be determined in the Wilderness Act. Absence of any standard for quantification is indicative of the fact that quantification was not meant to be determined. There is no language in the Wilderness Act compelling the conclusion that there must be reserved water rights to fulfill the purposes of the Act. There is no indication 'that without the water the purposes of the reservation would be entirely defeated.'"

Sawtooth. In the Sawtooth NRA decision, Trout's majority decision reversed Judge Hurlbutt's holding that implied reserved water rights exist for the area. She noted that "the district court ruled the United States is entitled to a federal reserved water right for the non-wilderness portion of the Sawtooth NRA, but required further quantification of the right."

In the October 27 ruling, the majority decided instead "we hold (1) Congress did not expressly claim or disclaim federal water rights in the lands designated by the Act; (2) the primary purpose of the Sawtooth NRA is to protect the non-wilderness portion from the dangers of unregulated development and mining, and to protect the wilderness portion from mining operations which would have been allowed under the Wilderness Act; and (3) the intent to reserve water in both the wilderness and non-wilderness portions of the Sawtooth NRA cannot be implied because, without water, the primary purposes of the reservations will not be entirely defeated."

Silak was the lone dissenter on this opinion.

Wild and Scenic Rivers. In its third ruling, the Supreme Court was unanimous in its more mixed ruling on rights associated with the Wild and Scenic Rivers Act.

Federal agencies claimed federal reserved water rights for the Middle Fork of the Salmon, the Middle Fork of the Clearwater (including the Lochsa and the Selway Rivers), the Rapid River and the main stem of the Salmon. SRBA Court agreed that those rights were reserved on the W&SR Act.

In this case, the Supreme Court said, "virtually everyone who has written in this area agrees that the Wild and Scenic Rivers Act reserves water. That is the ineluctable conclusion that attaches to the words of the Act, the Congressional history, and logic."

Specific amounts, however, still must be worked out by SRBA court, the high court said. ☒

FEDERAL LANDS PROCEDURES (4/2001) Judge Roger Burdick has outlined the process and procedure for handling wild and scenic river and the Hells Canyon National Recreation Area claims.

For **Wild and Scenic**, the process includes submission by May 1 of a proposed settlement moderator. Burdick noted, "If parties cannot stipulate to a moderator, then each party shall file with the Court a list of at least three potential moderators together with attached credentials. The Court will select a moderator from the lists submitted. Following selection of a settlement moderator, the Court will order an initial mandatory settlement conference."

For **Hells Canyon**, the judge said he will review the motion to participate at an April 10 hearing at Grangeville. As with Wild and Scenic, a May 1 deadline has. ☒

PARTICIPATION TURNED BACK (5/2001) Judge Burdick on April 23 turned back a request by a group of water organizations to participate directly in litigation over federal water rights in the Hells Canyon National Recreation area. The Harrison, Burgess and Peoples Canal & Irrigation Companies; Progressive, Enterprise, New Sweden, Snake River Valley and Idaho Irrigation Districts; Egin Bench Canals, Inc.; and North Fremont Canal Systems, Inc., and on behalf of A&B and Burley Irrigation Districts and Twin Falls and North Side Canal Companies, all represented by Rexburg attorney Jerry Rigby, sought to become intervenors in the case.

The request was the subject of oral argument at the SRBA status conference in Grangeville on April 10.

Burdick noted that "The Intervenors submit that the reason for seeking to participate in the subcases deals solely with the potential for any factual or legal precedent (law of the case within the SRBA) resulting from this Court's pretrial and trial rulings on these issues. The concerns expressed by the Intervenors deal with rulings regarding quantification methodology and science. The Intervenors express concern that any quantification methodology admitted or adopted by the Court in these subcases has the potential to become law of the case in quantification proceedings conducted in the future in which the Intervenors may have a direct interest. The Intervenors also agree that they do not intend to participate to present factual circumstances independent from, or different than, those presented by the State of Idaho."

Burdick said the intervenors' role in the subcase was too general, that their interests for the most part would be represented anyway by the state of Idaho, and would place a burden on the original parties. He said they would have other opportunities to challenge any decision, and did allow them to submit an *amicus* (friend of the court) brief. ☒

STIPULATIONS PROPOSED (9/2004) Negotiated agreements on settling remaining disputes over water rights in the Wild and Scenic Rivers and Hells Canyon National Recreation Area were filed with SRBA Court on August 20. Those agreements are large and complex, on an order comparable to the Nez Perce Tribe agreement released earlier this year. The Idaho attorney general's office summarized the key determinations as:

- "The issuance of water rights decrees for the six Wild and Scenic Rivers and for 32 tributary streams and lakes in the HCNRA; and

• "The subordination of these federal water rights to existing water rights and uses and to specified future rights and uses."

The Idaho River United conservation group noted that deal also:

• "Prevents out-of-basin transfers of water from the rivers.

•"Locks in minimum stream flows for each of the rivers.

• "Protects high water flows in each of the streams, which are necessary for maintaining the ecological health of rivers.

• "And requires the State of Idaho to actively protect the Wild & Scenic water right."

The Wild and Scenic Rivers cover 444 miles of river in the state.

In a decision reached in 2000, the Idaho Supreme Court held that the United States did have water rights for the Main Salmon, Middle Fork Salmon, Rapid, Selway, Lochsa and Middle Fork Clearwater River, and the Hells Canyon area. It said that entitlement was only for the minimum water necessary to fulfill the purposes Congress determined for those river stretches and the Hells Canyon area. How much that was, and how to determine that, was left unstated. ☒

Conservation claims

FILING FISH (3/1/1993) At the March 16 status conference, Judge Daniel Hurlbutt rejected Ketchum attorney James Kennedy's argument his clients – three conservation organizations as well as Snake River salmon and the river itself – be given intervenor status, on grounds the motion was premature. Hurlbutt did not indicate whether such a request would be rejected once the objection and response process is underway.

As Department of Water Resources Adjudication chief David Shaw pointed out, such an approval could open the door to a wide range of interested intervening parties, "a whole variety of special interests."

Kennedy appeared as both a staff and *pro bono* attorney for the Land and Water Fund of the Rockies, a conservation interest group. (Kennedy is an interim attorney for the group; permanent counsel is expected to arrive from California June 1.) He moved that it and four other named interests – two organizations, the others being salmon of the Snake River and the River itself – be admitted as formal parties to the Adjudication. Kennedy argued that intervention in the case, and standing in the case, are two separate issues. (The court did not specifically address that point.)

Kennedy used four legal bases for his argument:

• *Principle 10, the Rio declaration.* Adopted by the Rio de Janeiro conference on the environment (to which the United States was a party), it says water law has inescapable impact on the environment and economy and consequently calls for "effective access to judicial and administrative proceedings, including redress and remedy, shall be provided."

• *The McCarran amendment in federal law.* Kennedy suggested it called for comprehensiveness in water adjudication.

• *The Idaho SRBA statute* (42-1406A). Kennedy quoted one section calling for "effective management in the public interest of the Snake River basin" requiring comprehensive review of water rights, involving the rights of all "users of surface and ground water." Kennedy also noted that Sec. 42-

1420 also refers to a legislative intent that adjudication results will govern "persons" rather than "parties" to the action. That, he suggested, means that his interest groups have an automatic interest in the results of the adjudication, since they will be bound by it. In a point strongly opposed by other attorneys later, Kennedy suggested use of the water, not necessarily ownership of a water right, is enough to join the case.

• *Rule 24 of the Adjudication*, which covers admittance to the case.

Judge Hurlbutt questioned whether the two natural resources – river and salmon – already were represented by government counsel, since they are public property. Kennedy said various government agencies view those resources and their proper handling in very different ways. Hurlbutt replied in open session, "The state of Idaho is discordant and disorganized ... It seriously calls into question the State of Idaho as a sovereign body politic."

David Barber of the Idaho Attorney General's office said that the issues of standing and intervention were and should be separate, and said intervention by a natural entity was not appropriate. (He said his office did not oppose eventual involvement by the three organizations.) He did acknowledge that the Idaho Department of Water Resources is in an unusual position, being both defendant and advocate.

James Tucker of Rosholt, Robertson said that the adjudication is or should be focused on the identification of existing water rights, and that the idea certain persons or organizations are "users" of the river is not enough for standing. The issue, he suggested, is simply; are Kennedy's clients claiming an existing water right? He drew the distinction between a valid right to water and an ability to exercise that right and impositions on that ability to exercise it could be imposed from governmental policymakers. That public policymaking arena (mainly legislative) is, he suggested, where the public trust issue should be played out.

Judge Hurlbutt denied the motion to intervene (without prejudice) because, he said, "This motion is premature. … I think however at this juncture under 24-A-2 there is some deficiency in showing a particularized need." He said the entities would be free to file in specific cases as they arise, with appropriate pleadings. Appropriateness to intervene would be determined, he said, after all objections and responses are seen. ☒

WATER CONSERVATION (3/15/1993) The legislative debate over a bill designed to protect conservation of irrigation water crystallized in Senate Bill 1772, proposed by Sen. John Peavey (D-Carey) at the request of the Hagerman Water Rights Owners, Inc., at the Senate Resources and Environment Committee. Chairman Sen. Laird Noh (R-Kimberly) described it as "sometimes a rather heated controversy" and a "serious" issue. Asked later by Sen. Rex Furness (R-Rigby), "Is there any opposition?" Noh replied: "Oh, yes there is."

That was quickly evident. Sponsor Peavey pointed out that farmers who have invested heavily in irrigation equipment now, in many cases, face increased energy costs and a national push for conservation. If, however, they do use for irrigation (a declared "beneficial use") the water to which they have rights, they stand to lose it and could be in trouble if they need to switch back later to more water-intensive forms of irrigation. The bill would clarify that water rights would not be conceded because water is not used due to conservation measures. ☒

PUBLIC TRUST OUT (6/21/1993) For a second time, Judge Hurlbutt rejected an attempt by the Land and Water Fund of the Rockies, and associated Idaho conservation groups, to formally intervene in the adjudication.

His reasoning went to a key issue in the SRBA: whether public trust and public interest issues should be considered as a component. Hurlbutt said that public trust was not within the SRBA Court jurisdiction.

The Land and Water Fund had used the public trust doctrine as a key element of their rationale for seeking to intervene in the case. Because that doctrine, if accepted, could have exposed thousands (or maybe all) water rights in the basin to review and possibly reduction, attorneys for most of the major active players in the adjudication so far spoke against the motion.

The Land and Water Fund, on behalf of the Idaho Conservation League, Idaho Rivers United and the Idaho Wildlife Federation, had filed a motion to intervene November 25, 1992. That motion was heard in Court February 16; Judge Hurlbutt then denied the request "without prejudice," and noted that any future attempts should "identify the moving parties' particularized interest..."

The Fund, represented in Court June 15 by Laird Lucas in his first SRBA appearance, and with the Northwest Resource Information Center joining the effort, tried to do that in its second motion. This time pointed to five specific water rights, all in the Buhl-Hagerman area, which it contested with "non-conforming objections." The groups said their interest including fishing, rafting, swimming and otherwise using the waters, and that the public in general has interests which should be protected, but aren't, by existing SRBA participants. Lucas told the court that "what everyone is saying we're saying, is not what we're saying" – specifically, that he wasn't calling for specific minimum stream flows. "We're saying we don't know what the process should be, and we're willing to work responsibly with the Court."

The closest thing to support Lucas got from anyone else at the June 15 hearing was from Deputy Attorney General David Barber, who said of the public trust and related issues, "We would like to have it resolved." But the state, like an array of private parties, argued strongly against allowing the conservation groups their motion.

"The more I review the motion," said Don Olowinski of Hawley Troxell Ennis & Hawley, which represents irrigation companies, "the more I become convinced it is inappropriate in these proceedings. It is bad law and bad administration." Among other things, he said, it could require the Department of Water Resources and other participants to "go back to square one" in water adjudication. ☒

GROUPS OUT (8/2/1993) Judge Hurlbutt has rejected in a formal written order – as he did at the June 15 status conference – an attempt by the Land and Water Fund of the Rockies, and the conservation groups it represents, to formally intervene in the SRBA on grounds of public trust and interest.

Idaho Code 42-1411 defines the elements of a water right which the court will confirm by order of decree. The public trust doctrine is not enumerated as an element of a water right, Hurlbutt wrote. "In essence, this motion is for a writ of mandate requiring the Director to conduct investigations and make recommendations which would include the public trust doctrine as a judicially legislation element of a water right. The adjudication statutes do not so require and this court will not judicially legislate an element not specifically found in I.C. 41-1411." ☒

GROUPS IN (1/21/1994) In a decision January 14 Judge Hurlbutt has allowed the "conservation groups" (represented by Laird Lucas of the Land and Water Fund of the Rockies) to intervene in Basinwide Issue 1.

The groups, twice turned down by Hurlbutt on other requests, asked for reconsideration based in part on the "local public interest" standard. Hurlbutt said that local public interest is not an element of a water right to be resolved in the SRBA. Even so, he said, "Review of the SRBA statutes indicates that the legislature has required that the court apply the 'local public interest' standard as a precondition to confirmation of the right in a decree ..." So, he said, "where the 'local public interest' standard is determined to apply as a precondition to decreeing a water right in the SRBA, the conservation groups' motion for leave to intervene shall be granted."

That sounds expansive, but later Hurlbutt seemed to limit the participation by denying their request to participate on any groups other than through the presumption statute. The decision raised eyebrows, however. ⊠

SUPREME COURT ON CONSERVATION INTERVENTION (7/11/94) The Idaho Supreme Court has determined that the public trust doctrine has no place in the SRBA, blocking several interested conservation groups from their main (and preferred) entree into the adjudication. But the decision was sharply split 3-2, with Justices Byron Johnson and Stephen Bistline dissenting.

And one key sentence in the decision indicates that public trust may yet play a large role in water decisions even if not explicitly in the SRBA.

The decision generally reaffirmed an earlier ruling by Hurlbutt, but it added one new provision, the first interpretation of any of the pieces of the 1994 SRBA legislation. In that action, it vacated Hurlbutt's earlier ruling allowing the conservation groups to assert local public interest in one case, saying the new legislation ended the basis for making that allowance.

The majority ruling by Chief Justice Charles McDevitt (concurrences by Justices Cathy Silak and Linda Copple Trout), said Hurlbutt was right that "it had no jurisdiction to consider the public trust doctrine as an element of a water right because it was not so defined in Idaho Code 42-1411."

"The public trust doctrine has never been expanded in scope in the State of Idaho beyond its pre-constitution application to the beds of navigable waters below the natural high water mark," the high court said. "It has never been applied in the context of water appropriation by case law or statute. The public trust doctrine does not create an element of a water right to be determined by the adjudication."

More specifically, McDevitt wrote, "the public trust doctrine has never been expanded in scope in the state of Idaho beyond its pre-constitution application to the beds of navigable waters below the natural high water mark. It has never been applied in the context of water appropriation by case law or statute. The public trust doctrine does not create an element of a water right to be determined by the adjudication."

Johnson and Bistline wrote separate minority opinions. Johnson said that "the fundamental flaw in the Court's rejection of intervention by the Conservation Groups to assert the public trust doctrine is the misconception that the public trust doctrine in Idaho has never been applied in the context of water appropriation." He said the Idaho Supreme Court has referred to public rights in waterways in Idaho several times, in 1915 concerning the Salmon river, in 1935 in a water diversion case and in 1974 concerning Silver Creek.

"In my view, these cases provide irrefutable authority that this Court has applied the public trust doctrine in the context of water appropriation," he wrote. He said he would have granted intervention to the conservation groups and let the SRBA Court decide whether to grant attorneys fees under the Private Attorney General doctrine.

The main decision was, however, not all bad news for the conservation groups. The majority decision included the statement that "this opinion is issued with the Court's understanding from the parties that the respondents will not assert issue preclusion if the Conservation Groups assert a public trust doctrine claim in the proper form at the proper time." But the decision did not explicitly say what the form or time should be. ☒

SECOND TIME AT SUPREME COURT (9/11/95) In a tersely-worded statement, the Idaho Supreme Court a second time turned down the "conservation groups" in their effort to join in the SRBA. It also took away one narrow area in which the groups had been involved.

But the groups (the Idaho Conservation League, Idaho Rivers United, Idaho Wildlife Federation and Northwest Resource Information Center) did see a bright side (which in turn was seen as ominous by their opposition). The Court said specifically that the public trust doctrine has a basis for intervention, which the groups had strongly argued, and that the *Kootenai Environmental Alliance v. Panhandle Yacht Club* case from 1983 was relevant law in this instance.

That suggests, group attorney Laird Lucas said, that the environmental groups may be able to become active in water rights cases, if not specifically in the SRBA. As to what that might mean, he said, the groups are still unsure.

The revised decision said that "the SRBA court 'is in effect, a separate division of the district court and exercises the unique jurisdiction given it by the legislature.' ... That jurisdiction requires that the district court undertake 'a comprehensive determination of the nature, extent and priority of the rights of all users of surface and ground water' in the Snake River Basin. The state's ownership of the water that is the subject of the adjudication, is not before the SRBA court, nor is that ownership interest in any way diminished by the adjudication of claimants' rights."

The Court added, however, "The proprietary rights to use water, which are the subject of the SRBA, are held subject to the public trust. Kootenai, 105 Idaho at 631, 671 P.2d at 1094 ("[T]he public trust doctrine takes precedent even over vested water rights.") ☒

CLOSING THE DOOR (11/13/95) The Idaho Supreme Court on November 8 closed the door on a long-running case concerning possible involvement in the SRBA of several conservation groups. The case already had been reheard once by the high court, with a revised opinion. That revised opinion led to a second call for reconsideration of the case.

The high court in general said that the groups, which include the Idaho Conservation League and Idaho Rivers United, could not participate in the SRBA.

One element of the second opinion, however, concerned many of the central SRBA players: a reference to public trust as a component which apparently should be borne in mind in the SRBA; that was a key point underpinning the conservation groups' case. So a number of those SRBA participants, including A&B Irrigation, Nampa & Meridian Irrigation District, the state of Idaho and others, also asked for a rehearing. ☒

INDIVIDUALS IN BOISE STORAGE (12/2003) Snake River Basin Adjudication presiding Judge John M. Melanson on November 4 issued his first major order in the case, allowing participation in a key water right dispute near Boise by the state of Boise, the state of Idaho and four individuals associated with environmental interests.

"... participation is granted to Gene E. Bray, Thomas R. Stuart III, Thomas J. Cade and Amy Williams and the City of Boise," he wrote. "Because no party opposed participation by the State of Idaho, and also for the same reasons stated, participation is also granted to the State of Idaho."

The case grew out of water right claims filed by the federal Bureau of Reclamation, seeking rights for irrigation-related and other storage for Arrowrock Dam and Reservoir, and for Lucky Peak Dam and Reservoir, and Anderson Dam and Reservoir.

The water has, however, actually been used by an array of local water delivery organizations based mainly in Ada and Canyon counties. Those include the Nampa-Meridian Irrigation District, the Settlers Irrigation District, Pioneer Irrigation District, the Canyon County Water Company and many others. These organizations have distributed the stored water to farmers and others. Those groups together have also filed claims on the stored water.

In review, the state Department of Water Resources recommended rights be assigned to the Bureau of Reclamation.

Attorney Laird Lucas, who often represents environmental organizations in the SRBA and other matters, spoke in this case for water right holders including Tom Stuart, Gene Bray, Thomas Cade and Amy Williams. All are claimants in the basin, he said, and filed responses to the BOR and organization claims in the time set by former SRBA Judge Roger Burdick.

Their entry was opposed by attorneys for the districts and entities, who argued that the issue of ownership should be narrowly considered. The only question, they argued, is whether the Bureau or the entities own the rights, and the four individual claimants have no place in that dispute.

In reviewing the request to participate, Melanson noted the June 23 order issued by former SRBA Judge Roger Burdick (who has since moved to the Idaho Supreme Court). In that order, Burdick wrote, "Any party to the adjudication not already a party to one of the enumerated subcases in Exhibit A, seeking to participate in the consolidated subcase may do so by filing and serving a response setting forth their position on the issue. The response must be served on the parties to the consolidated subcase (listed in the attached certificate of mailing) prior to the date set for the hearing."

He noted that Bray, Stuart, Cade and Williams filed timely notices of intent to participate.

Melanson wrote, "It is readily apparent from the intent of the June 23, 2003, Order that Judge Burdick contemplated opening the consolidated subcase to allow for participation by parties to the adjudication not already parties to the consolidated subcase. This Court concurs for several reasons."

Some were procedural, involving the way the case was developed through and after the special master's review process. ☒

Shoshone-Bannock filings

TRIBAL FILINGS (3/29/1993) In-stream flows within the Snake River system were claimed March 25 by the U.S. Department of Justice on behalf of two Idaho Indian tribes. That came in the wake of a restraining order from U.S. District court in Washington, D.C., and a round of activity in the last two weeks involving Idaho's tribes and their claims on Snake River basin water.

The activity started with the March 15 motion by the Shoshone-Bannock Tribes to intervene in the adjudication. An attached memo, by attorney Candy Jackson, noted that "the United States in its role as trustee has been representing the interests of the Tribes along with the interests of other Indian tribes and of other federal entities in this adjudication." But she said that while the March 25 deadline for filing federal claims was fast approaching, the tribes have not been told whether their claims would be filed in time, so "the Tribes believe it is necessary for them to intervene on their own behalf in this adjudication. It is possible that the Tribes may find it necessary to file claims on their own behalf."

That latter point generated some dispute. Peter Monson, a Department of Justice attorney, said that the Department of Justice didn't oppose the tribe's participation in the adjudication noting that claimants of water rights need not obtain intervenor status to participate. "As claimants," he wrote, "the Tribes would be in a considerably different posture than applicants for intervention who wish to assert not a water right but rather a public policy interest, such as the recent motion to intervene filed by the Land and Water Fund of the Rockies, et. al., which was recently denied without prejudice by the Court." Monson also suggested that the tribes "would be unable to demonstrate inadequate representation by the United States."

At the March 16 status conference, Jackson asked Judge Hurlbutt for an expedited hearing on her request to intervene, prior to the March 25 federal claim deadline. At that point, the Nez Perce tribe, represented by Deputy Counsel Rebecca Craven, asked to appear in the Sho-Ban matter as *amicus curiae* (friend of the court), noting that it, too, planned to file water claims before March 25.

On March 22, Judge Hurlbutt approved both requests. But Ross indicated he might seek a temporary restraining order prohibiting filing of any federal-law based claims, despite the March 25 deadline, because the Idaho Department of Water Resources hadn't provided standard forms for such claims. (Standard forms do exist for state-based filings.) Ross also questioned if the March 25 deadline for federal reserved or federal law based claims applied to anyone other than federal government, such as the tribes.

On March 25, U.S. District Court issued a temporary restraining order ordering the Department of Justice to file for in-stream flows on behalf of the Nez Perce and Shoshone-Bannock tribes. About 1,100 claims in all, around the basin, were filed for. ☒

FEDERAL FOR TRIBES (4/26/1993) Waters in the Snake River system were claimed March 25 by the U.S. Department of Justice on behalf of two Idaho Indian tribes. That came in the wake of a restraining order from U.S. District court in Washington, D.C., and a round of activity in the last two weeks involving Idaho's tribes and their claims on Snake River basin water.

The activity started with the March 15 motion by the Shoshone-Bannock most heatedly-debated, partly because the disagreements over the Report grows out of local disputes that have gone on for generations.

The historic conflict developed between some surface water users along the river and groundwater users on Era flats. With the development of water storage facilities in the area, disagreements surfaced over the use of groundwater in the flats.

Hollifield's motion said that the Director's Report urges approval of a number of expanded water rights, and approval of a number of water rights where the department issued Cease and Desist orders in 1989.

Hollifield said that interim administration of water in the area by the department was needed to protect senior surface water rights. But he said a Water Management Proposal drafted mostly by David Shaw of IDWR said the water users agreed they would not try to limit junior ground water rights, at a time when ground water levels have dropped precipitously. "The continued use by junior ground water pumpers of the water as recommended in the director's Report to areas outside the District is substantially decreasing the groundwater level in Basin 34.

Shaw suggested that in effect "what Hollifield is asking is that wells be divided into two categories, those diverting public water and those rediverting original appropriators' water." Theoretically that could be done, but Shaw said that burden of proof for figuring out which wells fall into which categories would make the job very difficult. By that analysis, in effect, his proposal could shut off use of many wells in the area.

SHOSHONE BANNOCK FILING (6/20/1994) More than 200 objections have been filed to the Shoshone-Bannock water rights agreements. The filings were made under a lift of the general SRBA stay.

The filings have not yet been assigned to the judge or a special master, and their disposition is not yet clear. The filings also made a kind of legal history. They marked the first electronic filing in the case. ☒

FORT HALL OBJECTIONS (4/17/1995) Non-tribal water users in the Fort Hall water project are not water right holders and have no standing to participate in the SRBA, the federal government, the state of Idaho and the Shoshone-Bannock Tribes said in an April 11 court filing.

At stake: whether many water users in federal projects have water rights as such, or simply rights under signed contracts for delivery of water.

The federal and state agencies took the latter view, emphatically, even contending that at base, "the sole issue raised by the [Fort Hall Water Users] Association is whether the United States will continue to meet its contractual obligations to deliver water to the Association's members."

The Association and its spokesman, Kim Bodily, has sought to challenge the 1990 Fort Hall Water Rights Agreement.

But federal agencies noted that the rights to water which the Association's members use on contact is held by the U.S. Bureau of Reclamation, not by the users. The Association members have not filed claims in the SRBA and were not joined as parties in the action. "Thus," the federal/state reply said, "the only remaining issue relating to standing is whether there is some construction of the adjudication statutes that nonetheless gives the members of the Association the status of claimants." ☒

A PARTY IS A PARTY (8/1996) On a question that has arisen several times in the SRBA – participation of groups of parties in the case as groups – the

Idaho Supreme Court appeared on July 5 to conclude: To be a party in the case, you have to be a party.

The case – *Fort Hall Water Users Association v. United States* – was an SRBA appeal, from a decision by SRBA Judge Daniel Hurlbutt. The high court upheld Hurlbutt's ruling that the Fort Hall Water Users Association lacked standing to participate and object to the 1990 Fort Hall Indian Water Rights Agreement.

The decision by Justice Cathy Silak and unanimously agreed to, also dismissed the association's claims "for failure to state a claim upon which relief may granted."

The case grew out of the original 1985 state legislation which created the SRBA, and also included a separate resolution ordering the governor and attorney general to try to settle the water rights claims of the Shoshone-Bannock Tribes of the Fort Hall Indian Reservation through negotiations. After that, negotiations involved the federal government, the state of Idaho, the Shoshone-Bannock Tribes and the Committee of Nine (a group of irrigators that represents the non-Indian interests in Water District 01, which includes most of the southeastern portion of the Snake River basin.) That led to the 1990 Fort Hall Indian Water Rights Agreement which details the water rights of the Shoshone-Bannock Tribes upstream of Hells Canyon Dam, the rights of the Bureau of Indian Affairs, Fort Hall Agency, and the water rights of the Fort Hall Irrigation Project (which are operated by Indian irrigators). In the spring of 1991, that agreement was adopted by both the Idaho Legislature and the membership of the Shoshone-Bannock tribes.

In March 1994 the Idaho Department of Water Resources filed with SRBA Court a Director's Report abstracting the Agreement and containing a proposed consent decree; it concerned 25 water rights.

Two months later, the Fort Hall Water Users Association filed objections to seven of those 25 water rights. The FHWUA is an association of the 2,000 non-Indian water users in the Fort Hall Irrigation Project. In February 1995, the federal government, the state of Idaho and the Shoshone-Bannock Tribes asked the SRBA Court to dismiss the objections. The Twin Falls Canal Company and North Side Canal Company, which were involved in the negotiations to reduce the impact of the tribal claims on their water rights, filed a motion to participate in the disposition of the joint motions and the objections to protect their own interests.

Dismissal: A key to both the SRBA Court's and the Supreme Court's rulings concerned the nature of the request by the Association. Hurlbutt initially indicated that he would consider the issue as a summary judgment of the case; but apparently he changed his mind and considered it instead as a request by the government agencies and tribes to dismiss the Fort Hall association's objections. That meant he would considering the issue under a different set of rules and standards.

Hurlbutt said "the Motions to Dismiss are based on the record presently before the court, which consists solely of the pleadings."

Claimants: Supreme Court itself said "the standing issue in this case revolves around the statutory interpretation of I.C. Section 42-1401A(1) and the meaning of 'claimant.' The FHWUA asserts that it meets the requirements of being a claimant in the SRBA, not because it is itself claiming ownership of water rights, but because the United States filed the notice of claim on its behalf pursuant to the second half of the definition of 'claimant' under I.C. Section 42-1401A(1). We disagree." ☒

BURDICK REJECTS SPLIT RIGHT (8/2001) SRBA Judge Roger Burdick on July 24 turned back a proposal which would have broken apart a set of federal-related water rights at the Fort Hall Indian Reservation and the Fort Hall Irrigation Project.

Burdick said that "the rights have been decreed" effective with a 1995 subcase decree by former SRBA Judge Daniel Hurlbutt, and granting the new motion – for a filing of a late claim on water covered by the ruling – would mean that the partial decree would be reopened and reconsidered.

"The Court finds that extreme prejudice would result to all the parties that timely participated therein," he wrote.

The issue started with the 1990 Fort Hall Indian Rights Agreement, which among other things declared the federal government as trustee for the Shoshone-Bannock tribes' water rights at Fort Hall. That agreement was approved by Hurlbutt in August 1995 in a partial consent decree, and later by the Idaho Supreme Court.

Alan Oliver, a land owner within the Fort Hall area, said he is a tribal member – and is seeking a water right, though he acknowledged that his land is held in trust by the federal government. On March 2, he filed a motion to be allowed to file a late claim in the SRBA. He said he would seek a priority date of June 14, 1867, which tracks to the tribes' treaty date.

Oliver said he was not seeking a state-based right. Burdick said he "appears to be seeking a derivative or portion of the federal reserved water right contained in the 1995 decree. In other words, Mr. Oliver is asking this Court to designate or apportion a specific quantity of the federal reserved water right to his land." ☒

FACTS IN DISPUTE (6/2008) On May 2 Special Master Brigette Bilyeu rejected a request for summary judgment on a Fort Hall-area water right claim, saying "genuine issues of material fact remain for trial."

The subcase, 27-07320, involved a water right claimed by Connie, Michael, Beth, and Moroni Clawson; the IDWR recommended issuance, based on a license. However, the land involved was described by the Tribes as tribal land within the Fort Hall Indian Reservation, and the Shoshone-Bannock Tribes say a private person cannot have a water right on tribal land.

The Tribes asked for summary judgment in the case.

The tribes' objections were, Bilyeu said "based on a provision of the 1995 Consent Decree which decreed water rights within the exterior boundaries of the Fort Hall Reservation." That would seem to be a legal issue purely, but Bilyeu also notes: "The Tribes argue that this subcase raises an issue relating to the boundary of the Fort Hall Reservation. This subcase, however, is distinct from the boundary issue raised [in] 27-00016C. This subcase does *not relate to the realignment* of the Blackfoot River, which occurred in 1964. Instead, the issue in this subcase is whether a recent re-survey of the original reservation boundary shows some of the Clawsons' place of use to be on the Reservation. The Tribes contend that recent re-surveys show the land that was previously thought to be privately owned is now identified as on the Reservation. The area re-surveyed is near the Clawson's place of use."

Bilyeu: "The argument is that the Reservation boundaries have not changed, but recent surveys more accurately describe those boundaries." ☒

INTERIM ADMINISTRATION (3/29/1993) Judge Hurlbutt sharply shot down an Idaho Department of Water Resources request for reconsideration of his Interim administration order for Basin 34 (of December 12) at the March 16 status conference. In the process, he took aim at water administration in the Lost River area.

The Department is expected to return to court with a scaled-back, amended proposal.

From the perspective of Deputy Attorney General Peter Anderson, arguing the Department's case, the request for reconsideration amounted to a clarification of the elements of the maze of surface and ground water rights in the area, and of how they relate to each other. With such clarification, Anderson suggested, the Department could avoid being "whipsawed" between contesting parties disputing the Department's interpretation. Any action the Department takes on the difficult groundwater issue, he suggested, would be immediately contested.

Hurlbutt, however, saw it differently. "Everybody sort of picks and chooses what [rules] they'll follow up there," he said. "You don't need an interim administrative order if you're doing your job." he suggested that the IDWR was asking the court to determine how water should be delivered, an administrative matter he said the Court should not be involved in. (The Department said those same issues actually amounted to determination of components of water rights.) And, he said, "You don't want to apply the laws the legislature has decreed." ☒

"HOT TIME IN THE OLD TOWN TONIGHT" (4/26/93) That's how one state attorney sees the two-day hearing at the SRBA Courthouse starting May 4. And the only irony in the description is that the event will take place during daylight hours instead of at night.

The hearing grew from a motion by William Hollifield, Twin Falls, attorney for the Big Lost River Water Users Association, requesting changes in the IDWR Director's Report for the Big Lost area or "a restraining order requiring IDWR to administer water in Basin 34 according to Idaho law."

Since the Basin 34 (Lost River) Director's Report was one of the first issued, these proceedings could help set precedent for how others are handled. It also has implications for how groundwater-related disputes will be handled. But this is likely to be one of the stream flow be sent to local county commissioners and require approval by Legislature; application fails without legislative affirmation. ☒

INTERIM ADMIN CONTINUES (2/28/1994) Judge Daniel Hurlbutt granted an old request — more recently turned around — by the state Department of Water Resources for continued interim administration in Basin 34 (the Lost River area), on February 15. The decision could have a big impact on how water rights are handled in the SRBA in the wake of the unconstitutional ruling of the presumption statutes.

Deputy Attorney General David Barber noted that the Department had said it needed more time to continue interim administration of the area, a useful approach until Hurlbutt's ruling on Basinwide Issue 1 (the presumption statutes). Because a number of water rights were based at least in part on that statute, the department no longer has an accurate list of water rights, and wanted to hold off action in that area until the March 15 status conference so the department would have time for review.

At a steering committee meeting earlier in the day, Barber and other attorneys noted the difficulty of giving proper notice in the area's cases under current conditions.

One difficulty with continuance did arise from attorney Patrick Brown of Hepworth, Nungester & Lezamiz. His said the large San Felipe Ranch (one of his firm's clients) could run into a big problem if the matter is delayed, since the irrigation season in the Lost basin starts May 1. Some basic issues concerning rights need to be settled by then, he suggested.

That was echoed by Mitchell Sorensen, a farmer in the area representing himself in the case; he said he would need to know well before May 1 what water he could expect, because many seed purchasing and other decisions must be made well before May 1.

"It seems to me the difficulty we're facing now is the integrity of the list," Hurlbutt said. He acknowledged to Sorensen that his ruling on the unconstitutionality of the presumption statutes may have jeopardized some water rights in the Lost basin, and asked what sort of relief he wanted.

Sorensen said he is concerned now about harassment from other water users and challenges to his water rights claims. Up to now, he has been able to use the IDWR director's report for that purpose, and problems could result if that wasn't usable any more. That point may have been crucial in Hurlbutt's thinking, as he noted the Director's report is still the best list available, even after the presumption statute ruling. He said he saw no alternative but to continue state administration using it. ☒

SIX GENERAL PROVISIONS (6/2001) SRBA Judge Roger Burdick on May 9 ordered six general provisions included in Basin 34 water right permits.

They are:

• General Provision 1 "Definitions"

• General Provision 2 "2-B Gauge and Stockwatering During Non-irrigation Season"

• General Provision 3 "Rotation with Storage"

• General Provision 4 "Back Channel"

• General Provision 5 "Separate Streams"

• General Provision 6 "Howell Gauge – Connected and Unconnected River"

He noted that "The issue of "Conjunctive Management" was consolidated with Basin-Wide Issue 5, which involves recommended conjunctive management provisions for the entire SRBA and is not part of this Order."

Burdick on May 8 issued a separate order dismissing the season of use objections. The general provisions order grew out of a recommendation by the Idaho Department of Water Resources.

Burdick said "The basis for the recommendation stems from the unique and complex hydrologic conditions in Basin 34. These conditions include a highly variable water supply from year to year, as well as during the year, and a high degree of interaction between ground and surface water."

He said that the *Utah Construction Co. v. Abbott* decree indicated the federal district court declared a need for such provisions in administering rights in the Big Lost River area. A 1936 state 6th District court decision made a similar determination, and water in the area generally has been administered under those terms in the years since. ☒

INTERIM MANAGEMENT (12/2005) Judge Melanson on November 17 issued an order aimed at clarifying which Idaho Department of Water Resources actions could be properly taken before his court.

He held that, contrary to the views of some parties, the subject of a complaint over water administration by Rangen, Inc., legitimately could be brought there. He tossed the issue back to IDWR, saying court action is premature – but, depending on the department's next step, left the door open to reconsidering it in the future.

"Prior to the entry of a final unified decree all administration in the Snake River Basin will be pursuant to orders of interim administration pursuant to I.C. § 42-1417," he wrote. "In an abundance of caution and in the exercise of its discretion, this Court is reluctant to set a precedence for 'reviewing' the Director's decisions every time there is a dispute concerning administration under the ostensible purpose of enforcing compliance with its various orders granting interim administration. The SRBA Court is not the proper forum for hearing such disputes unless it is clear that the Director has acted in violation of one of this Court's orders. In this case, the basis for the Director's conclusion is not entirely clear."

Two state statutes were central in the dispute.

One was I.C. § 67-5271, a part of the Administrative Procedure Act; it provides that in-agency administrative procedures must be exhausted before an agency dispute can be taken to court.

The other was § 42-1401D, a limitation of the jurisdiction of the SRBA Court, barring it from jurisdiction over most IDWR agency actions. When the Idaho Supreme Court interpreted that section in 2003, it held that "the legislature enacted Idaho Code § 42-1401D to provide that judicial review of Department actions that are subject to review under the Idaho Administrative Procedure Act shall not be heard in the Snake River Basin Adjudication district court, but shall be heard in the district court authorized by Idaho Code."

Melanson concluded, "In an appropriate case, therefore, this Court would have jurisdiction to enforce its own orders not involving review of IDWR's actions under the Administrative Procedure Act." The distinction is crucial, since the orders of the SRBA Court are carried out, in the main, through the Department of Water Resources. ☒

ADMINISTRATION RELATIONSHIPS (1/2006) Judge John Melanson in December approved one request for interim administration but rejected a state request for accelerated action on another.

Those followed a November 17 order also related to interim administration but which was aimed at clarifying which Idaho Department of Water Resources actions could be properly taken before his court.

On December 13, Melanson agreed to an order requested by the Department of Water Resources for interim administration in Basin 37. That basin, which has relatively complex issues partly because of groundwater concerns, includes the Wood River basin. The state asked for administration in part so that the rights in the area could be included in a water district, and so that it can properly protect senior water rights.

Melanson noted that no parties had objected to the interim administration request though all had been served. Also, he noted, "The available water supply in all or portions of Basin 37, Surface Water, is currently not adequate to satisfy some senior surface water rights and is projected in the future to be insufficient at times to satisfy these water rights. The Court finds that interim administration is necessary for the protection of senior priority rights."

Melanson did however say he had a concern about the timing of the request at a relatively early stage in the adjudication process in the district:

"At the hearing, this Court expressed the concern that the State's *Motion* represents the first time an order of interim administration was sought solely based on the director's recommendations and prior to the expiration of the objection period. As such, parties may have not had adequate opportunity to review either their recommendation or the recommendations of others for purposes of determining whether to contest interim administration. Presumably, if a party objects to the director's recommendation, they would also object to the water right being administered according to the recommendation during the pendency of their objection being heard. Based on the number of claims reported in the *Director's Report*, Idaho Code provides for a 120-day objection period.

"Because of the expedited nature of the State's *Motion*, parties only had 25 days, including the service period, within which to review recommendations and determine whether or not to contest the States' *Motion*. This Court acknowledges that in most basins where orders of interim administration have previously been entered objections were also pending. However, in those situations, the objection period had expired, a case management report had typically been prepared, and the Court had the benefit of knowing the number of outstanding objections and the type and scope of issues raised by those objections." ☒

BASIN 27 ADMIN ON HOLD (4/2006) A proposal for state interim administration of water in Basin 27, a matter of debate since last fall, was put on hold in March for another 60 days.

"The suggestion of a continuance is not a surprise to me," said Judge John Melanson.

At dispute is not the idea of some interim administration (by the state Department of Water Resources) but rather the extent and terms of it, especially whether it should include just ground water rights or surface water as well. That latter point was the main consideration in a number of objections filed by the federal government. ☒

Deer Flat

DEER FLAT INQUIRY (7/5/1993) The single most striking question anyone asked at the June 25 Idaho Water Users water law seminar came from a legislator, House Majority Leader Bruce Newcomb. He wanted to know the status of actions concerning the federal Deer Flats water claims on the Snake River, near Ada County.

The short answer: No immediate action.

"This is the one that could upset the whole applecart," Newcomb, an irrigation farmer near Burley, said later. "To me, that Deer Flats is the scariest part of the whole thing ... I think its one of the biggest threats to the pumpers upstream from there."

Deer Flats has received little attention in the adjudication so far, but its prospective impact is enormous.

The reserved right claims at Deer Flat refuge are generated at islands in the Snake River below Swan Falls and continuing near headwaters of the Brownlee Dam. The United States seeks, through claims from the 1930s, a need for minimum flow through that area to prevent land predators from crossing to the islands and attacking bird nests and birds that use those islands as a bird refuge.

Those claims amount to about 8,000 to 8,500 cubic feet per second in the Swan Falls area at southern Ada County; 8,400 cfs is about what Idaho Power's water right at Swan Falls was at the time of the Swan Falls decision in 1977. The Swan Falls agreement subordinated those minimum flows to lower levels, allowing irrigation and other users upstream generally to maintain their uses. However, the U.S. claim on Deer Flats could amount to as much as Idaho Power's putting a vast number of upstream water rights at risk.

"So now that's becoming a component in the objections and response process," said Department of Water Resources attorney Phil Rassier. "It puts the Swan Falls bottleneck back in place." A number of in-stream water claims are included in federal filings in the SRBA. ☒

TALKS FAIL (6/1998) Attempts to reach an out of trial settlement in the Deer Flats case within the SRBA apparently have failed. Federal Department of Justice attorney Jim Dubois told Judge Daniel Hurlbutt at the May 18 status conference that "I'm sad to report that negotiations have irrevocably broken down as far as Deer Flats is concerned."

He suggested the court set up a time to review a prospective briefing schedule on the case. As a start, he said, the United States in early July might file a motion for summary judgment, to which objectors could respond by July 22.

He said that sequential briefing would be best, since everyone filing a brief would be able to respond to everyone else's arguments. ☒

DEER FLATS AT SRBA (10/1998) With the Idaho Supreme Court's recent decision on Public Water Reserve 107 weighing heavily over the courtroom, attorneys on June 15 soft-pedaled it and battled over whether a reserved water right should be issued for the Deer Flat Islands Wildlife Reserve.

It was a case of the federal government against an array of other parties, including the state of Idaho and various private water users. The request for an in-stream flow right is located in the main stem of the Snake River downstream from most Idaho water users (roughly, from Homedale to the Brownlee Dam). That right could affect all the rights upstream, so this outcome of this case could be extremely important for much of the state, a milestone in the SRBA.

But Judge Daniel Hurlbutt indicated the corner may already have been turned in the PWR 107 case.

In that case, the federal government maintained it had a reserved water right claim on certain isolated bodies of water which it needed to protect the water from monopolization by a single water user. Hurlbutt rejected that interpretation, but the Idaho Supreme Court, overturning Hurlbutt, accepted and even strengthened it, apparently making reference to not just a reserved but an "express" right.

The two kinds of rights are different. Tougher standards are required and more limited uses are allowed for "reserved" rights, which are taken to be implicit in the purposes of federal legislation. An express right, on the other hand, is relatively absolute (closer to the kind of water right granted in conventional ways through the state Department of Water Resources).

The PWR 107 case and that of the Deer Flats islands have some similarities. "I have this horrible sinking feeling we've been through all of this before," Hurlbutt said in noting the similarity of some arguments in the two cases. "I still think they [the Idaho Supreme Court] found an express reservation of water…. This is an historic decision. It places the federal government at a level that far supersedes anything I've seen before. I had addressed that very issue and was overturned."

The attorneys grappled with that, to some extent. Attorney Scott Campbell, representing several water user groups, said that "the concept is well established that each reservation of federal land under an authorizing statute or document or treaty has to be analyzed on it own."

Beyond all that, the Department of Interior on one hand and other parties on the other disagreed on fundamental points.

Asked (in clarification) if the primary purpose of the reservation was preservation of islands as islands, Federal attorney James Dubois replied, "Absolutely, your honor" – and that since islands, by definition, are lands surrounded by water, some water was implicitly reserved for the purpose of maintaining them that way.

The larger purpose, he said, involved protection of the many waterfowl that stop over on the islands in the river. Many species, he said, use the islands but specifically do not use the shorelines.

An array of other attorneys offered a string of counter arguments. They contended that the federal claims on the islands were broken by changes in their status. The federal reservation of land was changed over the decades.

Clive Strong, chief of the Idaho Attorney General's Natural Resources division – one of the attorneys opposing the federal argument – noted that the refuge has existed for 64 years as one of a string of federal projects, among them reclamation projects. The refuge, he said, was intended to be harmonious with those reclamation projects. He said that the state supports the refuge and that it clearly would continue in operation regardless of the decision in this case. ☒

DEER FLATS: NO RESERVED RIGHT (1/1999) In a major loss for federal water right claimants and a win for state of Idaho claims, SRBA Judge Daniel Hurlbutt (in his last day on the bench) rejected a series of federal arguments.

State attorney Clive Strong, the chief of the Attorney General's Natural Resources division, said that about a million acres of irrigated farmland in the Snake River Plain upstream from Brownlee Reservoir could be affected.

Governor Phil Batt called the December 31 decision "a watershed opinion for Idaho. It removes an ominous threat to Idaho's ability to manage its own precious water."

Federal agencies have claimed an implied reserved water right at Deer Flat, water which implicitly is needed for the primary purpose of the federal land reservation, and without which the purpose of the reservation would be "entirely defeated."

Hurlbutt did reject a contention by parties filing against the federal government that a change in land status by a 1963 public land order in effect altered the purpose of the reservation. "Application of the literal language in Public Land Order 3110 leads to the conclusion that the Deer Flat National Wildlife Refuge presently consists of all lands formerly part of the Snake River National Wildlife Refuge and the original Deer Flat National Wildlife Refuge." But, noting that he had earlier approved federal implied reservations of water rights, Hurlbutt said the language of the reservation executive orders in the Deer Flats case is different enough from those other orders that it "does not rise to the level of an implied reservation of water."

"The Deer Flat National Wildlife Refuge was not established by Congress with the same clarity of purpose. While Executive Order No. 7691, which reserves 'islands', conjures up images of water, it is equally as likely that the term 'island' was a fortuitous non-legal description of the land that comprised the reservation. This leads to the conclusion that there was an intention to reserve only those lands, described in shorthand as 'islands.' That Executive Order No. 7691 contains a relatively brief description of the exterior boundaries of the area while stating that all islands within those boundaries are reserved supports this interpretation. Similarly, a 'refuge' may be established simply by setting these lands apart from the less restrictive laws applying generally to federal lands."

He concluded: "A federal reserved water right may only be implied if absolutely necessary to fulfill the primary purposes of the reservation. Unlike other implied reserved water rights granted by this court, the purposes of the Deer Flat Wildlife Refuge do not clearly necessitate water to be fulfilled. There is no enabling or authorizing legislation for the Deer Flat National Wildlife Refuge which requires water. Therefore, there is no legal basis upon which an implied federal reserved right may be based." ☒

SUPREME COURT RULES AGAINST FEDS (3/2001) The Idaho Supreme Court on February 22 upheld an SRBA Court decision rejecting federal water rights claims in the Deer Flats area. The high court decision generally backed the reasoning of the last decision by former SRBA Presiding Judge Daniel Hurlbutt, in December 1998.

In the new decision, the Supreme Court said, "The existence or absence of a reserved water right is a matter of federal law. In its prior decisions this Court has relied solely upon United States Supreme Court cases and relevant federal executive and legislative history. Reliance of this Court upon its prior decisions is intended simply to incorporate reasoning based upon federal law, not imply that there is applicable state law. In order to determine whether there is a basis for a federal reserved water right the Court will assess (1) whether there has been a reservation of land, and, if so, (2) whether the applicable acts of Congress contain an express reservation of water, and (3) if not, whether the applicable acts imply a reservation of water."

The court noted "There is no dispute that the United States withdrew land from the public domain in 1937 and 1963 respectively by reserving the islands in the Snake River. At the time the reservations were made, the purpose was to create sanctuaries for migratory birds to protect them from hunters and trappers so they would not become extinct and so they could continue to benefit husbandry." ☒

FEDS WON'T APPEAL (10/2001) The Department of Justice said in September that it will not appeal to the U.S. Supreme Court an Idaho court ruling greatly limiting federal water rights at the Deer Flat National Wildlife Refuge in southwest Idaho. The agency's deadline for filing a request that the U.S. Supreme Court review the state decision came and went on September 24. An appeal from the Idaho Supreme Court had been expected, but the U.S. Department of Justice opted not to pursue it.

Laird Lucas, an attorney for the Land and Water Fund of the Rockies, said it was "taking the federal government to task for not seeking cert." He said that conservation groups has been satisfied with the federal defense of water right claims in the area, and did not try to intervene partly for that reason. Now, he suggested, "They've shown they can be influenced by politics." ☒

City Rights

CITY REQUIREMENTS (6/1996) Another issue on the SRBA horizon is the impact of a new measure passed by the 1996 Idaho Legislature: loosening requirements for cities seeking to secure their water rights.

The measure (1996 Idaho Session Law 297) was drafted by the Idaho Department of Water Resources. It allows cities, municipal water providers and related entities to obtain water right permits which would meet anticipated as well as current needs, and in an expanded as well as the current service area. It also allows cities to purchase water rights (that are sold voluntarily) and hold them for a time without using them, without risking their forfeiture.

All this marks a substantial change in law. Existing Idaho law provides for forfeiture of unused water rights, and for water rights only which are in beneficial use at present, not prospectively in the future.

Backers of the measure, including the law firm Givens Pursley & Huntley (whose clients include several municipal water users), note that Idaho law intended to ban speculation in water by holders of the rights, and the new measure includes provisions designed to prevent that. Those include requirements that cities using the new provisions could not profit from them, build the infrastructure to carry water around the city, and have to show a clear future need for the water and show it is consistent with local planning.

"Three court decisions in Idaho suggest that the law recognizes the unique needs of municipalities to plan for the future," a Givens Pursley flyer on the bill noted. "However, the case law is not well developed or fully tested in Idaho. Moreover, some read Idaho's water code… [up until passage of this bill] as in conflict with the right of municipalities to hold water rights for future needs." ☒

ARCO FILING REJECTED (9/1997) A request by the city of Arco to file a late claim was rejected by Judge Hurlbutt March 14.

Attorney William Hollifield, representing the city, noted that it had experienced deep divisions on whether to file for the in-stream flow claims, which were bitterly opposed by a number of water users in the area. "The city council has been subject to much pressure," he said.

But Department of Water Resources attorney Dan Steckel noted that the city had specifically considered and rejected filing the claim once before. A change in membership on the city council resulted in the change of heart.

Judge Hurlbutt agreed with Steckel, saying that if he approved this request, he could be stuck with approving late requests (or canceling old ones) whenever a governing board changes membership and philosophy. ☒

POCATELLO CLAIMS REJECTED (11/2006) SRBA Judge John Melanson on October 10 rejected an unusual city of Pocatello claim to water rights – a claim it said the federal government effectively awarded it more than a century ago. The decision upheld an earlier special master decision.

The use of federal reserved rights is not unusual for federal and tribal claims, but highly unusual for those claimed by anyone else.

The city specifically cited the Pocatello Townsite Act, Act of September 1, 1888, Ch. 936, 25 Stat. 452, Section 10. The act was central in the formation of the city of Pocatello, located near the Fort Hall Indian Reservation.

The city noted that the act says, "That the citizens of the town hereinbefore provided for shall have the free and undisturbed use in common with the said Indians of the waters of any river, creek, stream, or spring flowing through Fort Hall Reservation in the vicinity of said town, with right of access at all times thereto, and the right to construct, operate, and maintain all such ditches, canals, works, or other aqueducts, drain and sewerage pipes, and other appliances on the reservation, as may be necessary to provide said town with proper water and sewerage facilities."

The legal issue was: Did that language include an award of a water right (or more than one) to the new city of Pocatello?

The dispute grew out of the June 1867 establishment of the Fort Hall reservation, and a followup treaty dated the next year which required that land could not be carved away from the reservation without approval of a majority of the adult male tribal members. In 1878, the Utah Northern Railway built a railroad north and south across the reservation, without permission. It did get permission to build another rail running west (toward Boise), but when non-tribal members started settling at the junction of the two lines – on reservation land, at what is now Pocatello – trespassing issues erupted, and nearly led to considerable violence. At one point federal Indian Affairs officials ordered the settlers at the junction to leave, but they refused, and armed conflict seemed likely.

In negotiations in 1887, Melanson noted, "The Indians said they did not want to sell their land but they were persuaded by [Indian Agent Peter] Gallagher that they should sell in order to get money to build irrigation ditches to irrigate their land. The Indians agreed and a Cession Agreement was signed by which the Pocatello Townsite was to be conveyed by the United States with the Railroad to receive a right-of-way for its existing tracks 'together with necessary grounds for station and water purposes'."

The piece of federal law the city of Pocatello relied on, however, was not part of that agreement but instead a separate congressional action, proposed by Commissioner of Indian Affairs, J.D.C. Adkins. His explanation of it to the then-Interior secretary said, "Inasmuch as conflicting opinions seem to prevail as to the source or sources from which the town will derive its supply of water, I have deemed it advisable, as a matter of precaution, to insert in the bill a clause providing for the use by the citizens of the town, in common with the Indians, of the water of any river, creek, stream or spring flowing through the reservation lands in the vicinity of the town with the right of access at all times thereto, and the right to construct, operate, and maintain all such ditches, canals, works or other aqueducts, drain and sewerage pipes, and other appliances on the reservation as may be necessary to provide with proper water and sewerage facilities."

Melanson added "two examples where in the past Congress has expressly granted a water right without a reservation of land. However, because none of the parties to this subcase dispute the fact that Congress would have had the authority under the Property Clause to convey a water right to the City had it intended to do so, the Court need not address the issue."

He pointed out too that "Section 10 expressly and unambiguously applied to "the waters of any river, creek, stream, or spring flowing through Fort Hall Reservation in the vicinity of said town. ... Of the City's thirty-eight (38) state-law based claims for which the City filed an alternative claim based on federal law only five of those claims are to surface sources. The remainder are groundwater claims."

And he concluded that even if he were to approve all other elements of the city's request, a city right under federal reserved right provisions would not work the same way as it does under lands covered by federal reserved. Some of the reason is a matter of chronology: "in 1888, Congress could not have intended that the City share in a portion of the Tribes' federal reserved water right because the concept of a federal reserved water right did not yet exist and would not exist for another twenty years. Therefore, it would be error for this Court to impute that Congress intended by section 10 that the City share in a portion of the Tribes' federal reserved water right." ⊠

NO RESERVED FOR POCATELLO (3/2008) A unanimous Idaho Supreme Court held in February that the city of Pocatello has no claim to a federal reserved water right, a claim it maintained in filing in the SRBA in 1990.

The city maintained that a provision of a law passed by Congress in 1888 gave it a reserved water right, which was comparable to rights claimed by federal agencies for federal lands such as national forests. Such rights can be extensive, since they can stretch to meet the needs or objectives outlined in the federal law establishing the territory or usage. The city later adjusted its legal reasoning, abandoning the reserved right claim but still arguing that the statute specifically gave the city a federal water right.

But in the decision written by Justice Jim Jones the Idaho Supreme Court said (as the master and SRBA Court did) that, while Congress could have established a specific water right for Pocatello, it didn't do that.

The decision laid out in blunt language the origins of Pocatello, originally a place called Pocatello junction located in the middle of the Fort Hall Indian Reservation. Two sets of railroad tracks, one authorized by the tribes and one not, were built through the reservation; they met at Pocatello, and a railroad support community was created there. Federal officials at one point ordered the non-tribal residents to leave, but eventually entered into negotiations with the Shoshone-Bannock Tribes for a cessation of the land in and near Pocatello, so the new community could remain. The tribes eventually agreed, and in the act of Congress ratifying the deal a provision concerning water was included:

"That the citizens of the town hereinbefore provided for shall have the free and undisturbed use in common with the said Indians of the waters of any river, creek, stream, or spring flowing through the Fort Hall Reservation in the vicinity of said town, with right of access at all times thereto, and the right to construct, operate, and maintain all such ditches, canals, works, or other aqueducts, drain, and sewerage pipes, and other appliances on the reservation, as may be necessary to provide said town with proper water and sewerage facilities."

The city of Pocatello claimed that provision gave it a federal reserved water right. It was opposed by, among others, the Shoshone-Bannock Tribes and the federal government. In the SRBA, the claim went to a special master and then to SRBA court, and both rejected the city's reasoning.

The Idaho Supreme Court concluded, "The question presented is whether Section 10 of the 1888 Act granted a federal water right to the City of Pocatello. We hold the Act created no such right. Rather, it granted the City access to surface water sources on the Reservation, along with the opportunity to establish a water right under state law." ☒

POCATELLO RETURNS TO SRBA (1/2009) A string of Pocatello city-related water right cases that were appealed all the way to the U.S. Supreme Court are back in SRBA Court, after the nation's high court denied certiorari – acceptance of the case for review.

Proceedings on 30 Pocatello water right cases had been stayed while appellate efforts were underway. But SRBA Judge John Melanson said on December 16 that he had been informed the U.S. Supreme Court had declined to consider the case.

"So, my thought is our next step were the court to issue a scheduling order," he told the attorneys involved in the case. ☒

Nez Perce tribal claims

NEZ PERCE NEGOTIATIONS (1/10/1994) State and Nez Perce tribal officials started negotiations on December 17 concerning the tribe's water claims in the SRBA. The claims mainly concern use of water on the reservation, though some in-stream flow claims also are included. ☒

CLAIMS: LET THE LITIGATION BEGIN (4/97) The long attempts at hashing it out through negotiations are over. The litigation is about to begin. And the stakes, in the cases involving Nez Perce Tribal claims to in-stream flow rights on the Snake River, are as high as any in the SRBA.

Usually low-key Boise attorney Don Olowinski put it this way in his March 14 memorandum on scheduling in the case: "As to the significance of the claims by the United States and the Tribe, there can be no doubt. The Tribal in-stream flow claims in the main stem of the Snake River essentially ask for all water in the river as of the year 1855. If granted, the Tribal claims could eliminate much of southern Idaho civilization."

That's one point of view, anyway; the claimants suggest nothing quite so drastic. But the effects of whatever rights the tribe is granted clearly could be important. Objectors in these in-stream flow cases, and direct contestants of the tribe, include a string of Idaho powerhouse organizations, including the J.R. Simplot Co., Idaho Power Co., A&B Irrigation District (based in Rupert) and a long string of irrigation districts (most of the major Idaho districts), Amalgamated Sugar Co., Ore-Ida Foods and the city of Pocatello. ☒

NEZ PERCE LEAD COUNSEL (6/1997) The organization of the massive Nez Perce water right litigation may be determined by the many rather than by the few. Following sharply conflicting arguments about how to structure this litigation within the SRBA – a litigation by the Nez Perce tribe that could impact water rights throughout western and southern Idaho – Judge Hurlbutt decided, before making a decision, to find out how many people exactly plan to participate in the litigation. The number theoretically could be hundreds, although several key participants at the May 20 Twin Falls status conference suggested it likely would be much smaller. ☒

MANY OBJECTIONS DROPPED (7/1997) As of July 19, there were 2,376 fewer objections to those claims. That is because Judge Hurlbutt did what he had said he would do: he dismissed them, all in one action. That in turn grew out of negotiations over how to proceed with the complex Nez Perce litigation. Because literally thousands of parties have an interest of some kind in the Nez Perce claims, the court and attorneys have been concerned for months with how to organize that portion of the case. Most favor some kind of "alignment" of parties, but fashioning such an alignment would be complex. To get a handle on who planned to participate and how, Hurlbutt on May 23 sent a mailer to the hundreds of parties who objected to some part of the Nez Perce claims.

That Notice of Active Participation gave objectors the option of participating actively (which would include attending most of the meetings and legal conferences over a period of years), or of retaining the objection but being a passive participant in the Nez Perce activities, or of dropping their objection. Failure to respond at all, Hurlbutt noted, would mean the objection would be dismissed. No response was received from the people and organizations – 223 in all. ☒

EVIDENCE DISPUTE (9/1997) As actions swirling around the Nez Perce claims grind on toward commencement of major litigation, the debate over submissions of evidence and documents – mainly involving the state of Idaho, the federal government and the Nez Perce tribe – moves on toward acrimony. On August 18, Department of Justice attorney Peter Monson and attorneys for the Nez Perce Tribe objected to the sheer number of inquiries from the state of Idaho for detailed evidence information.

Monson wrote (as did the tribe, in similar language): "Before the United States and the Tribe should be required to respond to any more discovery from any of the objectors, it is our position that the objectors, including but not limited to the State, must fully and completely respond our discovery requests. Regrettably, judging by the responses which we have received to date, such full and complete responses have not yet been provided by any objector."

The response from the state, on August 25, cast a light on some of the back-and-forth activity dominating the Nez Perce section of the SRBA this summer. Idaho Deputy Attorney General Steven Strack (the lead state attorney on the matter) replied to Monson and to Steve Moore of the Native American Rights Fund. "First," he wrote, "allow me to apologize for not following up on our promise to supply you with calibrated data. I have been in contact with Tom Payne, and they're working to gather the data. The problem is that the primary custodians of the data are currently in the field and are not expected to return to the office for some time. Tom Payne initially indicated it would take six weeks to gather the data. We are working to expedite that process. Of course, this delay works no prejudice to you, since you have refused to supply your calibrated data until you receive ours. I hope you will be patient, as we have been with you.

"For example," he said, "we have yet to receive any data from you regarding the extrapolation process Mr. Reiser used to determine flow recommendations on non-studied streams. Under the rules, that response was due June 1, 1997. Additionally, we have not yet received a comprehensible response to our request that you identify, for each claim, the months in which the claimed flow is based on passage flows, rather than in-stream habitat flows. That response also was due June 1."

He added: "In reviewing your responses, we had a number of concerns. First, in your response to Request for Admission No. 1, you indicate that the question is not within the scope of the proceeding. How can that be? *United States v Adair* describes a federal reserved in-stream flow right as "the right to prevent other appropriators from depleting the streams waters below a protected level." Request for admission No. 1 mirrors the Adair language. If you are not seeking an Adair-type right, what exactly is it that you are seeking?" ☒

A LITIGATION PLAN (7/1998) SRBA Judge Daniel Hurlbutt has set in motion a summary judgment schedule and a plan for bringing the massive Nez Perce water right claims to trial. While noting that "settlement has certain advantages," he also indicated that he may resolve some preliminary issues through summary judgment this summer.

As for the final court event, probably to occur in the year 2000, "anybody who expects a six-month trial" should find another trial to watch, he said.

The new round of activity was sparked by attorney James Tucker of Rosholt, Robertson & Tucker, representing Idaho Power Co. In following up on a March 17 Nez Perce ruling by Hurlbutt, he said, he'd prepared a motion for summary judgment – not to slow down the process, he said, but to "put some focus on it."

He acknowledged federal concerns that the case is not ready yet for summary judgment, since many facts (and the means for obtaining them) are still in dispute. Tucker suggested that shouldn't stop consideration of whether to start the summary judgment process; those disputed issues can be considered on their own merits as the process goes on, he suggested.

He pointed out that informal settlement efforts begun a year ago have failed, and raised the idea that summary judgment of some issues – or even raising the prospect of imminent settlement of certain issues – might revive that process.

Tucker said that parties in the group have talked with a mediator, Francis McGovern, who has agreed to participate in helping mediate the case. So, he said, "this is a package process in a sense; it entails continued litigation of these claims." ☒

MEDIATION LIVES (10/1998) Mediation apparently isn't yet a dead letter in the massive Nez Perce Tribe subcase. Failed efforts at mediation lasted through 1996 and 1997, but in June this year the central parties to the case, including Idaho Power, the tribe, the federal government and a coalition of objectors to the Nez Perce claims, agreed to take another stab at it.

Since then, attorney James Tucker said in an August 24 memo signed by attorneys for the various sides, "the Parties have reached agreement on the broad contours of a mediation process." He went on to say: "This mediation will differ from the initial negotiations in, at least, two distinct ways. First, a mediator, chosen by the parties, will be involved at the outset."

That is Francis E. McGovern, a professor at the Duke University School of Law in North Carolina, has agreed to serve as mediator, and won approval from all parties.

"Second," Tucker wrote, "the parties, with the assistance of the mediator, have agreed to explore the mediation process for an initial period of approximately 90 days. During this time, the parties intend to identify the issues that will be subject to the mediation and develop a procedure for proceeding with the mediation along with a time line for its completion. At the conclusion of this initial review period, the parties will assess the pros and cons of continuing with the mediation process and either agree to continue or else close the process. This litigation [of the claims] would proceed during this initial review period without deviation from the schedule the Court has previously set." ☒

MEDIATION ORDER (1/1999) Judge Daniel Hurlbutt issued the mediation and appointment order in December: "Professor Francis McGovern is appointed as Mediator, pursuant to Rule 16(k) of the Idaho Rules of Civil Procedure, for the purposes of the mediation of the claims that are the subject of these consolidated subcases, along with such other matters that necessarily relate to the resolution of those claims. This appointment shall continue until further order of this court. Should the Mediator, prior to January 15, 1999, advise the court that successful mediation of the claims is not possible within a reasonable period of time, this order shall be reconsidered."

It said that he will be compensated by assessments imposed on claimants and objectors, with half the cost to be paid by each side. Up to that point, McGovern's expenses had been picked up by Idaho Power Co. and its coalition, attorney James Tucker said. He also set up a schedule for action through 1999. Much of this grew out of a hearing on December 21, when Hurlbutt called for an update on mediation.

McGovern said that he had met with between 125 and 150 people so far, and "I have concluded relatively firmly that there seems to be a sincere interest to proceed with a mediation approach."

The week before, he said, he met with 10 legislators and Governor-elect Dirk Kempthorne. "It is somewhat difficult for the state to espouse a position at this moment" because of the transition of administrations, he said, "but I think within the next several weeks it will be possible to do so. I have no reason to believe there will not be a willingness by anyone to proceed on the mediation track."

That was seconded by a string of attorneys. "I think our position is as it always has been, that we're willing to consider negotiating or mediating these claims, said federal attorney Peter Monson. ☒

NO EXTRA-RESERVATION WATER (12/1999) In the first major ruling in the massive Nez Perce Tribe water right case within the SRBA, Judge Barry Wood held that the Nez Perce Tribe does not have off-reservation water rights for the purpose of preserving fish runs.

Wood said that he specifically was not ruling on tribal rights within the reservation. But some elements of this decision could prospectively be applied to future Nez Perce decisions, and it is likely to be parsed closely.

The case drew involvement from a significant number of parties. The claimants were the Nez Perce Tribe and the federal government, with the Shoshone-Bannock Tribes of southeast Idaho and the Native American Rights Fund weighing in as well. Objections came from the federal claims coalition, a collection of a large number of parties, and the Idaho Power Company.

The case was most recently argued in court on October 13. Wood said that he considered it fully submitted as of November 4, and delivered his decision just six days later. Wood said:

• "That pursuant to the 1855 Treaty (between the United States and the Nez Perce), the Nez Perce Tribe reserved among other things, the 'right of taking fish at all usual and accustomed places in common with the citizens of the territory.'

• "That the Nez Perce Tribe or the United States did not specifically intend to reserve an off-reservation in-stream flow water right for purposes of maintaining said fishing right.

• "That the scope of the 'right of taking fish in common' does not also confer an off-reservation in-stream flow water right.

• "That pursuant to the 1893 Agreement and its subsequent congressional ratification, the Nez Perce Tribe ceded all interest in unallotted lands not expressly reserved to the Tribe.

"That by the savings clause the Tribe again reserved its off-reservation in common fishing rights.

• "Therefore, the Nez Perce do not have Indian reserved in-stream flow water rights extending beyond the boundaries of the present Reservation, where ever those boundaries may be. This Court makes no ruling on the extent of on-reservation water rights of any kind."

Wood examined the history of treaties and other legal developments between the tribe and the federal government, and concluded that the tribe's rights are more limited than it and the federal government had suggested.

He noted that the center of the Indian claims comes from a provision in the 1853 Treaty providing for "the right of taking fish at all usual and accustomed places in common with the citizens of the territory…."

The "fishing in common" language, he said, has been interpreted by courts to mean that neither tribal or non-tribal fishermen can deprive the other of fishing opportunities.

But, he said, "the Supreme Court's interpretation is inconsistent with the creation of a water right. The off-reservation fishing right does not guarantee a predetermined amount of fish, establish a minimum amount of fish, or otherwise require maintenance of the status quo. Rather, the right extends to a proportionate share of the available fish run, whatever that run may be. Implicit in the ruling is the recognition the fish runs will vary or even be subject to shortages. This recognition is therefore inconsistent with the assertion that a water right is necessary for maintenance of fish habitat or fish propagation. Simply put, the Nez Perce do not have an absolute right to a predetermined or consistent level of fish."

He concluded that: "The Nez Perce contend that a water right must necessarily be implied to give effect to the Tribe's off-reservation fishing right. The Nez Perce admit that the Tribe did not intend to reserve a water right in 1855 because fish habitat was not contemplated," the judge wrote. "As such, the scope of the treaty fishing right must be ascertained to determine whether the application of canons of treaty interpretation imply a water right necessary to give effect to that treaty right." ☒

CHENOWETH-HAGE AND THE MEDIATION (12/2000) Outgoing U.S. Rep. Helen Chenoweth-Hage in November released an opinion piece, published in Idaho newspapers, expressing concerns about the mediation process intended to at least partially resolve disputes surrounding the Nez Perce Tribe claims in the SRBA.

Mediation negotiations have been underway for many months, and progress so far has been described as limited at best.

"But a lot of Idahoans do not understand what sorts of deals affecting those [water] rights are being made between state, federal and tribal officials in the Snake River Basin Adjudication process," Chenoweth-Hage wrote. "The reason is simple. The negotiations are being conducted in secrecy, behind closed doors. All Idahoans should be concerned about these negotiations. Not only are their vital water rights being affected, but the unintended consequences of some of the decisions could leave taxpayers holding a very large bill."

She said that, "Early in this process, the Nez Perce Tribe announced its position that the tribe has a right to virtually all the water in the Snake River watershed. This outrageous position would have placed the tribe's interests ahead of every other individual, business, municipality and irrigator in the state. Clearly, there were serious differences of legal opinion here. In December of 1998, a state district judge [Daniel Hurlbutt] ordered the parties into the current closed mediation process. Idahoans need to demand these negotiations be opened to public scrutiny."

In another argument likely to be sharply disputed by adjudication participants, she warned that, "If the state is held liable, owing compensation to these property owners, it is the taxpayers of the state who will pay the bill. If the state continues down this process, thousands of water right holders will lose their property. When these property owners realize that the state has negotiated away their property, they may seek to hold the state liable for 'takings.' These families and businesses would have strong grounds on which to pursue these claims. With water rights selling for between $500 and $1,500 per acre foot, the cost to Idaho taxpayers could be enormous." ☒

BURDICK ENDS MEDIATION (3/2003) Judge Roger Burdick on May 7 sent a letter to Francis McGovern, the mediator in the Nez Perce water rights dispute, saying that he will call a halt to mediation efforts effective June 2.

The mediation has been active for the five years since it was ordered into effect by then-SRBA Judge Daniel Hurlbutt in 1998.

"For some period of time I have been mulling the continued efficacy of the mediation on the Nez Perce issues in the Snake River Basin Adjudication," Burdick wrote McGovern, in a letter posted on the court's Internet web site.

He noted that "to try this lawsuit within a reasonable period of time, many years of preparation will be necessary. In addition, the Idaho Supreme Court has stayed [former SRBA] Judge [Barry] Wood's Nez Perce decision while awaiting results from this mediation. I have tried to move other issues forward in the Nez Perce case, but while Judge Wood's opinion is on appeal, the consensus has been that nothing can go forward."

That stoppage may have had rippling effects elsewhere in the SRBA.

Burdick wrote, "I tried to energize it [the mediation] with certain scheduling and status conferences in 2002 and there was some progress as a result. I know that many outstanding attorneys have tried their hardest to bring this mediation to a fruitful conclusion. I have immense respect for those individuals who see the greater good and try to bring their clients to it. I cannot imagine the amount of time and energy some of these great attorneys have put into this mediation. That is the main reason that I have kept a hands off attitude and allowed the mediation to progress at its own pace."

But time has run out, he suggested:

"I believe it is necessary to order this mediation to end on June 2, 2003. After that date I will not entertain any further motions to restart the mediation prior to trial. This Court expects to put this on a pure litigation track.

"I understand the costs the parties might be put to by this decision; however, I believe that this issue must come to some conclusion."

He thanked McGovern and praised him, and other participants in the process, for their efforts. ☒

SETTLEMENT? (4/2004) All they need, they said in mid-March, is a little more time to "memorialize it in writing." And SRBA Presiding Judge John Melanson agreed to give them that much. The occasion was the March 16 SRBA status conference in Twin Falls, when attorneys were scheduled to report to the judge on whether they have been able to make progress on the long, difficult negotiations over the Nez Perce tribal in-stream claims on the Snake River – one of the most significant developments so far in the SRBA.

(Ironically, though a large number of attorneys participated in the meeting, it went unrecorded by stenographer since no stenographer was there. It was, however, recorded on audio tape, with approval of all the parties)

"We've had conversations throughout the weekend, Monday and this morning as well," lead state attorney Clive Strong said at the meeting. "We believe we are approaching [an agreement] and we would like to proceed with the protective order remaining in place." The point, he said, was to turn conceptual understandings into a firm document.

"We have the litigation track moving," he said, but hoped to get the judge's approval to continue a few more steps on negotiation as well.

However far the agreement reached, it did appear to cover the situation as Strong described it: A line of other attorneys said they had the same understanding of the state of affairs.

Steven Moore, an attorney for the Native American Rights Fund and the Nez Perce, said "we essentially concur with the summary of where we're at …" He said he is, however, unsure what Strong was proposing concerning the separate springs and fountains claims or the stay of a key subcase.

"If we are unable to reach agreement in next week or 10 days we would come back to court," he said, and seek a litigation track for reporting of springs and fountains claims.

Department of Justice lead attorney Peter Monson agreed: "There has been significant progress made in negotiations since we last met with the court. We're close, and we need to get to the goal line …An additional week or 10 days would be in order to allow the parties to try to encapsulate an agreement in principle on some of the last remaining issues." ☒

SETTLEMENT RELEASED (6/2004) One day ahead of deadline, parties in the Nez Perce water right claims negotiations released the terms of the proposed deal. The "term sheet" was complex enough to be of a piece with one of the most important remaining components of the Snake River Basin Adjudication. Parties involved included the Nez Perce Tribe, the federal government (through the Department of Interior and Department of Justice), the state of Idaho, and a wide range of private parties (including many water users) across Idaho.

A press conference announcing the terms of the agreement was attended by Governor Dirk Kempthorne and Interior Secretary Gale Norton.

A summary sheet outlines the key components of the agreement:

• **NEZ PERCE TRIBAL COMPONENT** which, among other things, quantifies the Tribe's on-reservation, consumptive use reserved water right at 50,000 acre feet a year with a priority date of 1855; establishes a $50 million multiple-use water and fisheries resources trust fund; provides $23 million for the design and construction of a water supply and sewer system on the reservation; transfers management authority of Kooskia National Fish Hatchery to the Tribe; and transfers a portion of Bureau of Land Management-administered land within the reservation valued at $7 million to the Tribe.

• **SALMON/CLEARWATER HABITAT MANAGEMENT AND RESTORATION INITIATIVE** which, among other things, provides that in-stream flows will be established and held by the Idaho Water Resources Board for selected streams of importance to the Tribe; requires the State of Idaho to administer a cooperative agreement under the Endangered Species Act; and establishes a Habitat Fund to provide funding for habitat improvement projects.

• **SNAKE RIVER FLOW COMPONENT** which, among other things, provides that certain minimum flows will be decreed by the SRBA Court to the Idaho Water Resources Board; requires the State of Idaho to extend the provisions of State law for the term of the agreement to allow the Bureau of Reclamation to lease up to 427,000 acre feet of water from Idaho water banks for flow augmentation; and allows Reclamation to acquire up to 60,000 acre feet of consumptive natural flow water rights from the Snake River, with compensation to local communities for impacts caused by this acquisition.

Meeting the conditions set out in the agreement will be a major challenge. The backers said they plan to have that work wrapped up by April 2005, but acknowledge that is an ambitious goal.

That is true in part simply because of long list of "to-do" items. The mediator's term sheet, a concise description of what must be done, runs 49 single-space pages. A selection of some of the items noted:

• "The United States will establish a $50 million multiple-use water and fisheries resource trust fund for the Tribe to use in acquiring lands and water rights, restoring/improving fish habitat, fish production, agricultural development, cultural preservation, and water resource development or fisheries-related projects."

• "The SRBA court will decree the instream flows established by the IWRB on the streams listed in Appendix I, Lists A and B. In the event the State proposes to change any instream flow listed in Appendix I, Lists A and B, the State agrees to: 1) provide 6 months advanced written notice to the parties of any proposed change, including the basis for the proposed change and an analysis of the impacts, if any, resulting from the proposed change to fish and wildlife resources; and 2) to consult with the Nez Perce Tribe on a government-to-government basis prior to making the change."

• "The State will develop a program to provide incentives for improving fish habitat." ☒

CLEARING CONGRESS (12/2004) After a couple of months in which the Nez Perce package seemed stuck in Congress until at least next spring, developments took a big jump in November, and a bill containing all the congressionally-required provisions of the deal cleared Congress in November. ➲ *The measure was signed into law December 8.*

Idaho Senators Larry Craig and Mike Crapo, who worked on passage of S.2605 (the Snake River Water Rights Act of 2004) in the Senate, said on October 26 that action on federal legislation to help carry out key portions of the Nez Perce water rights agreement covering the Snake River probably had been stopped at least until early in 2005.

The measure did pass through the Senate Indian Affairs Committee and appeared to be ready for passage. But another senator – Craig and Crapo said they did not know who – then put a "hold" on the measure, freezing it in place, and keeping it from Senate floor consideration.

As late as the November 16 SRBA status conference, key advocates said they were doubtful the bill would make process this fall.

Then in late November an opportunity arose when the Senate and House considered the Fiscal Year 2005 Omnibus Appropriations bill, the main national budget bill. On request from Craig, the SRBA bill was incorporated in the budget bill and, swallowed whole, was passed along with all the rest through both Senate and House.

Craig remarked afterward, "Craig said, "This bill directs the federal government to facilitate compliance with the terms of the Settlement Agreement by authorizing federal funds and land exchanges. When this bill is signed into law, the Idaho State legislature will have the responsibility of determining whether this agreement should be executed. The Idaho Delegation also is very pleased with the cooperation we received from the Chairman and Ranking Member of the Senate Indian Affairs Committee, Senators Ben Nighthorse Campbell and Daniel Inouye." ☒

AT THE LEGISLATURE (3/2005) Three bills collectively providing for final state approval of the Nez Perce water rights agreement in the Snake River Basin Adjudication in late February took early steps toward final approval.

The bills, introduced in mid-February, are House Bills 152, 153 and 154.

They did not meet universal acceptance. But the votes on February 25 in the House Resources & Conservation Committee – 14-4 for one bill and 15-3 for the other two – appeared to foreshadow acceptance on the House floor, where Speaker Bruce Newcomb is one of the deal's prime advocates. Representatives voting no in committee were Ken Roberts, Lenore Barrett and Paul Shepherd for all three and Ken Andrus for one of them.

Not all of the favorable votes were enthusiastic. Representative JoAn Wood of Rigby said she voted in favor because of strong sentiment that way by water users in her district. At the same time, she was quoted as saying, "Never more than today do I regret the vote that I must make. In my heart I know, I believe this is wrong. I am pressed by my water users to vote for what they believe will protect them from further jeopardy, at the cost to others who stand in just as much jeopardy of their private property rights."

The Nez Perce Tribe has not yet acted on the proposal, and its approval, like that of the legislature, is needed by the end of March to ensure the agreement goes into effect.

There, as at the legislature, approval seems probable though not certain. A number of tribal members have said they think the tribe could prevail in court and win control of massive volumes of extremely valuable water rights.

Rebecca Miles of the Nez Perce Tribal Executive Committee told the Idaho Statesman in its February 26 edition that, "This agreement is emotionally difficult for me and my people," and she said she would not speculate whether the nine members of the tribe's governing council would approve it.

The deal has the backing of Governor Dirk Kempthorne and many key legislators including House Speaker Bruce Newcomb. But a number of legislators, notably in northern Idaho (Senator Skip Brandt of Kooskia has taken a lead role) and in the Boise area, have expressed concern about the state committing to the deal. And the Idaho Farm Bureau, one of the strongest lobbies in the state, has gone on record in opposition. ☒

AGREEMENT REACHED (4/2005) The long-running effort to resolve Nez Perce tribal claims on the main Snake River was resolved in March, as both the state of Idaho and the tribe formally approved the complex agreement released about a year ago.

Three bills collectively providing for final state approval of the Nez Perce water rights agreement in the Snake River Basin Adjudication, introduced in late February, were approved in March in the Idaho Legislature, and quickly signed into law by Governor Dirk Kempthorne, who had supported them.

The bills, introduced in mid-February, are House Bills 152, 153 and 154. The first was the measure specifically ratifying the agreement with the tribe and the federal government. HB 153 provided authority for water augmentation to assist with salmon runs, and HB 154 sets conditions for minimum stream flows which also are part of the agreement.

The last approval work occurred within the Nez Perce tribe, where members were divided over whether to give up claim to much of the Snake River water. The agreement did provide substantial benefits for the tribe, including direct financial compensation, fish enhancement and timberland assets. But the deal nonetheless led to considerable in-tribe soul searching, and the decision apparently was not a given.

But on March 29, the Tribal Council voted 6-2 to approve the agreement.

Kempthorne remarked after that decision, "This was the final step in a long journey. Think about the significance of this agreement, which resolved issues from documents signed by President James Buchanan in the 1850s and for decades to come will provide certainty and predictability for all of us, while preserving state water rights. With this very positive vote by the Nez Perce Tribe, now we know we can begin implementing the to-do list and the terms of the historic agreement."

Although all of the terms of the agreement now have been met, that does not necessarily foreclose the possibility of legal challenge later on. That prospect was raised during the in-tribal debate on the matter, and other possible attacks on the deal also are possible.

But for the time being, it appears likely to be approved by SRBA Presiding Judge John Melanson, and incorporated into the water rights system of the state. ☒

SHOSHONE-BANNOCK STANDING (7/2005) The first and to date major challenge to the Nez Perce Tribe water right agreement – whose terms have been met by federal and state entities and other parties – was turned back on June 27 by the Idaho Supreme Court.

That challenge was filed by the Shoshone-Bannock Tribes, in the form of 56 objections to the agreement. During the implementation process over the last year, the Southeast Idaho tribe warned that it had a number of concerns that were not addressed.

The Supreme Court decision does not necessarily mean they won't be.

The high court noted, "The 56 objections of the Shoshone-Bannock Tribe to the Nez Perce claims have never been litigated nor are they the subject of this appeal. Technically, they are still in the trial court. If there are questions concerning their efficacy in light of the Nez Perce Settlement Mediator's Term Sheet, those are proper matters for the trial court to create appropriate factual and legal records."

They could, in other words, be litigated in full in SRBA Court. ☒

NON-DISCLOSURE (9/2005) Mediation on the Nez Perce claims in the SRBA may be long over, but judicial orders banning disclosure of those discussions remain in force, Judge John Melanson ruled on August 22.

The issue arose on August 8, when William Bacon, an attorney for the Shoshone-Bannock Tribes, filed a motion asking for permission to "disclose limited draft portions of the proposed settlement agreement that may be covered by the Protective Order for Mediation dated July 21, 1999 to the Court."

Other parties opposed the motion, saying that the Shoshone-Bannock motion didn't indicate which documents were intended for release, and in any event violated the rules of evidence on release of draft settlement agreements. Melanson generally sided with those parties. He noted that a protective order imposing confidentiality applied to everyone participating in the Nez Perce talks, and that it had not yet been lifted. ☒

SHO-BANS END OPPOSITION (11/2005) The Shoshone-Bannock Tribes of eastern Idaho, which have expressed concern with a number of provisions of the Nez Perce water right claims deal, said in late October they will drop their opposition to the agreement.

Opposing parties in either the minimum stream flow claims or the multiple use claims had until November 1 to deliver their objections in what is anticipated to be the final round of activity in the Nez Perce arena.

The Idaho Supreme Court on June 27 remanded many of the tribe's issues to SRBA Court, and denied the Shoshone-Bannock Tribe's objection. The final court action, needed to lock the agreement into legal place, began last summer when SRBA Judge John Melanson set a schedule for handling any remaining objections to the agreement. ☒

OBJECTION TO SPRING (4/2006) An objection to the sensitive Nez Perce water rights has been scheduled for a hearing on May 18.

The objection, which relates to use of a spring, is not in itself part of the big Nez Perce Tribe agreement which is still in final stages of settlement. But it does affect tribal water rights, and it marks a point of potential conflict between the tribe and some of its neighbors.

"My concern," said Judge Melanson, "is that the Nez Perce agreement is really of historic significance." While noting that his court has not yet formally acted on it – one of the conditions before the terms of the deal become final – he suggested, "my thought was that protracted litigation, with a virtual certainty of an appeal by one side or the other, should be avoided."

Noting that the parties had been in discussion, he urged that effort to continue. ☒

REDDEN BLASTS DEAL (10/2006) U.S. District Judge James Redden, sitting at Portland, on September 27 followed up earlier decisions on salmon recovery and Snake River water use by holding that the Endangered Species Act trumps all other water rights considerations – possibly throwing out pieces of the long-negotiated Nez Perce Tribe water rights agreement on the Snake River basin. Specifically, he ordered federal agencies to rewrite their salmon protection plans. He criticized federal agencies for drawing environmental plans intended to match terms of the Nez Perce agreement.

The Idaho congressional delegation, including Senators Larry Craig and Mike Crapo, and Congressmen Mike Simpson and C.L. "Butch" Otter, in turn blasted Redden and said they "would take whatever action is necessary and possible to turn back this explicit threat to Idaho's water and future."

The implications of the Portland judge's decision were not clear, but the delegation warned that it "could lead to the dewatering of millions of acres of irrigated land in the name of salmon recovery, much as an earlier ESA decision did to Oregon's Klamath Basin in 2001. That would ruin the economy and individual livelihoods in rural communities throughout southern Idaho."

The Nez Perce agreement does include provisions intended to help the fish. It lets the U.S. Bureau of Reclamation send 487,000 acre-feet of water from areas around the upper Snake River to increase downstream flows for salmon migration. Redden suggested in his decision that was not enough. ☒

A LAW REVIEW MENTION (12/2006) Much of the current *Idaho Law Review* quarterly (published on November 3, as Volume 42, by the University of Idaho College of Law) was devoted to the settlement of one of the key issues in the Snake River Basin Adjudication in recent years:

The Nez Perce tribal water right claims on the Snake River. The years-long process involved a large number of both governmental and private entities, and whole squadrons of attorneys. A number of those participants contributed chapters to the *Review*. ☒

NEZ PERCE PROVISION PULLED (1/2008) The Idaho congressional delegation and possibly the Nez Perce Tribe water right agreement took a hit in December when a provision aimed at fulfilling terms of the sweeping water agreement was deleted from an appropriations bill, at the request of California Senator Dianne Feinstein. Senator Larry Craig attempted to restore the provision, but was unable to do so before its passage.

The full Idaho delegation had supported inclusion of the provision.

The provision would have incorporated a biological opinion covering governance of several dams; passage of it is a part of the Nez Perce agreement, which resolved a massive water right dispute covering much of the Snake River Basin. But it may have run afoul of recent rulings by U.S. District Judge James Redden at Portland, who has said that federal agencies have not been properly acting to preserve salmon runs in the region. ☒

Sho-Pai rights

RULING ON SHO-PAI RIGHTS (1/2007) Judge Melanson on December 12 issued a final order and approval of a consent decree on the long-running set of subcases of the Shoshone-Paiute water rights.

"... the court has determined that there is no just reason for delay of the entry of a final judgment and that the court has and does hereby direct that the above judgment or order shall be a final judgment upon which execution may issue and an appeal may be taken as provided by the Idaho Appellate Rules," Melanson wrote.

The case goes back to a 1998 filing by the federal government on behalf of the Shoshone-Paiute tribes, claiming what became 363 claim numbers. With later amendments, the total grew to 369.

Objections came from the state of Idaho, the J.R. Simplot Company and the Riddle Ranch, which is located near the reservation. Negotiations between the parties went on for years, but in October 2005 the three objecting parties made an offer to the federal government to settle. A month later, the offer was accepted, and the matter went to court.

Melanson eventually accepted much though not all of the agreement. He found some errors in the original reports, and ordered those corrected.

The parties agreed (and Melanson accepted) on federal reserved water rights, which as the judge noted "are not subject to loss through non-use."

And, he said, "These water rights describe purposes of use, points of diversion and places of use, which are not intended to preclude the Tribes' ability to change those purposes of use, points of diversion and places of use within the Duck Valley Indian Reservation pursuant to a tribal water code, provided however, that any change shall not enlarge the right.... the Parties agree that the remaining claims asserted by the United States as trustee for the benefit of the Shoshone-Paiute Tribes in the SRBA within the State of Idaho will be decreed as disallowed."

Melanson also agreed the deal would not set any other precedents:

"Nothing in this Consent Decree shall be construed or interpreted to establish any standard to be used for the quantification of federal reserved water rights or any other Indian water claims of any other Indian Tribes in any judicial or administrative proceeding. This Consent Decree is the result of good faith negotiations between the Parties for the purpose of implementing the United States' conditional acceptance of the Objectors' offer of judgment regarding the United States' claims for the benefit of the Shoshone- Paiute Tribes. The Parties agree that no offers and/or compromises made in the course thereof shall be construed as admissions against interest or be used in any legal proceeding and nothing in this Consent Decree shall be read as an admission or determination by the Parties that any of the actions anticipated by this Consent Decree are necessarily required under any federal or state law." ☒

Private adjudications

NOT CONCLUSIVE (10/97) The Hagerman group and the SRBA Court had held that a prior decision was conclusive evidence of the nature of a water right. The Supreme Court disagreed, noting that nowhere in Idaho law "is the Director 'obligated to accept a prior decree' issued in a private adjudication "as being conclusive proof of the nature of a water right.' This is especially true in light of longstanding decisions in Idaho that decreed water rights, although protected like any other water right, are not insulated from re-examination by the court and may be lost or reduced based on evidence that the water right has been forfeited."

The Court concluded that "While a decree issued in a private adjudication is evidence of a legal right, the Director is not obligated to accept the decree as conclusive proof of the extent and nature of the water right and the district court's decision is reversed in this respect." ☒

Joyce and the LU Ranch

LAND TITLE AND DIVERSIONS (5/2000) In 1992 the LU ranching company filed water right claims for stock watering with an 1872 priority date; some of those claims were located on federal land. It based the claims on earlier claims by its predecessors at the property. The Bureau of Land Management challenged the claims.

Former Special Master Fritz Haemmerle said in April 1999 that the earliest priority date LU Ranching could claim is 1976, that being when company was founded, since there was no record of a conveyance of an earlier valid right from someone else.

The case presented three questions, Judge Wood wrote:

• "Did the subject state-law based water rights, used for in-stream stockwatering on federal grazing allotments, transfer via the instruments (deeds) conveying the privately owned base property to which the grazing preference is attached?"

Master Haemmerle held in a summary judgement that the water right had not been passed from earlier holders to LU. Wood took some issue with that, and said material questions of fact exist, and therefore should still get its "day in court" to go over those matters.

"In this Court's view," Wood wrote, "it is error to create a "hard and fast rule" that water rights perfected on federal public land are as a matter of law *per se* appurtenant to the federal public land, particularly under the facts of these subcases. In Idaho, it is well established that the ownership of a water right can exist independently from the ownership of the land on which the water right is used." And, he suggested, the fact that the land involved was not the location of the water right cut against the idea of inheriting the water right through buying the property. He did not rule out the possibility, however, suggesting several ways that could have been done.

• "Is Idaho Code §42-113(2) unconstitutionally retroactive as applied in these subcases?"

• "Did the Special Master err in refusing to consider LU's motion for summary judgment regarding the United States' claims for stockwater rights on the grazing allotments?"

LU AND NOTICE (12/2001) Are water users being unconstitutionally denied access to the Snake River Basin Adjudication, and losing their water rights because they were never given a chance to participate?

SRBA Court officials have for years devoted extensive effort to ensuring adequate notice in the massive case. But on November 6 LU Ranching Inc. mounted a challenge to those procedures with the Idaho Supreme Court, filing suit against the state of Idaho and the federal government.

Those parties originally were expected to respond to the opening brief by the end of November, but asked for extensions which would allow for filing on December 20.

"At issue in this appeal," it said, "is whether default decrees can be entered against known adverse parties in the SRBA without first giving them notice of the proceedings against them."

LU Ranching, a cattle ranching firm, has lands scattered in a number of locations. It operates in part on Bureau of Land Management lands, in grazing allotments (including the Cliffs, South Mountain, Cow Creek Individual, McKay FFR, Lowry FFR allotments).

The brief said "In this capacity, LU Ranching timely filed numerous claims for stockwater rights in the SRBA … The Idaho Department of Water Resources issued a director's report for LU Ranching's claims."

The BLM filed objections to those claims, and also its own competing claims.

"LU Ranching was not given notice of the filing of these claims, and it was unaware of the United States' actions in this regard," the brief said.

Eventually, the company said, "The United States obtained partial decrees on the water rights at issue without notice ever being given to LU Ranching of the underlying claims. Moreover, other procedural safeguards allegedly in place to prevent injustice in the SRBA proceedings apparently were never employed. With respect to the United States claims, it appears that the IDWR conducted no investigation and reported the claims in the United States' director's report simply with a statement of the claimed elements."

LU Ranching filed a motion in September 2000 to set aside those partial decrees; SRBA judge Roger Burdick denied that motion in May 2001. The appeal to the Idaho Supreme Court sprang from that denial.

The appellant said that "Those opposing LU Ranching's motion to set aside [the partial decrees] have relied on what can only be described as a diversionary tactic to promote their position, claiming that notice by mailing would require mailing of billions of documents. This rationale for denying LU Ranching's motion to set aside was adopted by the district court."

Beyond the specifics of that case, the LU Ranching brief charged, the whole notice procedure in the SRBA's administrative order – and for that matter in the Idaho Code – is flawed and unconstitutional.

Both, it said, "fail to meet the minimum due process requirements mandated by the Idaho and United States Constitutions because they permit parties to obtain default decrees without first giving notice of proceedings to known adversary parties." It cited the 14th amendment of the United States Constitution and Article I, Section 13 of the Idaho Constitution. ☒

NOTICE WAS SUFFICIENT (5/2003) The Idaho Supreme Court on April 3 held that ample notice was given the LU Ranching Company in a contest over federal water right claims. The case had broad prospective impact. If the decision had gone the other way, numerous claims in the Snake River Basin Adjudication, especially many federal claims, probably would have had to be re-litigated. Some case observers speculated such a decision could have upended the whole SRBA.

The unanimous high court decision upheld a ruling by SRBA Judge Roger Burdick. Essentially, the high court said, LU is challenging the constitutionality of several of the statutes governing the SRBA and of the court's operating rules for the case.

"LU Ranching contends that requiring parties to sift the Director's Reports so that they notify themselves as to claims potentially or actually adverse to their own is too onerous and risks the deprivation of water rights, maintaining that water right claimants who object to or knowingly file conflicting claims against other known and identified water claimants must personally serve such parties when pursuing adverse decrees," the court noted.

However, it said, "there is no doubt that LU Ranching was aware of the commencement of the SRBA and aware that action concerning its claimed rights and the rights of others in the region would be adjudicated. It received notice of the Director's report, the nature of that report, its location, and the way to access the report, as well as the offer of technical assistance if necessary. AO1 (6)(d) allows one to subscribe to the SRBA docket sheet for a nominal fee. The method of notice given was reasonably calculated to give LU Ranching and all other claimants the information to pursue and protect their rights. In fact, LU Ranching found the information when it examined the Director's report. Requiring personal service of all potentially adverse claims could well involve a flood of paper that would do no more than what is done by existing procedures ...

"Despite claims that following the procedures in the SRBA would require a Herculean effort, LU Ranching was able to recognize the conflicts and get notice of the objections to its water claims once it actually looked at the Director's Report. LU Ranching simply looked too late. Its difficulties arise from a lack of timely attention, not inadequacy of notice." ☒

LU: NO RECONSIDERATION (6/2005) Judge Melanson on April 29 declined to reconsider his order on water rights covering public grazing lands, as LU Ranching had requested.

The question concerned whether a rancher who had a permit to graze – and water – cattle on public lands could convey the water rights as an appurtenance of his land if he sold his property. The judge held that such a transfer was an issue of fact which might vary case by case.

LU Ranching had sought priority dates for its grazing on public lands that preceded enactment of the Taylor Grazing Act in 1934. In his original decision, Melanson held that they were not entitled to the early dates.

"LU argues that the Department of Interior would not have awarded a grazing permit unless the applicant had shown prior use before 1934. According to LU, the only way for applicants to obtain a preference grazing right was to demonstrate prior use of the same rangeland. LU argues that because the Department of Interior awarded grazing permits based on prior use, the granting of the permit is proof that prior use occurred. It is true that the Department of Interior did award permits to users showing prior use. However, as the regulations and cases interpreting those regulations make clear, prior use, although the preferred criterion, *was not the only criterion* for awarding grazing permits," Melanson noted (italics his).

"The regulations certainly gave preference to landowners who showed prior use of the rangeland. However, a landowner who did not show prior use could also gain a grazing permit, as could a nomadic herder (which was not the case here). Because of this, it cannot be said that, as a matter of law, the awarding of a permit would only follow a proof of prior use by the grazing applicant. The regulations governing the order of preference listed three different preferences, with the highest being land ownership and prior use. It is not logical to state that any permit issued *must* have been, as a matter of law, pursuant to that first preference."

But the key to this particular case, Melanson suggested, was the lack of any paper document transferring the water right:

"...even if it is established that a predecessor grazed in a particular area for purposes of establishing a water right, the next issue is whether the predecessor intended to transfer the water right with a place of use on public land as an appurtenance to a parcel of private or base ranch property. The issue in these subcases turns on the satisfaction of the statute of frauds. LU introduced no instruments in its chain of title expressly conveying or otherwise even referring to the existence of water rights on the subject public lands. Nevertheless, LU was given the opportunity, at trial, to put on evidence to show that a grantor of private base ranch property intended that the instrument of conveyance included, as an appurtenance, a water right with a place of use located elsewhere." ☒

JOYCE PRIORITY DATES (9/2005) SRBA Judge John Melanson on August 3 reversed a special master ruling and said that Joyce Livestock had established 1935 priority dates for three water right claims by the federal government. He disallowed the claims for 55-11061, 55-11385, 55-12452 and, instead of remanding the case to the special master as has sometimes happened, declared it settled, at least for purposes of appeal.

Perhaps more significantly, Melanson stepped back from the narrow issues and, in making his ruling, took a larger look at the matter of stockwater rights. It has to be considered, he said, in the larger context of the management of public lands: "This dispute over water rights has less to do with the administration of water than the contemporary administration of public lands."

The case grew out of a water right claim by Joyce Livestock Company for .23 cfs from Jordan Creek in Owyhee County; the firm claimed a very early priority date of 1865, for the purpose of watering livestock. The federal government filed conflicting claims, noting that the rights were located on federal land, and objected to the Joyce claim.

The federal government objected to the priority date, points of diversion and places of use. The state of Idaho then argued that the priority date should not be earlier than the enactment of the Taylor Grazing Act, in 1934, which was when the federal government began administering public lands used for grazing. When the federal government agreed with that, the state withdrew from the subcases.

The Taylor Grazing Act date point has been an important factor in stockwater grazing right issues in the SRBA.

The case went to then-Special Master Fritz Haemmerle, and in October 2003 he found in favor of the federal agencies. Joyce challenged that finding before Melanson.

Melanson: "The Special Master ruled that Joyce's predecessors-in-interest did not appropriate water rights by simply grazing cattle on open public rangeland or on defined grazing allotments following the implementation of the Taylor Grazing Act. The Special Master ruled that grazing cattle in common on the public rangeland was insufficient to establish the requisite intent needed to establish a water right. The Special Master held "the preponderance of the evidence is that none of Joyce Livestock's grantor's intended to appropriate the water of Jordan Creek for in-stream watering." The Special Master recommended that Joyce therefore failed to acquire a stockwater right from any of its predecessors-in-interest." ☒

SUPREME COURT UPHOLDS JOYCE (3/2007) In a long-running subcase of the Snake River Basin Adjudication closely watched by water attorneys, the Idaho Supreme Court in February held that a livestock company which grazes on federal range land has water rights on that public range land.

In *Joyce Livestock Company v. United States*, written by Justice Daniel Eismann and released February 9, the court generally affirmed an SRBA Court decision on the matter, but sent it back to district court for a redetermination of the rights priority dates, which the high court rejected.

Joyce Livestock, based in Owyhee County, owns about 10,000 acres of property, including what once were 29 homesteads and small ranches. It runs cattle on much of that land and also on federal lands.

Patents on the Joyce property date back to 1898, and the ranch filed for in-stream stockwater rights in Jordan Creek that same year. United States claims filed in the SRBA for some of that same area – area where Joyce grazed cattle on federal property – but taking in federally-owned land where the Joyce cattle were grazed, date to 1934, when the Taylor Grazing Act was passed by Congress.

When the dispute came before an SRBA special master, he recommended the Joyce rights be denied because there was no evidence that Joyce Livestock's predecessors had attempted to exclude other ranchers from using that same water source. He wrote that the water right claimed by the United States should be granted with a 1934 priority date.

SRBA Judge John Melanson, however, said the special master was wrong in his analysis that Joyce Livestock's predecessors lacked the intent required to obtain a water right, that the necessary intent could be inferred from the act of watering livestock.

But Melanson also held that the Joyce predecessors could not have obtained water rights on federal land unless their applications for grazing permits filed under the Taylor Grazing Act showed that they understood or believed they had acquired such water rights. Since that evidence was lacking from the grazing permit applications, the district court held that the earliest priority date Joyce Livestock could establish was April 26, 1935, when one of the predecessors filed an application for a grazing permit.

The SRBA Court awarded Joyce a water right with a priority date of April 26, 1935, and denied the federal claims. The district court also denied Joyce Livestock's request for an award of attorney fees against the United States, holding that it was not entitled to an award.

Neither side having gotten what they wanted – Joyce its 1898 priority date, and the federal government any right at all – both appealed to the Idaho Supreme Court.

Water rights on federal land. The Idaho Supreme Court agreed with Melanson that Joyce Livestock had acquired a water right on federal land. It based that on more expansive findings:

- An appropriator can obtain a water right in non-navigable waters on federal land.

● Under the constitutional method, an appropriator could obtain a water right for stock watering without diverting the water from the water source.

● Joyce Livestock's predecessors obtained water rights on federal land for stock watering simply by applying the water to a beneficial use through watering their livestock in the springs, creeks, and rivers on the range they used for forage.

● The water rights that ranchers obtained by watering their livestock on federal land were appurtenant to their patented properties.

● A water right appurtenant to real property is conveyed with the real property unless it is expressly reserved or the parties clearly intended that the conveyance not include the water right.

Priority dates. The high court said Melanson erred, however, on its assessment of priority dates for Joyce Livestock. The Supreme Court said the priority dates to be considered for the Joyce predecessors should relate to their beneficial use of the water: that is, by grazing livestock where they would have access to the water sources at issue.

"As such," a court release said, "the Court held the district court erred by: 1) Refusing to recognize in-stream water rights on federal rangeland unless subsequent applications for grazing permits identified those water rights; 2) Holding that the failure to list a water right in the application for a grazing permit constituted abandonment or non-use of the omitted water right; 3) Failing to give consideration to the fact that a predecessor was issued a grazing right permit that demonstrates an earlier use."

Federal in-stream rights. The Supreme Court agreed with Melanson on his analysis of in-stream water rights for stock watering. The federal agencies had claimed in-stream rights, relying on federal ownership of the lands, alongside the Bureau of Land Management administration of the property under the Taylor Grazing Act.

The district court held that simple ownership or management did not rise to beneficial use of the water, as defined by the Idaho Constitution, and said it therefore had no state-based water rights. The Idaho Supreme Court agreed with that analysis.

The high court noted, "Under Idaho law, an appropriator need not have a possessory interest in the land upon which the water source is located in order to obtain a water right."

LU UPHELD TOO (3/2007) On the same day it released the Joyce decision, the Idaho Supreme Court released another, related, opinion, on *LU Ranching Co. v. United States*. Here too, a private party contesting with the federal government over water right claims saw its side upheld.

As in the case of Joyce, the high court generally upheld a decision by Judge John Melanson to award rights to the private party, in this case LU Ranching, and agreed with its denial of an attorney fees request. But it similarly returned the case to the district court level for a re-determination of the priority date for the claims.

This decision was also written by Justice Dan Eismann, and it also was unanimous.

The LU Ranching operation in Owyhee County, which since 1976 has owned about 5,000 acres of land, is a successor to a series of smaller ranching interests. Those interests had rights with an 1872 priority date. Among the LU's interests were three grazing allotments (called the South Mountain, Cow Creek and Cliff) – where cattle could be grazed on federal land – on Bureau of Land Management land, set up under the Taylor Grazing Act. As in the case of Joyce, the federal government maintained that it properly owned water rights for the federal portion of that property.

At the special master level, the first determination was that patents and affidavits of homestead were enough to establish that they had been using federal land and the water on it as soon as the first person began living there. The earliest of these patents was issued on September 29, 1886, to Ezra Mills, who said he had lived on and worked the homestead since June 10, 1876. With that as a basis, the special master held that LU Ranching was entitled to a priority date of June 10, 1876. As with Joyce, both sides wanted district court review.

It concluded, "We affirm the judgment of the district court holding that LU Ranching has established water rights and denying its request for an award of attorney fees. We vacate the district court's determination of the priority dates of LU Ranching's water rights and remand this case for redetermination of such priority date(s) in a manner consistent with our opinion in *Joyce Livestock Company v. United States*. We deny LU Ranching's request for an award of attorney fees on appeal." ⊠

U.S. SUPREME COURT ON FEES (12/2007) The attempts by LU Ranching Company and Joyce Livestock to recover attorneys costs in their long-running water rights case against federal agencies—a case in which they prevailed in the Idaho Supreme Court—hit a roadblock in November, when the U.S. Supreme Court declined to hear the case.

The courts have said that although the ranchers were legally correct, the federal case was reasonable, not arbitrary or flimsy although "a serious misunderstanding of water law." ⊠

Idaho Power challenges Swan Falls

SWAN FALLS II? (6/2007) In May Idaho Power said its proper rights at the Swan Falls are being impinged upon. Former House Speaker Bruce Newcomb was quoted as calling the new case "Armageddon." Attorney General Lawrence Wasden called it "big, very big."

The 1984 settlement preserved nearly all water use upstream of Swan Falls but guaranteed flows to Idaho Power at the dam, a winter flow of 5,600 cfs and a summer flow of 3,900 cfs – well below its original allowance, but accepted as a de facto guarantee of flow, which water rights generally are not. However, the company pointed out in its new filing, water flows at the dam have frequently fallen below that level.

The new filing said the state had acted in bad faith by allowing at the time, and continuing to allow, upstream water users it knew would impinge on Idaho Power's rights. It argued that "… the state of Idaho does not hold legal title to Idaho Power's water rights, and title to the water rights referenced in the Swan Falls Agreement is quieted … ."

State attorneys say the state has managed the original deal as agreed, and that the utility now is trying to in effect change its terms.

In an analysis in the *Idaho Statesman*, reporter Rocky Barker outlined the next steps as Idaho Power sees them: "The company wants the state to aggressively reduce the depletion of the Eastern Snake Plain Aquifer, which has led to lower flows in the Snake River. It also wants the state to pay the company when it tries to reduce this depletion by recharging the aquifer — seeping surface water into the aquifer— for the hydropower it says it would lose.

"It could force the state to shut down many more of the groundwater users who are threatened with loss of water now in a legal struggle with the state and surface water users over continued pumping from the aquifer for crops, dairies, food-processing and city water. It could force the state to dry up hundreds of thousands of acres of farmland, primarily in the Magic Valley, unless the farmers reached their own accommodation with Idaho Power." ☒

SUING THE FEDS (11/2007) Idaho Power Company on October 16 filed in U.S. District Court a long-anticipated lawsuit against the U.S. Department of Interior, saying it long has been in contravention of a 1923 agreement concerning the release of water at American Falls Dam.

The utility said the federal agencies (including the Bureau of Reclamation) have managed their water in ways that have denied Idaho Power water it ought to have.

No federal response to the claims was immediately available. Nor was there an immediate indication of whether the case might properly be lodged in the Snake River Basin Adjudication court.

The company has sought about 300,000 acre-feet of water, mainly for hydropower purposes. ☒

OVERTURN REJECTED (5/2008) Presiding Judge John Melanson on April 18 delivered a consequential ruling – which may be appealed to the Idaho Supreme Court – rejecting Idaho Power Company's arguments seeking to overturn parts of the Swan Falls water agreement from the 80s, claims that if upheld could dramatically change the shape of water rights in Idaho.

The holding: "Granting state of Idaho's motion for summary judgment on different grounds. Holding Idaho Power's rights exceeding the minimum flows are held in trust pursuant to the October 25, 1984 Swan Falls Agreement, which the Court finds to be unambiguous. As a term and condition of the agreement, Idaho Power agreed to the regulatory authority of the State as is now codified at I.C. 42-203B. The Court makes no ruling regarding the scope of the State's regulatory authority other than as agreed by Idaho Power in the October 25, 1984 Swan Falls Agreement. Holding that trust res contains water rights is dispositive of cause of action for mutual mistake."

The whole of the Snake River Basin Adjudication evolved from that agreement, between Idaho Power, the state of Idaho and other parties including Congress, in 1984. The agreement (which in turn followed a state Supreme Court ruling which appeared to give broad control over Snake River water to the utility) did award Idaho Power a substantial amount of water which it could use for hydropower generation at dams it operates on the Snake; those dams include Swan Falls, the legal centerpoint.

More recently, however, Idaho Power challenged the validity is parts of that agreement. Among other things, it noted that water flows (including groundwater flows) are much better understood now,and that a number of water shortages have ensued in recent years. It sought a revision of the deal in SRBA Court.

Several of these issues had arisen in 26 Idaho Power water rights claims, which the SRBA Court consolidated into one case. But Melanson pointed out that "Partial Decrees were issued for the three hydropower claims in the name of Idaho Power on November 11, 1997, and did not contain subordination remarks." Last May, it sued the state of Idaho with those contentions in hand, arguing both sides had made a "mutual mistake." A mass of briefings ensued, and an oral hearing was held on February 15.

Melanson rejected those arguments. The Twin Falls *Times-News* said in an editorial about the decision, "Turns out Idaho Power doesn't get to rewrite history. On Friday, 5th District Judge John Melanson declined to turn the world upside down."

It added, "Other water users think Idaho Power's attempt to rewrite history was cynical, and they're right. Like it or not, the utility is stuck in the same boat on the Snake River as the rest of us."

The company said a few days after the decision that it was engaged in a review of the case before deciding what it would do next. It did suggest that the Melanson decision is "taking water away from our customers."

Melanson's 50-page opinion included a detailed legal history of hydropower water rights in Idaho, noting that the issue was considered even before statehood in 1890.

He summarized the current dispute: "At issue in these cross-motions for summary judgment is the title to Idaho Power's hydropower claims or portions of the claims which exceed the minimum flows at the Murphy Gauge located below the Swan Falls Dam. The state of Idaho argues that pursuant to I.C. 42-203B, the portions of the claims exceeding the minimum flows are held in trust by the State of Idaho for the benefit of Idaho Power and the citizens of the state of Idaho. The result is that the state of Idaho owns legal title and Idaho Power and the citizens of the state of Idaho share equitable title to rights held in trust..." Idaho Power, he wrote argues instead that two legal cases (*Idaho Power Company v. State of Idaho*, and *Idaho Power Company v. Idaho Department of Water Resources*, both 1990) serve to define its rights – more broadly.

In reviewing the claims, Melanson took a detailed look at the original Swan Falls agreement, which he said is "the starting point" of a legal review. That agreement, he wrote, is clear as to the rights of the state and the utility.

"Idaho Power argues that it never would have entered into an agreement where it assigned or transferred its water rights to the State," Melanson wrote. "In response, the Court makes the following findings. First, the agreement was carefully drafted so that Idaho Power would not be directly assigning or transferring its water rights to the state. Rather than transferring or assigning the rights, they were placed in trust pursuant to the state's regulatory authority. Idaho Power was simply conceding to and agreeing not to challenge the state's regulatory authority...Finally, this Court finds it inconceivable that Idaho Power would enter into a contract with one of the conditions of the contract being that the state pass legislation entirely inconsistent with the body of the contract or the intent of the parties." ☒

SETTLEMENT (4/2009) The Idaho Power Company challenge to the terms of the 1984 Swan Falls agreement ended on March 25 when the company, together with state officials and others, agreed to a "reaffirmation" of the deal, with a few adjustments.

One quick result of the agreement was introduction in the Idaho Legislature, two days later, of Senate Bill 1169, aimed at locking the new framework agreement into place. The measure said the "Public Utilities Commission shall have no jurisdiction to consider in any proceeding, whether instituted before or after the effective date of this act, any issue as to whether any electric utility, including Idaho Power Company, should have or could have preserved, maintained or protected its water rights and hydroelectric generation in a manner inconsistent with the Framework Reaffirming the Swan Falls Settlement entered into by the Governor, Attorney General and the Idaho Power Company dated March 25, 2009."

The measure had not progressed to hearing by month's end. The Idaho Legislature was expected to adjourn sometime in mid- to late April.

The agreement also is expected to be delivered to the SRBA court, which has been considering the Idaho Power challenge, soon.

The new proposed settlement resolves the litigation by clarifying that the water rights held in trust by the State are subject to subordination to future upstream beneficial uses, including aquifer recharge. It also commits the State and Idaho Power to further discussions on important water management issues concerning the Swan Falls agreement and the management of water in the Snake River Basin.

In addition, the proposed settlement recognizes water management measures that enhance aquifer levels, springs and river flows—such as aquifer recharge projects—benefit both agricultural development and hydropower generation. The parties anticipate that the role of such water management measures will be developed in the implementation of the Comprehensive Aquifer Management Plan (CAMP) recently approved by the Idaho Water Resource Board. Idaho Power also is cooperating in the development and implementation of a recharge project below American Falls Reservoir. ☒

Bureau of Reclamation

THE WATER BUREC HOLDS (10/2004) In a potentially key ruling on federal/local district water ownership issues, SRBA Presiding Judge John Melanson on September 2 ruled that the rights to water held in several Boise River Bureau of Reclamation storage facilities should be held directly by BuRec – but that "equitable title" also belongs to several local irrigation entities. As Melanson summarized the background of the case:

"The United States Bureau of Reclamation filed water right claims for irrigation storage, irrigation from storage, and other storage rights from Arrowrock Dam and Reservoir, Lucky Peak Dam and Reservoir, and Anderson Ranch Dam and Reservoir. All three projects were authorized and developed pursuant to the Reclamation Act of 1902 and its subsequent amendments.

"The various parties comprising the Irrigation Entities, which have contracts with the BOR for the storage and delivery of the project water, also filed separate claims to the same water rights consistent with their individual respective uses. The Idaho Department of Water Resources recommended the water rights in the name of the BOR, substantially as claimed by the BOR. The corresponding claims filed by the Irrigation Entities were recommended as disallowed. The Irrigation Entities individually filed objections to IDWR's recommendations, all alleging, inter alia, that the water rights should be decreed either in the name of the contracting entity or alternatively, that the partial decree should also recognize the entity's beneficial ownership interest in the water right."

Since water rights are held subject to beneficial use, the question arose: Who undertook the beneficial use – the Bureau, the irrigation entities, or someone else?

The case initially showed up in SRBA Court in 2003, before then-Judge Roger Burdick (now a member of the Idaho Supreme Court). The Bureau received some support from conservation and other groups, and the irrigation companies from local business and agricultural interests.

Early in this case, Melanson noted, "The BOR and the Conservation Objectors both argue that the Irrigation Entities lack standing to participate in the proceedings based on the holding in *Fort Hall Water Users Ass'n v. United States*, 129 Idaho 39, 921 P.2d 739 (1996). *Fort Hall Water Users Ass'n,* like this case, involved a federal irrigation project where the United States had delivery contracts with the Fort Hall Water Users Association for the delivery of irrigation water. The United States filed claims in the SRBA for the project water rights that were eventually included in the Fort Hall Indian Water Rights Agreement consent decree. The FHWUA filed objections to some of the water rights claimed by the United States. The Supreme Court ruled that the FHWUA lacked standing to file the objections."

But Melanson said the comparison is apples and oranges.

"In Fort Hall the FHWUA never filed claims to the water rights nor even asserted an ownership interest to the rights in its objections. In the objections the FHWUA stated that its only interest in the water right was a contractual right to use the water. The ownership interest in the rights was never contested or at issue. In this case ownership is the issue: the Irrigation Entities filed separate claims to the water rights and objected to the director's recommendations regarding ownership. Consequently, unlike the situation in Fort Hall Water Users Ass'n, the Irrigation Entities are "claimants" and therefore meet the definition of "party to the adjudication."

As to the Bureau's right to water, Melanson pointed out "the Reclamation Act is somewhat vague as to the specifics of the ownership of water rights. However, it is still apparent from the original version of the Act, its subsequent amendments, accompanying regulations and the early practices of the BOR that landowners within the project were intended to have an interest in the water right, even though the right for the entire project was licensed or decreed in the name of the United States." ☒

HIGH COURT ON BUREC (4/2007) The Idaho Supreme Court tackled that question on March 9 in two companion cases, the *SRBA Case No. 39576* (Subcase 91-63) / *United States v. Pioneer Irrigation District*, and *SRBA Case No. 39576* (Subcase 91-63) / *Gene F. Bray v. Pioneer Irrigation District.* Both were appeals from SRBA Judge John Melanson.

As the high court sums up in the first *Pioneer* case, "The United States Bureau of Reclamation filed water right claims for irrigation storage, irrigation from storage, and other storage rights from Arrowrock Dam and Reservoir, Lucky Peak Dam and Reservoir, and Anderson Ranch Dam and Reservoir. These three projects were authorized and developed pursuant to the Reclamation Act of 1902 and its subsequent amendments. The irrigation entities have contracts with the BOR for the storage and delivery of the project water. The irrigation entities filed separate claims to the same water rights consistent with their respective uses. The Idaho Department of Water Resources recommended that the water rights be in the name of the BOR and that the claims filed by the irrigation entities be disallowed. The irrigation entities filed several objections to IDWR's recommendations."

In a unanimous decision, the Idaho Supreme Court came down squarely on the side of the local water users, largely on grounds that the local water users, not the federal agency, actually put the water to beneficial use – a key prerequisite for obtaining and keeping a water right in Idaho.

Sundry issues

WHAT IS "OTHER"? (6/1999) Just as a celebrated national court case recently involved the meaning of the word "is", so one brace of subcases may turn on the meaning of "other."

The dispute at immediate issue involves just 10 subcases (all in Basin 36, numbers 00006, 00007, 00008, 00033, 00047, 00068, 00069, 00099, 00100 and 00106). The implications of the dispute could possibly run much further.

The claims (all in the Hagerman area) grew out of the 1932 *New International Mortgage Bank v. Idaho Power Co.* case, which allowed water for the beneficial purposes of domestic and irrigation "and other" uses.

The claimants, in SRBA proceedings, have asserted beneficial uses including fish propagation, irrigation maintenance, recreation, wildlife and aesthetics, all under the terms of the 1932 decree, noting that the decree referred to "other" uses, and said they had a legal right to amend them.

Those uses do not, apparently, go back as far as 1932; most of those uses seem to have started in the 1940s. The Idaho Department of Fish & Game, in a March 5 filing this year, said those new uses "constitute unconstitutional enlargements to the rights decreed."

In an order on the case, Special Master Fritz Haemmerle said that he would not consider purposes of use as they were in 1932; he denied the Fish & Game objections on expanded use on grounds that current Idaho law (Idaho Code 42-1427) limits consideration of expanded use issues to purposes of use in effect as of 1987. (He also said that Fish & Game did not specifically say whether the expanded purposes, such as fish propagation, in fact came into effect after the New International decree, or before.)

Fish & Game, in turn, said that ruling was based on an "erroneous" reading of the law. Following up on this, Twin Falls attorney Patrick Brown (representing some of the claimants) pressed for a change in the Department of Water Resources report on the filings. On May 12, Haemmerle agreed to issue an order requiring the IDWR to show cause (at a hearing set for May 19) why the court should not order it:

• "To change the director's reports in each of the above enumerated subcases in order to recommend all purposes of use and the quantities and purpose of each being made of water, as of the commencement of the SRBA ...

• "To establish why the Director ... has recommended the purposes, priorities and quantities of use in the above enumerated subcases under standards of criteria different than those used by the Director to make recommendations in subcase 36-00133."

That prompted an IDWR filing by attorney Peter Anderson – itself an unusual occurrence, since the department by law is not a party to the SRBA but only a technical assistant. Anderson said that Haemmerle's order exceeds the scope of his authority as a master.

Maybe more significantly, Anderson pointed out: "A director's report [on a subcase] is prima facie evidence of the nature and extent of water rights. The claimants are requesting the special master to issue an order to IDWR that would create the very evidence that the Special Master and District Court is charged with weighing in these subcases." ☒

FORFEITURE BY CANAL COMPANY? (7/1999) The Idaho Supreme Court held on May 26 that the non-use of water by a customer of a canal company doesn't mean the canal company has forfeited that part of its water right.

In *Aberdeen-Springfield Canal Co. v. George and LaVaudis Peipers*, the Court upheld summary judgements in SRBA Court (by then-Judge Daniel Hurlbutt) and in seventh district court.

The case stems from 1969, when the Peipers bought farm property in Bingham County which was located in the ASCC irrigation system. The previous owner of the Peipers' property was a stockholder of the canal company.

The Peipers' relationship with the company became considerably more distant. Although Aberdeen-Springfield's by-laws say the transfer of a stockholder's land in effect also constitutes a transfer of stock and the right to use ASCC water, "whether expressed therein or not," the Peipers apparently never participated. They found that, by the time they moved into the property, the irrigation water for it came from a well installed by their predecessor. The Peipers discovered that the ditch which linked the property to the ASCC headgate had been destroyed a few years before they bought the property. When the Peipers asked for permission to install a new ditch, the owner of the land located between the Peipers and the canal replied that they "could forget about putting in another [ditch]."

After that, the Peipers sought no water from Aberdeen-Springfield (which had delivered no water to the property since 1962).

Even so, Aberdeen-Springfield imposed maintenance charges against the Peipers, who Peipers refused to pay. The company filed suit in December 1986 seeking foreclosure of liens for assessments levied against the property for 1983, 1984 and 1985. In October 1992 the company filed suit for non-payments from 1984 to 1990. Later, 1991-93 payments also were sought.

The case moved slowly, bounced between 7th District Court before Judge James Herndon, and 5th District (SRBA) Court Judge Hurlbutt.

On the forfeiture issue, the Supreme Court noted "This [forfeiture] statute was recently held [in 1997, in *State v. Hagerman Water Right Owners*] to provide for partial forfeiture of water rights where an appropriator 'cannot apply a portion of a water right to beneficial use during any part of the statutory period.' The SRBA court held as a matter of law that since ASCC was the appropriator who held legal title to the water rights, only ASCC could forfeit the portion of its water right appurtenant to the Peiper property."

The Supreme Court pointed out that, "this Court has never addressed the question of whether a stockholder's decision not to use the water provided by a Carey Act operating company triggers the forfeiture provision."

The Supreme Court's analysis:

"A finding of forfeiture in this case, where the appropriator did nothing to cause the nonuse of the water, would have troubling consequences for all Carey Act operating companies. Such a ruling would give stockholders, who are not appropriators, the power to determine the fate of ASCC's water rights. If a number of stockholders chose not to use their share of ASCC's water for the statutory period, ASCC's water right would gradually revert to the state through partial forfeiture. If the Peipers' argument were valid, ASCC could only watch helplessly while its water right was lost." ☒

FISH PROCESSING (1/2000) In a case which could have large implications for Idaho aquaculture, Judge Barry Wood backed decisions by the SRBA masters that special measures of water use were not needed in describing water rights for fish breeders.

That conclusion also had been reached by the each of the three masters then working in the SRBA; each had presided over relevant subcases, and issued recommendations on them. Those subcases were consolidated on appeal for two issues: whether "facility volume" should be – as the Idaho Department of Water Resources has contended – a required component of a water right decree for fish producers; and whether certain related evidence should be admitted.

Wood noted that "facility volume" is not included in the state water rights statute as a normal component of a water right. He went on to note that "IDWR has historically admitted that fish production (pounds of fish raised) is, in reality, not dependant on the size of a given facility, rather production is mostly dependant on the flow rate of available water. ☒

CONTINUOUS FLOW (1/2001) The Idaho Supreme Court on December 28 vacated a 7th District court order enforcing a policy of the Aberdeen-Springfield Canal Company setting a "continuous flow" policy of irrigation.

The ASCC sends water to shareholders through its extensive canal system, generally operated by gravity flow. That flow is delivered continuously for twenty-four hours until a ditch-rider readjusts the head gate. This is termed a "continuous flow" turnout.

Some of the shareholders have converted from gravity irrigation to sprinkler systems and installed pump lines in their turnouts that draw water directly from the ASCC canal system. These turnouts are known as "non-continuous flow" turnouts. Shareholders using non-continuous flow turnouts can cause flows in the ASCC canal system to fluctuate when they turn their pumps off after water is ordered.

In 1994, the ASCC board adopted a uniform "continuous flow" system of irrigation. A majority of shareholders voted to abolish the "continuous flow" policy, but the board reinstated it despite the shareholder vote. In April 1994, several shareholders filed suit in 7th District court against the board and five of its nine directors, seeking a temporary restraining order and a preliminary and permanent injunction, enjoining the board from implementing and enforcing the "continuous flow policy."

In April of 1994 District Judge James Herndon granted summary judgment in favor of the board. Later, two new members were elected to the board, which rescinded the "continuous flow" policy.

Alan DeGiulio is a shareholder who experienced problems in the delivery of water because of ASCC shareholders operating pumps in nearby non-continuous turnouts. He filed a motion to enforce the district court's 1994 judgment and amended restraining order, asserting that certain shareholders and the new board had failed and refused to comply with the district court's 1994 order. The district court found that the board's rescission of the continuous flow policy was in contravention of the court's 1994 order and ruled that the order and injunction were still in effect, estopping the board and all shareholders from "claiming, demanding or seeking the right to use a non-continuous flow policy."

The Idaho Supreme Court vacated the district court's order, saying the board had the authority to manage the canal system and that the order entered in 1994 enforced the authority of the board.

When the company's board changed the policy, the Supreme Court said, the injunction that had been entered should have been vacated. ☒

BOUGHT PROPERTY FORFEIT (2/2001) The Idaho Supreme Court held on January 24 that water rights to recently-purchased property had been abandoned or forfeited. The decision affirmed rulings by Special Master Brigette Bilyeu and former SRBA Judge Barry Wood.

The property, in Basin 34 (the Lost River area) was farmed and irrigated by Gerald "Doug" Storer from 1973 to 1984, when he transferred it to the Farmers Home Administration, which held a mortgage on it. From then to 1992, the agency leased the property for farming or cattle grazing.

In May 1992, the Idaho Department of Water Resources filed a director's report recommending water rights on the property be disallowed because of abandonment. The federal government objected to that report. Three years later John and Matea McCray bought the land from the FHA and substituted themselves in objecting to the IDWR report.

The special master, and Judge Wood, held that most of the water rights in fact had been abandoned. The McCrays appealed.

The Supreme Court said the special master applied the correct standard of evidence and made sufficient findings to support the conclusions of the district court, and that the McCrays failed to prove that their nonuse of the water right was caused by conditions beyond their control. ☒

ACCOMPLISHED TRANSFER (4/2001) A Glenns Ferry subcase centering on an enlarged use of water was remanded on March by Judge Roger Burdick to Special Master Thomas Cushman, saying the master hadn't properly applied the accomplished transfer statute.

The statute was created in the course of litigating the SRBA.

The case concerned two groundwater right claims by Magic West, a food processing company at Glenns Ferry. One of them bore a 1939 priority date and a diversion rate of 0.40 cubic feet per second, with the period of use set from April 1 to November 1. In 1997, the company amended its claim, changed to indicate industrial use and full year period of use. The other claim followed a similar pattern: a level of 0.67 cfs and use for 10.5 months a year. In 1989, the firm's SRBA filing claimed a priority date of 1974, diversion rate of 0.67 cfs, industrial use, and use from August 15 to July 1 (10.5 months). In 1990, the court noted, "the right was licensed with a diversion rate of 0.67 cfs and an annual diversion volume of 12.9 acre-feet per year."

There were more increases. In 1999, the Department of Water Resources agreed to increase the volume for the two rights from13.7 to 66 acre feet per year (combined). In February 2000, Special Master Cushman agreed with the increases. Burdick mostly agreed too.

"If the Batruels wished to contest the stipulation, they should have done so through a trial before the Special Master," Burdick said. "While reasonable minds may differ as to the import of the season of use set forth in the original Notice of Claim, it could be concluded that because Magic West amended its claim and sought to increase the season of use contained in the license, that the information in the original Notice of Claim was incorrect but the facts stipulated to by the parties was correct. Therefore, this Court finds that the Batruels have failed to show that the Special Master's findings of fact were clearly erroneous." ☒

MOUNTAIN HOME (5/2001) Uncontested water right claims usually move directly through the Adjudication to approval, but on April 6 Judge Roger Burdick disallowed several uncontested federal water right claims at Mountain Home Air Force Base. Burdick noted that while uncontested claims based on state law have gone through an investigation by the Idaho Department of Water Resources, those based on federal law have not. Because of that, he said, federal uncontested claims do not carry a presumption in their favor, but have to be persuasively argued.

His decision said "water right claims 61-11783, 61-11784, and 61-11785 are hereby disallowed with prejudice."

The water in question is groundwater obtained from – as of last October – a dozen wells. Another has been under recent construction. The amount of water used on the base has been substantial. Federal briefs said it amounted 832.2 million gallons in 1999, and is estimated to reach 845.2 mgal in 2006.

Burdick's decision on the case follows the trend of other decisions but may break new ground in its central finding, that federal reserved water rights do not extend to land purchased or condemned by the government – only to lands withdrawn for a specific purpose from the public domain.

He wrote, "A federal reserved water right originates with a reservation of land. If established, the related reserved water right becomes appurtenant to that land. It follows that federal reserved waters cannot be applied to or used in conjunction with non-reserved (non-appurtenant) lands. The use of reserved water on non-reserved land would in effect be creating a separate water right. Because federal reserved water cannot be applied to non-reserved land, implicit in establishment of the Mountain Home facility was the acknowledgment that the water supply needs would have to include state-based water rights. The United States' conduct in constructing improvements on the acquired land where reserved water cannot be applied is testament to that acknowledgment. The United States has not attempted to demonstrate where and to what extent a federal reserved water right can be used and to what extent federal reserved rights would have to be supplemented with state-based water."

The base was founded in 1943, when land was set aside for a wartime "airport"; the Department of Defense uses that date for its priority for groundwater rights. The base was redesignated over the years, and expanded. Almost half of the base's 6,741 acres was obtained, through condemnation or other means, from private land owners who in turn had obtained it from the federal government. A federal brief argued that "For purposes of a functioning Mountain Home Air Force Base, there is no distinction between acquired land, and reserved public land. The acquired land and the reserved public lands are intermingled and both underlie the runways and structures necessary to the military base... Because of the jigsaw puzzle fit of the pieces, and the nature of the air force base requiring long runways and geographically expansive operation, the water needs for the acquired and reserved land *cannot* be divided."

Burdick countered that argument: "Simply put, because of the intermingling of the withdrawn and condemned land, the primary purpose of the reservation cannot fail without a federal reserved water right. The United States had to acknowledge that at least some of the water supply for the facility would be state-based."

There were no other parties in the subcase. The J.R. Simplot Company was denied permission to participate directly, but briefs from it and from the state of Idaho were accepted on an *amicus* (friend of the court) basis. ☒

TRANSFER-ABANDONMENT (1/2002) A Department of Water Resources hearing is set for January 30 on the contested transfer of a water right critics say has been forfeited. The case is attracting attention not only because it could affect construction of an Idaho Power generation center at Mountain Home, but also because this kind of case could emerge more frequently in the SRBA in years ahead.

The property in question is located near Mountain Home; farmer Peter Nielsen in December 1979 obtained a license for groundwater use there, for diversion of 3.494 cubic feet per second for irrigation purposes. The groundwater came from a well which was built in 1966.

Nielsen participated normally in the SRBA process; the IDWR developed a director's report (subcase 61-02168) based on water use in 1987, and in October 2000, based on that report and no contests to it, SRBA Judge Barry Wood issued a partial decree for it.

There matters might have ended except that Idaho Power, seeking water for its new generation facility in the area, reached a property sales agreement with Nielsen. In June this year, Nielsen signed an agreement to sell 320 acres and the associated water rights to Idaho Power for $66,240, and they applied to the Department of Water Resources for a transfer permit.

Several of Nielsen's neighbors were opposed to the new power center, however, and filed their opposition to the transfer.

One of them, Mark Sukup, is out of the country on Operation Enduring Freedom. His wife Trudy Sukup wrote on August 6, "The proposal for the power plant well threatens the already critical water table here in Mountain Home. The new location of the power plant, built within a half-mile of my residence without my knowledge, would most likely dehydrate my residential well. Without water, my family would have to relocate and possibly lose our home based on poor assessed market value due to water extinction."

The key problem facing the transfer, however, lay elsewhere. Several documents in Department of Water Resources files on the case suggest that the water right may have gone unused for more than five years – the period of nonuse which can constitute abandonment.

In his sales agreement with Idaho Power, Nielsen said the water in his right "has been placed to beneficial use in the past five years."

However, filings from Idaho Power Company on November 16 indicated that the pump connected to Nielsen's well was last operated in July 1986. Another document suggested that irrigation of the property ended in 1988 or 1989. On October 15, Nielsen filed with IDWR an application for extension of time to avoid forfeiture of the water right. That application is pending before the department.

David Tuthill of IDWR has advised the SRBA Court on several occasions that, since the department bases its director's report reviews on water use as of 1987, non-use of water in the years since aren't yet reflected in the SRBA process – but may be as water rights are transferred or challenged. ☒

RECAPTURED IS JUNIOR (7/2005) The Idaho Supreme Court on June 21 upheld an SRBA Court decision that recaptured waters cannot be included in an "enlarged" water use but have to be considered junior and therefore subject to senior water right holders.

The unanimous decision grew out of *A&B Irrigation District v. Aberdeen-American Falls Groundwater District et al.* It developed from an application by A&B for a groundwater right which included an expansion of a 2363.1-acre right which included recaptured excess runoff water. After a state law change, A&B withdraw that application, but it later filed another, and in 1992 the state Department of Water Resources recommended approval of its enlargement, but its proposed later priority dates were disputed by A&B. The situation was further complicated by state Supreme Court decisions which invalidated some of the surrounding law.

Eventually, the special master in the case determined that the seepage water was groundwater, and proposed a relatively late priority date. A&B appealed; the SRBA Court upheld the decision; A&B appealed; and the Supreme Court again upheld the decision.

The Supreme Court said that the SRBA Court properly treated the water in question as groundwater. But it also said that whether the water was groundwater or runoff, it still had to be subordinated to senior rights. ☒

STREAMFLOW MAINTENANCE LICENSE VALID (10/2008) Judge Melanson on September 23 held that a controversial water license on the Boise River is valid, saying the Idaho Minimum Stream Flow Act does not cover the stream maintenance water license.

In his conclusion, he said that "this Court holds that the streamfiow maintenance claim at issue is outside the scope of the IMSFA. IDWR did not act outside its authority in the license for a streamfiow maintenance purpose of use and, therefore, the license is valid. Objections to the purpose of use therefore constitute impermissible collateral attacks to the license. The Court holds further that a remark in the partial decree is necessary to acknowledge and administer the interests held in Lucky Peak that are related to contract rights held in Anderson Ranch and Arrowrock Reservoirs."

Melanson certified the decision as final, meaning that it is cleared for appeal, if one of the losing parties chooses to appeal.

The case grew out of the water flow developed after construction of the Lucky Peak and Arrowrock dams, involving a series of contracts and memorandums of agreement between the Bureau of Reclamation and local water delivery organizations, including irrigation districts and other entities. Later, when BuRec contemplated a couple of additional projects, protests from a number of those entities were filed. The new decision noted that, "Ultimately, the BOR resolved the protests through the filing of an amendment to the permit application. The application was amended to provide that 'Lucky Peak stored waters will be utilized in the Boise Valley on presently irrigated lands for supplemental irrigation water'" and additional terms. Further water agreements involving federal and local entities have followed, and the detailed terms of these were considered in the new decision.

Generally, the decision said that the federal Bureau of Reclamation claimed and the Idaho Department of Water Resources proposed "year 'round streamflow maintenance storage and streamfiow maintenance from storage in the amount of 152,300 AFY. The streamflow maintenance is for the channel of the Boise River downstream from Lucky Peak Dam to the confluence with the Snake River. The recommendation is based on and consistent with the license issued by IDWR in 2002 for this claim." ☒

8 | Concluding the SRBA?

Some water adjudications never end. Literally. In some western states, a number of water adjudications have been started but put on hiatus, possibly never to be resolved.

The SRBA was too big for that: Once started, something had to be done with it. Many of the legislators who voted to begin it had hopes it would be complete within a decade or so. No large water adjudication in the West has been completed so quickly; many which are far smaller have been ongoing for much longer than the SRBA, and seem farther from resolution.

There is however some reason to think that the bulk of the work of the SRBA, at least, can be completed within about 20 years of its beginning. What follows is a progress report current in the spring of 1999, suggesting what's been done and what may happen over the next few years.

Test basins

The most time-consuming work in the SRBA may have been on the three "test basins" – 34 in the Lost River area centered around Butte County; 36 in the central Snake River north side, mainly including Jerome and Minidoka counties; and 57 in western Owyhee County. Here many of the trickiest issues have been argued over and in many cases settled.

The Department of Water Resources early on developed its reports (and recommendations) covering water rights in these basins. Once that was done, special masters were assigned to the basins (one to each of the three basin) and the claims were worked through. In many cases, disputes were resolved before they got to the master; in other cases, short trials were held.

As of 2009, these basins are nearly complete.

Domestic and stockwater

In 1997 the SRBA Court and the Department of Water Resources decided on a "double track" approach to resolving cases in the SRBA. They would divide water rights cases in two: "domestic and stockwater" and "irrigation and other."

The idea was that tens of thousands of small and relatively simple domestic and stockwater claims could be resolved relatively quickly, letting a majority of claimants in the SRBA off the hook, and clearing the decks for the more difficult irrigation and other claims. That process has moved speedily ahead, and worked in general as intended.

The SRBA hit a milestone in March 1999 when it issued the last of its reports for all the domestic and stockwater water rights cases in the SRBA. By then, the department had issues its reports for more than half of all the cases in the SRBA, and most of those were domestic and stockwater.

As a group, these are relatively easy cases to resolve. The amount of water involved is ordinarily not large, and the disputes over them are relatively few.

Irrigation and other

After 1999 – and leaving aside a few special cases such as the Nez Perce water rights – most of the story of the SRBA will be told in the resolution of "irrigation and other" water claims: The largest, most complex claims.

Department of Water Resources schedules (which apart from occasional minor delays have been met rigorously so far) call for completion of departmental reports on all these claims by the end of 2005.

Of course, all this refers to work by the Idaho Department of Water Resources, not to decreed rights.

Experience in the test basin suggests, though, that the large majority of decrees may be issued not long after the department's work is done. During the months when objections can be lodged and resolved, most cases (certainly in the test basins) seem to be settled that way.

In the basins

What level of progress has been made on recording claims to water rights, objections to them and settlement of them? The Department of Water Resources tracks thoe changes every month, and reports on them to the SRBA Court. Here is what those reports said, eight years apart.

February 2001

	decreed	total
34 (Lost River)	5,502	5,961
36 (Central North Snake)	6,942	7,564
57 (Central Owyhee)	2,575	2,737

Department of Water Resources Adjudication Administrator David Tuthill said that Basin 36 appears likely to be fully resolved soon.

Developments in other basins:

• **32** (Medicine Lodge Creek area in western Clark County) – Of the 413 rights recommended by the IDWR, most have been resolved. Tuthill said that most of those remaining, in the Reno Ditch, concern the permissible place of use. Just seven subcases still are contested. "This basin is moving forward," Tuthill said.

• **33** (Howe-Clyde area east of Arco) – In the 55 contested subcases (water right claims) here, the 1,716 objections initially filed have been resolved. Almost all of the objections came from a group of stockholders over mainly small domestic and stockwater claims.

• **35** (NW of Snake River from American Falls area to Rigby area) – More than 2,300 unresolved objections remain here, mainly from federal agencies.

• **41** (mainly western Power County) – 41 objections remain (in a basin with 210 subcases), from canal companies. The issues are similar to those in Basin 35.

• **55** (Owyhee River, SW corner of Idaho) – Of 367 recommendations in the director's report, 18 remain at issue, and Tuthill said he is hoping for an early resolution. "It's on a trial track at this point," he said in February.

• **65** (Payette River Basin) – The three parts of this basin are proceeding at various speeds. Hearings on Part I (northern fork around Cascade Reservoir and Payette Lake) were held November 30 and December 6.

• **71** (Stanley area south) – Of the 288 recommendations in the director's report, just seven remain at issue, Tuthill said. He said that he is hoping to "close out" the basin soon. A "basin order" has been drafted (in working draft form) and the department is now considering how to "finalize" the basin.

• **72** (Challis area) – Just 41 objections appear to remain in this district (of 727 department recommendations), but Tuthill said that a trial may yet come out of these. ☒

February 2009

Adjudication staff said that as of February 5, while work remains on some late claims, all submitted in the ordinary timely fashion through the SRBA process (starting in 1988) are reported in director's reports.

So far, 139,365 decrees in the SRBA have been assigned (about 900 more than last month), and 11,219 have been submitted and are awaiting decrees (about 900 fewer—reflecting significant progress in December and January).

Areas where timely objections are resolved are basins 23, 25, 31, 32, 33, part 1 (groundwater) of 37 in the Wood River area, 43, 51, 55, 57, 61, 63 part 1, 65, 69, 71, 72, 79, 81, 82, 83, 84 and 86. That is the same as last month.

In Basin 34 an objection remains to one recommendation; the initial hearing was held on November 17. There is also a late claim and a motion to set aside a decree.

In Basin 36, one issue remained for the city of Burley; a settlement meeting has been set for the spring.

Action in other basins:

• **01** (part 1, Snake River from Wyoming down to around Blackfoot): A director's report filed in May 2006 listed 178 state-based claims and one federal-based claim; also a major objection from Monsanto Corporation, and two from the city of Burley. Most recently, there were 384 objections to 110 recommendations (down four each from last month).

• **01** (part 2, Snake River downstream from Blackfoot): There are 156 objections (one down from last month) filed to 63 recommendations (also one down) in the director's report, which was filed last December; there's been no change here for several months. The largest single share of findings for which claims are unresolved (51 of them) involve Bureau of Land Management claims, though there are 60 varying cases involving conflicts over ownership and competing rights.

• **02** (Snake River from eastern Magic Valley to Oregon): The objection deadline was December 5, and response deadline was February 5. Earlier this year 223 objections were noted to 109 recommendations; two months ago, the number of objections fell from 180 to 171, to 144 recommendations.

• **03** (Snake River north of Hells Canyon): Of 182 (one recently added) state law recommendations, 12 objections (eight of those private) developed. Five of those remain (same as last month), four of those involve the city of Weiser and the other concerns Idaho Power Company.

• **21** (Henry's Fork area, Fremont County): The director's report on 745 claims originally drew 46 responses. Currently, 380 objections (same as last month) are filed to 126 recommendations (same as last month). Most (78) are private-based.

• **22** (northern Teton basin, eastern Madison County/Teton County): Numbers in Part 1 of this basin have held since last month, at 37 objections (30 of those private) to 15 rights, same as last month. Those are still being worked on, following an August hearing. The Part 2 set currently has 362 objections (down six from last month) to 181 recommendations (down six from last month).

• **24** (NE Caribou County, Freedom area): For 186 state-based recommendations, just one private objection remains, from the RVG Trust (down from nine several months ago). A status conference was held in October.

• **27** (Blackfoot River basin): This basin once appeared headed for easy settlement but has turned complex; 438 objections (same as last month) reflecting three settlements in tribe-related matters) are on file to IDWR recommendations, and those objections are all over the map. The largest portion of objections (223 at present) is from the Shoshone-Bannock Tribes.

There are also objections from the Bureau of Land Management, from the Bureau of Indian Affairs, and at least two departments in state government: Lands and Health & Welfare.

• **29** (Portneuf River Basin): With resolution of the Pocatello city claims, just two unresolved objections (one additional from last month), of the city of Lava Hot Springs, remains.

• **35** (NW of Snake River, American Falls area to Rigby area): Recovered water subcases, 101 of them, have been stayed. There are four private objections to three recommendations, 10 objections to the Aberdeen-Springfield ADR. Private class 1 recovered water subcases have been stayed here.

• **37** (Wood River basin), Part 1: 20 objections remain in 15 subcases; those numbers have been dropping substantially this year). Many of the Idaho Power Company subcases, which were the largest issue here, have been resolved.

• **37** (Wood River basin), Part 2: 39 objections (two fewer than last month), in 33 subcases. Most of the cases involve the Speck and Flying Triangle claims, and several scattered federal and private claims.

• **37** (Wood River basin), Part 3: A prospectively massive effort here, currently with 622 subcases (up from 565 subcases last month) reporting 2,875 objections (same as last month). Initial hearings were held last fall in Hailey.

• **41** (Raft River area): Two objections have been filed to late claims on the director's report. There were 215 state-based claims. The department reports that, "settlement is progressing."

• **45** (Oakley area): This is one of the most complex basins in the system, and one of the most difficult to resolve. Of 2,028 IDWR recommendations (all but one state-based, and down one from last month), Bedke ranching claims are the largest group (down to 66 this month, same as last month). Objections now number 113, the same as last month, in 75 subcases.

• **47** (South central Magic Valley area): Some 323 objections have been filed and 315 remain (four fewer than last month), an estimated 188 from the Twin Falls Canal Company and 61 from the Bureau of Land Management.

• **63 (Part II)** (Ada County): Much work still remains on this complex area, the largest share of which involves private claims and objections. A wide variety of disputes have arisen here among the 1,576 state-based claims, and 14 federal reserved claims. There are currently 131 objections remaining.

• **63 (Part III)** (Canyon County and nearby area): 264 objections (down 21 from last month) were filed to 226 (down 21) subcases, the largest category being private objections, and another large group of irrigation district objections.

• **67** (SW Idaho): After the objection deadline in August, 30 objections (down four from last month) remained to 28 recommendations (down three). Most (22) are private.

• **73** (SW Idaho): At present, there are 160 objections (down one from last month) to 135 subcases, mostly private but about a third related to Bureau of Land Management claims.

• **74** (Lemhi River): 816 objections originally were filed, now reduced to 646 (down three from last month) in 325 subcases, slightly over half from federal agencies, and most of the rest from the Nez Perce Tribe.

• **75** (Salmon River near Salmon): Of the 286 objections filed to 116 recommendations, 233 objections (two below last month) remain in 192 subcases. An early corner may have been turned in this basin, although matters seemed to slow this winter.

• **77** (upper Salmon River, Dixie, Big Creek, Landmark): The director's report notes 291 state-based claims, and 23 federal. Some 98 objections remain in 22 recommendations.

• **78** (northern Idaho): The IDWR records four current objections to four recommendations (each measure down one from last month). All of those objections are private.

• **82** (Southern Clearwater River area): From 216 state recommendations just two objections remain.

• **85** (Western Clearwater River area, including Lewiston): Only seven objections (same as last month, all involving the Lewiston Orchard Irrigation District) remain from the 564 original state recommendations; most of them involve various federal agencies and private parties. There have also been 20 motions so far to file late claims. ☒

9 | The Northern Adjudication

Planning the Northern Adjudication

PANHANDLE ADJUDICATION LIKELY (4/2006) The Idaho Legislature in March passed a measure which would order adjudication of all water rights in northern Idaho which haven't been adjudicated in the SRBA.

That would mean everything north of the Clearwater River system – roughly, everything from central Latah County north to Canada.

Specifically, House Bill 545 says, "the director of the department of water resources shall petition the district court to commence adjudications within the terms of the McCarran amendment, 43 U.S.C. section 666, of the water rights from surface water and ground water sources in northern Idaho through initiation of three (3) proceedings. Separate petitions shall be filed for water rights adjudications for each of the following river basins, and related ground water sources whether or not hydraulically connected to a surface water source, within Idaho: the Coeur d'Alene-Spokane river basin, the Palouse river basin, and the Kootenai and Clark Fork-Pend Oreille river basins. The filing of each petition shall be contingent on legislative funding approval. Each petition shall describe the boundaries of the water source or water sources to be adjudicated." ☒

ASSIGNMENT (11/2006) The Idaho Supreme Court on September 29 assigned the three new water adjudications in the Idaho panhandle to SRBA Presiding Judge John Melanson, and based those adjudications at his court in southern Idaho's Twin Falls.

The north Idaho adjudications were authorized in the last term of the Idaho Legislature. They were started with the filing of petitions by the director of the Department of Water Resources. Karl Dreher chose to do just that for the Spokane, the Palouse and the Clark Fork-Pend Oreille river basins. The legislation also said that jurisdiction for those adjudications would go to the same court handling the SRBA – that of District Judge Melanson in the 5th district, based at Twin Falls.

The measure did leave open the option for the Supreme Court to locate the case elsewhere, but it chose not to – at least for a while. If local panhandle activity grows, however, some adjustment might be made.

The Supreme Court did say in its order, however, that "prior to the filing of petitions, in conjunction with the planning stages for the three general adjudications, the district court anticipated to be assigned to preside over the adjudications in conjunction with the Idaho Department of Water Resources, will be required to begin various logistical administrative matters including the incurring of related expenditures, and which in order to proceed with accordingly, require from this Court a provisional order confirming special jurisdiction, determining venue and assigning a district judge."

SUPREME COURT order:

IT IS HEREBY ORDERED, that the presiding judge of the Snake River Basin Adjudication District Court, an office held at present by District Judge John M. Melanson, be and is hereby, assigned as the presiding judge over these actions as general adjudications of the water rights in the Coeur d'Alene-Spokane River Basin, the Palouse River Basin and the Clark Fork-Pend Oreille River Basins.

IT IS FURTHER ORDERED, that pursuant to I.C. § 42-1406B special jurisdiction for these general adjudications is confirmed and shall reside in the Snake River Basin Adjudication District Court of the Fifth Judicial District of the State of Idaho, in and for the County of Twin Falls.

IT IS FURTHER ORDERED, that pursuant to I.C. § 42-1406B and I.C. § 42-1407 the Court does hereby designate the Snake River Basin Adjudication District Court of the Fifth Judicial District of the State of Idaho, in and for the County of Twin Falls, as the county and court of venue for these general adjudication proceedings and that all pleadings and documents with regard to these general adjudications shall be filed with the clerk of that court. Notwithstanding this designation of venue, hearings may be held by masters and the presiding district judge at such places within the State of Idaho as are designated by the masters or presiding judge for the convenience of the parties and witnesses.

IT IS FURTHER ORDERED, that this Provisional Order shall remain in full force and effect until further order of this Court. ☒

Launching the adjudication

STAFFING UP (4/2007) The planned new adjudication for Northern Idaho is taking another step forward with the addition of special language in the Department of Water Resources budget bill which moved though the legislature. Special language was included in IDWR appropriation:

The changes include several new positions in the state office to accommodated the northern adjudication.

Department officials said in March that during the month they had interviewed two agents for the planned northern regional office. ☒

PROJECTING CLAIMS (5/2007) Just how large a project will be the newly underway North Idaho Adjudication? The earliest estimate now indicates it will review about a sixth as many water right claims as the SRBA has.

Development of a North Idaho adjudication was approved by the Idaho Legislature as an offshoot of the Nez Perce Tribe water rights settlement.

IDWR Water Rights Manager Don Shaff said at the April information meeting that his agency has developed projected counts for the nine basins in the Panhandle area, which IDWR and the SRBA Court will consider next.

The grand total: About 24,500 water rights. ☒

That compares to somewhere around 140,000 water rights in the SRBA.

SESSIONS (7/2007) Two public meetings were held – June 13 at Sandpoint and June 14 at Plummer – updating Panhandle residents on the coming North

Idaho adjudications. Local news reports did note substantial skepticism among local water users, concerned about some of the difficulties southern Idaho water users have encountered recently. ☒

IN REVOLT (11/2007) A local government revolt against the about-to-begin Northern Idaho Adjudication was slowed but not halted in October, as most but not all Panhandle county commissioners declared their opposition to the water cataloguing effort. The dispute led Idaho Department of Water Resources Director David Tuthill to send a letter to legislative leadership asking for suggestion on what path to take. An abridged version of the extensive letter appears in this issue of the *Digest,* starting on page 6.

Commissioners in Boundary, Bonner, Shoshone and Benewah counties asked the state to drop its plans for adjudication in the northern basins. But commissions in Kootenai and Latah counties went the other way, arguing that the adjudication would be helpful.

Commissioners in the four dissenting counties said they would send a letter to Governor C.L. "Butch" Otter asking the state effort be suspended.

The Northern Idaho adjudication, launched with legislation passed in 2006 and supported by the Panhandle delegation, is intended to cover the northern part of the state which hasn't been covered by the Snake River Basin Adjudication. Water rights are less thoroughly recorded in many areas of this region than they have been in the more arid south; by some estimates, only a third or fewer of water rights in the region have been formally recorded. The subject and practice of water rights management is less familiar to many northern Idahoans than it is in the south.

The Spokane *Spokesman-Review* on October 24 said that "sentiment about the adjudication has been mixed in North Idaho, with strong opposition in more rural areas where some residents don't want the government asking about their water use, and support in more rapidly developing areas where water conflicts are increasing." ☒

IN THE LEGISLATURE (2/2008) The fate of the North Idaho Adjudication was a key topic when the Idaho Legislature convened. After numerous complaints from Panhandle residents, the Department of Water Resources slowed its proposal for a general stream adjudication there. Some proposed legislation would cut the Kootenai, Clark Fork and Pend Oreille basins from the adjudication. Some streams in areas where public support for an adjudication is greater, as in the Palouse River area, may go forward.

Senate Bill 1277 would "make the participation in the northern Idaho water adjudication of individual domestic water users voluntary. In other water adjudications Idaho has undertaken domestic water users were not mandated to participate." It was sponsored by Senators Joyce Broadsword and Shawn Keough, and Representatives Eric Anderson, George Eskridge, Mary Lou Shepherd and Dick Harwood, all from the Panhandle area. In late January, it was in the Senate Resources & Environment Committee.

Another measure, SB 1279, would cancel the North Idaho Adjudication completely. Sponsored by Broadsword, Harwood and Shepherd, it also is lodged in Resources & Environment. ☒ [*It failed.*]

ADJUDICATION PETITIONED (8/2008) The Idaho Attorney General's office petitioned the Northern Idaho Adjudication District Court in July to begin work adjudicating surface and ground water rights in much of the Idaho panhandle. As directed by the Idaho Legislature, the Northern Idaho Adjudication will proceed in three phases. Phase 1 begins this year with

Basins 91-95 (Coeur d'Alene and Spokane River Basins). Contingent on funding, Phase 2 will address Basin 87 (Palouse River Basin) and Phase 3 will deal with Basins 96 and 97 (Clark Fork-Pend Oreille River Basins).

IDWR held a series of town hall meetings from July 21st to July 24th in seven northern Idaho cities to provide information about the adjudication.

The 2008 Idaho Legislature changed the original Northern Idaho Adjudication plan. Those changes include reducing the fees charged for water right claims to match the fees set for the Snake River Basin Adjudication. Many water right holders will pay a filing fee of only $25 dollars to have a small domestic water right adjudicated.

Other amendments included removing the Kootenai River Basin in the northernmost part of the state (Basin 98) from the adjudication. Changes also included direction by the legislature that small domestic and stock water claims be deferred. If approved by the NIA District Court, holders of these rights will have the option of filing claims in the Northern Idaho Adjudication or deferring filing to a later date. However, IDWR recommends that they file in this proceeding to protect their water right. ☒

ADJUDICATION LAUNCHED (9/2008) The initial commencement hearing in the Northern Idaho Adjudication was held at the federal courthouse at Coeur d'Alene on August 28. The event had been ordered on July 11 by SRBA Judge John Melanson, also is presiding over the Panhandle adjudications.

Phase 1 of the adjudication begins this year with Basins 91-95 (Coeur d'Alene and Spokane River Basins). Contingent on funding, Phase 2 will address Basin 87 (Palouse River Basin) and Phase 3 will deal with Basins 96 and 97 (Clark Fork-Pend Oreille River Basins).

The 2008 Idaho Legislature changed the original Northern Idaho Adjudication plan. Those changes include reducing the fees charged for water right claims to match the fees set for the Snake River Basin Adjudication. Many water right holders will pay a filing fee of only $25 dollars to have a small domestic water right adjudicated.

Other amendments included removing the Kootenai River Basin in the northernmost part of the state (Basin 98) from the adjudication. Changes also included direction by the legislature that small domestic and stock water claims be deferred. If approved by the NIA District Court, holders of these rights will have the option of filing claims in the Northern Idaho Adjudication or deferring filing to a later date. However, IDWR recommends that they file in this proceeding to protect their water right. ☒

FILINGS (2/2009) Filings in the brand-new North Idaho Adjudication are underway. The Idaho Department of Water Resources said that 38 claims have been filed, seven of those on-line. It did not specify where they were.

About 1,300 first-round notices were mailed in mid-January. About 50,000 notices were expected to be delivered in Kootenai County. On-line filing is allowed. ☒

Appendix | SRBA Chronology

1983

March 31 – Idaho Supreme Court ruling on the Swan Falls case, declaring that Idaho Power Company has water right interest at the dam.

July 25 – Swan Falls settlement involving the Idaho Department of Water Resources, and James Bruce for Idaho Power Co., to resolve the Swan Falls dispute.

1984

Gov. John Evans kills the initial agreement, and negotiations begin for a few Swan Falls document. Swan Falls is a major topic in legislative elections that year.

1985

March – After much debate, the Idaho Legislature passes a measure accepting the "Swan Falls agreement".

1987

January 3 – Keith Higginson takes over as director of the Idaho Department of Water Resources.

June 17 – Petition to commence the Snake River Basin Adjudication filed by the Department of Water Resources, determine all water rights in the Snake River Basin.

June 19 – The Idaho Supreme Court assigns the SRBA to the Fifth Judicial District at Twin Falls and to District Judge Daniel Hurlbutt.

June 25 – Judge Hurlbutt sets out initial procedures for the commencement hearing in the SRBA.

September 8 – Hearing on the petition begins in Twin Falls; discussion of how to begin in the case gets underway.

November 17 – The SRBA is formally commenced in Judge Hurlbutt's court. The lawsuit is formally joined.

December – Congress passes, and President Reagan signs, a bill forcing the Federal Energy Regulatory Commission and other federal entities to agree to the Swan Falls settlement.

1991

December 24 – Notice of Appearance for Candy Jackson, Shoshone-Bannock Tribal attorney; interpreted as indicating formal entry of the tribes into the SRBA.

1992

April 21 – Plans for filing director's reports with the SRBA court are due in court, and filed.

1993

March 25 – U.S. District Court issued a temporary restraining order ordering the Department of justice to file for in-stream flows on behalf of the Nez Perce and Shoshone-Bannock tribes.

February 16 – A general attempt by conservation groups to intervene in the SRBA was turned back by Judge Hurlbutt.

May 3 – The U. S. Supreme Court in *United States v. Idaho*, ruling against the Idaho's attempt to collect standard fees.

June 16 – Idaho Supreme Court rules in Young Harvey Walker case that most water disputes in the Snake River Basin should be run through the SRBA Court.

July 1 – Terry Dolan becomes the first special master in the SRBA.

July 12 – Brigette Bilyeu becomes the second special master in the SRBA.

July 13 – Judge Hurlbutt formally designated the first basin-wide issue in the Adjudication: the constitutionality of the presumption statute.

August 5 – Writ of Mandate from Judge Hurlbutt to Department of Water Resources ordering delivery of water in the Musser case.

October 1 – Second Basin Wide Issue declared, concerning the role in the Adjudication of the state Department of Water Resources.

October 15 – Judge Hurlbutt clarified BW2 and for the first time approved use of the Private attorney general doctrine which allows an attorney for a private interest to be paid by the state for raising an issue of general public importance.

October 25 – New Mexico attorney Richard Simms is third special master.

November 12 – Panel appointed to review "steering committee" in the SRBA.

November 26 – The U.S. Department of Justice files for removal of Simms as a special master, arguing he has displayed anti-federal bias in the past.

December 17 – Special Master Richard Simms resigns.

1994

January 4 – Special Master Bilyeu begins the first subcase hearings in Basin 34.

February 4 – Decision on Basin Wide Issue 1 by Judge Hurlbutt: declaring most of the presumption statutes as unconstitutional.

February 28 – Idaho Supreme Court decision upholding Judge Hurlbutt on the Musser delivery of water case.

April 1 – Idaho Legislature passes legislation changing parts of the structure of the SRBA, declaring the Department of Water Resources is no longer a party.

April 7 – SRBA legislation is signed into law by Gov. Cecil Andrus.

April 19 – Judge Hurlbutt stays all action in the SRBA (with a few exceptions) pending consideration of how to deal with the new 1994 SRBA legislation.

May 3 – Judge Hurlbutt appoints a committee (chaired by former Chief Justice Robert Bakes) to consider how the SRBA should proceed.

June 28 – Idaho Supreme Court declares that the "public trust doctrine" does not apply to the SRBA, turning back an effort by conservation groups.

July 6 – The steering committee chaired by Robert Bakes signs off on its report on how to proceed in the SRBA, placing top priority on the role of the director, the validity of the amnesty statutes and attorney fee issues.

July 15 – Judge Hurlbutt lifts the general stay on the SRBA and declares Basin Wide Issue 3.

July 26 – The A&B Irrigation District (through attorney Roger Ling) files a "call" on groundwater covering a vast area in eastern Idaho.

December 7 – Ruling by Judge Hurlbutt in Basin Wide Issues 2 and 3, in effect throwing out the 1994 legislation as unconstitutional, except for the new "amnesty statutes," which he referred to a newly-created Basin Wide Issue 4.

1995

January 9 – At his first State of the State address, Gov. Phil Batt refers to a "water quagmire" in the state.

February 8 – The Legislature seeks to intervene in appeal of Issues 2 and 3.

March 17 – Hurlbutt upholds the 1992 "amnesty statutes" as constitutional, and provides an interpretation of them.

May 3 – Judge Hurlbutt strikes down the "general provisions" in the Department of Water Resources report on water rights.

June 1 – Karl Dreher of Colorado takes over as the new director of the Idaho Department of Water Resources.

June 23 – The Idaho Supreme Court upholds most of the 1994 SRBA legislation.

September 29 – Northern Idaho action in the SRBA takes a step forward when several north-central communities said they plan to join the suit through an attorney.

October 1 – Fritz Haemmerle, a prosecuting attorney at Blaine County, fills the long-vacant third special master position.

October 4 – The U.S. Forest Service drops many water right claims.

November 21 – Judge Hurlbutt considers an unusual request to establish three new basin wide issues (proposed by attorney Scott Campbell) all at once.

1996

February 14 – Federal attorneys file a proposed basin wide issue seeking to determine what information should be included in a water right decree.

March 4 – Judge Hurlbutt formally names the Department of Water Resources as a special expert to the court in the SRBA.

March 8 – Hurlbutt designates Basin Wide Issue 9, "whether Public Water Reserve 107 is a valid basis for a federal reserved water right."

April 26 – Hurlbutt again rejects inclusion of a number of "general provisions" in Department of Water Resources-drafted reports.

April 26 – Hurlbutt declares that "partial forfeiture" of water rights is not provided for under Idaho law.

July 5 – Idaho Supreme Court turns back a request by a water users group at Fort Hall to participate in the SRBA, declaring that it is not a party.

September 25 – David Tuthill named new administrator of the Department of Water Resources Adjudication Bureau, replacing administrator David Shaw.

1997

May – The SRBA Court web site, including the IWATRS database, goes on line.

October 3 – Idaho Supreme Court delivers a mixed opinion on special provisions (Basin Wide Issue 5).

October 6 – Hagerman Water Right Owners, for whom attorneys pushed basin wide issues and repeatedly shaken up the SRBA, departed the case.

October 10 – The Idaho Supreme Court held that partial forfeiture of water rights is allowed under current Idaho law.

1998

April 22 – Idaho Supreme Court revisits its decision on Basin Wide Issue 5 (general provisions).

April 26 – Idaho Supreme Court holds that the federal government does have Public Water Reserve 107 water rights.

June – A state Republican Party platform plank calling for ending the SRBA is considered but rejected at the state party convention.

June – Judge Daniel Hurlbutt has set in motion a summary judgment schedule and a plan for bringing the massive Nez Perce water right claims to trial.

September 15 – Judge Hurlbutt on September 15 said a reserved water right exists for the Sawtooth Wilderness Area, with a priority date of August 22, 1972.

October 14 – Initial SRBA Judge Daniel Hurlbutt says he will resign from the bench at the end of the year.

December – Karl Dreher reappointed by incoming Governor Dirk Kempthorne as director of the Department of Water Resources.

December 21 – Last open court session for Initial SRBA Judge Daniel Hurlbutt.

December – 5th District Judge Barry Wood named to take over the SRBA.

December – Judge Hurlbutt appoints a mediator, Francis McGovern, in the SRBA Tribe water rights case.

December 31 – Initial SRBA Judge Daniel Hurlbutt leaves the bench. He delivers substantial decisions just before his departure. In a major loss for federal water right claimants, he rejected a series of federal arguments.

1999

February – An initially short-term appointment to the SRBA for Judge Barry Wood is extended by the Supreme Court.

May 26 – The Idaho Supreme Court held the non-use of water by a customer of a canal company doesn't mean the canal company forfeits that part of its water right.

August 25 – Judge Wood said he plans to restructure the gradually splintered Basin Wide Issue 5.

August 31 – Special Master Fritz Haemmerle departs the SRBA.

September 1 – Tom Cushman replaces Fritz Haemmerle as special master.

October 1 – A sharply divided Idaho Supreme Court held that the United States does have implied reserved water rights for wilderness areas in Idaho – and those rights include all the water that naturally flows through those areas.

2000

February – Nez Perce tribal interests challenge Judge Wood, contending that he has a conflict of interest in some or all of the SRBA.

March 9 – The Idaho Supreme Court unanimously held that the federal government could not use the state's "constitutional appropriation" method to claim non-diversionary water rights for anything other than stock watering.

March 23 – In a written statement, Judge Wood declares that he has no conflicts of interest in the SRBA.

June 14 – Judge Barry Wood on June 14 ordered a type of mediation, and named a mediator, in an attempt to resolve a number of conjunctive management issues. The mediator, however, later was withdrawn.

July – At the Idaho Water Users Association, long-time Executive Director Sherl Chapman is replaced by attorney Norm Semanko.

August – The three SRBA special master deliver statements relating to prospective conflicts of interest.

August 31 – Idaho Supreme Court removes Judge Barry Wood from the SRBA, after Wood's brother in law Daniel Eismann is elected to the Supreme Court.

October 22 – 5th District Judge Roger Burdick is named the third SRBA presiding judge, by the Idaho Supreme Court.

October 27 – The Idaho Supreme Court partly reversed itself on an earlier key federal water rights decision, and held in general that Congress must explicitly reserve water for a federal reserved water right to exist for wilderness areas.

December 15 – Judge Burdick takes charge of the SRBA.

2001

February 22 – The Idaho Supreme Court on February 22 upheld an SRBA Court decision rejecting federal water rights claims in the Deer Flats area.

April 23 – Judge Burdick on April 23 turned back a request by a group of water organizations to participate directly in litigation over federal water rights in the Hells Canyon National Recreation area.

May – Department of Water Resources proposes reducing from 120 to 60 days the claim objection period.

June 25 – Judge Burdick sets revised procedures for filing appeals in the SRBA.

July 24 – Judge Roger Burdick on July 24 turned back a proposal which would have broken apart a set of federal-related water rights at the Fort Hall Indian Reservation and the Fort Hall Irrigation Project.

September – The Idaho Department of Water Resources took more direct control of groundwater diversions in two regions of the Snake River Plain.

2003

April 3 – The Idaho Supreme Court on April 3 held that ample notice was given the LU Ranching Company in a contest over federal water right claims.

April 10 – Idaho Supreme Court decides the Sagewillow case, turning back a resumption-of-use defense offered by the Idaho Department of Water Resources.

May 7 – Judge Burdick orders an end to mediation in the Nez Perce Tribe water rights issue.

August 1 – SRBA Judge Roger Burdick joins the bench of the Idaho Supreme Court, after having been appointed to replace Justice Jesse Walters.

October – 5th District Judge John Melanson appointed to preside over the SRBA, becoming the fourth presiding judge.

November 4 – Judge Melanson issued his first major order in the case, allowing participation in a key water right dispute near Boise by the city of Boise, the state of Idaho and four individuals with right claims but also associated with environmental interests.

2004

May – Settlement documents in the Nez Perce Tribe water issue are released.

July 1 – Special Master Tom Cushman retires.

August 23 – Judge Melanson designates as a basin wide issue the question of incorporating terms of the Swan Falls agreement into the SRBA.

September 2 – Judge John Melanson ruled that the rights to water held in several Boise River Bureau of Reclamation storage facilities should be held directly by BuRec, but that "equitable title" also belongs to several local irrigation entities.

October 1 – Ted Booth starts as a special master, replacing Tom Cushman.

October – Department of Water Resources moves from its central headquarters in Boise on Orchard Street to the Water Center near downtown.

December 8 – Legislation passed in Congress was signed into law, to comply with terms of the Nez Perce water rights settlement.

2005

March – State legislation needed to meet terms of the Nez Perce Tribe water rights settlement, is passed and signed into law by Governor Dirk Kempthorne.

November – An unusual water right claim at a highway rest stop is received.

November – Adjudication Chief David Tuthill is named administrator of IDWR Water Management Division. Don Shaff replaces him in charge of adjudication.

November 17 – Judge Melanson issued an order aimed at clarifying which Department of Water Resources actions could be properly taken before his court.

2006

July 1 – SRBA filing fees are increased.

September 27 – U.S. District Judge James Redden, sitting at Portland, said that the Endangered Species Act trumps all other water rights considerations – possibly throwing out pieces of the long-negotiated Nez Perce Tribe water rights agreement.

October 10 – SRBA Judge John Melanson on October 10 rejected an unusual city of Pocatello claim to water rights – a claim it said the federal government effectively awarded it more than a century ago.

November – Incoming Governor C.L. "Butch" Otter said he will not reappoint Karl Dreher as director of Water Resources.

2007

January – David Tuthill, administrator of water management, is named by Governor Otter as the new director of the Department of Water Resources. The appointment, originally interim, later was made permanent.

February – The Idaho Supreme Court in February held that a livestock company which grazes on federal range land has water rights on that public range land.

March 5 – Idaho Supreme Court upholds Department of Water Resources rules on conjunctive management.

October 16 – Idaho Power Company filed in U.S. District Court suit against the U.S. Department of Interior, saying it long has been in contravention of a 1923 agreement concerning the release of water at American Falls Dam.

2008

February – A unanimous Idaho Supreme Court held in February that the city of Pocatello has no claim to a federal reserved water right, a claim it maintained in filing in the SRBA in 1990.

April 18 – Judge Melanson delivered a ruling rejecting Idaho Power Company's arguments seeking to overturn parts of the Swan Falls water agreement from the 80s.

June – Judge Melanson indicates designation of a new basin wide issue covering aesthetic, wildlife and recreational water rights.

2009

January 29 – A comprehensive Snake River aquifer plan is approved by the Idaho Water Resources Board.

March 25 – Idaho Power Company challenge to the terms of the 1984 Swan Falls agreement ended on March 25 when the company, together with state officials and others, agreed to a "reaffirmation" of the deal, with a few adjustments.

NEED MORE?

Additional copies of this book are available from Ridenbaugh Press, and so is the ***SRBA and North Idaho Digest*** – keeping you up to date on the adjudication as continues to develop.

UPSTEAM: Adjudicating the Snake River Basin

____ copy/copies, $15.95 each

THE SNAKE RIVER BASIN
& North Idaho ADJUDICATION DIGEST

Keep up with the SRBA every month with the ***SRBA Digest***, the independent review since 1993 of key developments in the adjudication – and the soure for what you read in this book.

____ Subscriptions: e-mail $99/year. Print, first class mail $129/year.

Name ____

Address ____

City ________________ State ________________ Zip __________

Email ____

Ridenbaugh Press
Box 843, Carlton OR 97111.
Order by phone (503) 852-0010.
Order by e-mail stapilus@ridenbaugh.com
World Wide Web at http://www.ridenbaugh.com

Made in the USA
Monee, IL
04 November 2026

67382838R00128